# Goddess

# Consciousness

## Women's Mysticism & Sacred Arts

## Marlaina Donato

Ekstasis Multimedia
Blairstown, New Jersey

*Goddess Consciousness* ★

Ekstasis Multimedia: www.booksandbrush.net

Goddess Consciousness/Marlaina Donato
Blairstown, New Jersey: Ekstasis Multimedia, LLC, 2014
ISBN-13: 978-0692286869
ISBN-10: 0692286861

Cover art and design: Marlaina Donato
*Interior art and images: Marlaina Donato
*with the exception of the Yoni mudra: public domain

References by the author: excerpts from the article *Sweet Seduction: Magic, Superstition, and Our Romance with Food* (Demeter's Emerald, Summer 1990) and the book *Naked Soul: Astral Travel and Cosmic Relationships* (Llewellyn Worldwide, 1998)

For the late Michelle Hillekamp,
teacher, Spirit Sister, and dearest Friend
for visiting my life on her way Home.

...Winifred Druhan, my incomparable and exquisite
guru-mother for her Goddess soul, eternal wisdom, and
our barefoot twilights in the garden. Thank you, Mama, for
holding the mirror for me, then and now.

...and Goddess-centered authors Shekhinah
Mountainwater, Barbara Walker, Judy Grahn, Diane Stein,
Mary Daly, Merlin Stone, and Z. Budapest for their
invaluable work in my early 20s that showed my wounded
self the shimmering truth beneath the rubble. If not for
these brave women who reopened a spiritual path lost
and overgrown for centuries, I can say with certainty that
I—and countless others—might not be here today. To
these women, I am indebted.

Also by Marlaina Donato

*Fiction & Memoir*

Broken Jar
Hollow Bread

*Body-Mind-Spirit*

Spiritual Famine in the Age of Plenty
Birthing Fire: Meditations on the Sacred Feminine
Naked Soul: Astral Travel & Cosmic Relationships

*Children's Literature*

The Silver Ladder: Children's Stories for the Magical Years

*Poetry*

A Brief Infinity
Alabaster
Cup of Fire
Angel of the Dawn

# *Table of Contents*

### I
## *Feminine Foundations*

Introduction......8

1: The Flower's Thunder: Woman's Sacred Energy......18

2: Goddess Rising: Visualizations and Self-Blessings......30

3: A Corner of the Universe: Goddess Altars and Sacred Space......42

### II
## *Feminine Spirit*

4: Woman in the Moon: Goddess Ceremony.....81

5: Earth Psalms: Goddess Prayers, Chant, and Sacred Sound......113

6: Whispers of the Goddess: Second Sight and Creative Divination.....129

7: Women's Wings: Dreams and Spirit Journeys......155

8: Shadow of the Sword: Calling the Dark Mother......167

### III
## *Feminine Arts*

9: Sacred Beauty: Ancient Mysticism of Cosmetics and Adornment......172

10: Soul Sustenance: Sacred Herbs, Food, and Goddess Kitchens......234

11: Touching the Universe: Woman's Sexual Fire......312

### IV
## *The Sacred Feminine Four*

**12: Elemental Identity: Finding Yourself in Earth, Air, Fire, and Water......329**

**Conclusion......373**

**Resources......376**

**Recommended Reading......380**

**Bibliography......384**

**Index......389**

**About the Author......402**

I

# Feminine Foundations

## *Welcome...*

From this page forward, this book is designed to be your special place. Here, you are not your clothing or bra size, age, or vocation. Rather, you are a woman the Sufi poet Rumi calls "A ray of God; creative, not created." Here you are also a *ray of Goddess*.

*What* is Goddess? *Who* is She? There are many answers to these questions, but in simplest terms, Goddess is the creative aspect of Deity; Her body is manifested in the physical world as our planet Earth. Her soul is the productive mystery of the universe and the infinite capacity to conjure life from the void. She is autonomy within every living being in its purest and most uncompromised form. The Divine Feminine Force is not all flowers, light and beauty, but also the blood of birth, the fierce heart of the tempest, and the dance of survival. Her force is simultaneously creative and destructive. This law of opposing equals is seen in the lava that destroys all life in its path but fertilizes soil for new growth. She is an artist who paints over an old canvas to begin anew. She gives her children the courage to cut through dense illusions about self and find the jewel of immeasurable value, the pearl that sleeps inside each of us and is ultimately our most valuable currency for evolvement.

From the Hindu Durga to the Gnostic Sophia, the Christian Blessed Mother to the Wiccan Triple Goddess, the feminine aspect of Deity is an ancient model that runs through all cultures around the globe. Her worship pervaded Europe, the Middle East, Northern Africa, India, and Pakistan, and according to some sources, can be traced to 30,000 BC. Civilizations up until 6,000 BC. saw Deity primarily as feminine, the male principle a later model that eventually extinguished the Sacred Feminine. Until then, ancient cultures saw nature in all of its fierce majesty as female and women as Her embodiments. Early matriarchal societies celebrated the Sacred Feminine and observed this force in the earth's fertility, woman's capacity to bring forth life, and in the cyclic, lunar correspondence of menstruation. Humankind's earliest calendars were created by women who tracked their menses along with the moon's phases. Our foremothers in long buried cultures knew the connection between themselves and the earth's cycles of abundance. Ancient structures of community honored the feminine divine in many aspects of living and revered women as incarnations of the feminine aspect of God, the all-encompassing Great Mother. These societies preferred peace over strife, nurtured female empowerment, and honored the fruitful earth. Still used today, the term *Mother Nature* is one of the few linguistic remnants of these matriarchal times.

According to recent, extensive archeological findings and contrary to previous assumptions, ancient priestesses of the Hellenic world held honored positions both spiritually and politically in patriarchal Greek society. And there was a time in early Christianity when women officiated as respected priests who baptized, blessed, and prophesized as dedicated followers of Christ.

Once war-centered patriarchal peoples fragmented matriarchal ethos and organized religions restructured or snuffed out former spiritual cultures, women and the Goddess were demoted to inferior rank. Eventually, Her significance was forgotten, save for a precious few who kept Her presence and rituals alive by going underground or disguising them in plain sight within the confines of established religion.

The Creative Life Force manifests in patterns of regeneration and degeneration, birth and death, and the cellular workings of the body's metabolism seen in the second-to-second balancing act of anabolism and catabolism. Whether we acknowledge this energy in spiritual terms or scientific explanation, it affects all living beings on this planet and is present in the seasons, tides, elements, light and dark, and female and male. Women's biological rhythms mirror the earth's fertility—our monthly blood comes with each lunar cycle; our genitalia clearly resemble the anatomical structures of fruits and flowers; our hormones ebb and flow like the tides. When we observe these biological synchronicities, it is easy to understand how ancient peoples saw the female body reflected in the macrocosm. Parts of the body held symbolic significance and related to the mystical workings of nature and the universe.

Today in our modern age we, as women, hunger for connection to something wild and beautiful—to unearth the sanctity of our bodies and help us to remember our lineage as priestesses and healers. In our age of rampant feminine self-hatred, eating disorders, addiction, and body dysmorphia, this cultivation of Goddess consciousness is needed now more than any other time in history. What if we could rise above the demons of society and see ourselves not through cultural whim but through the eyes of the Goddess? What if we raised our daughters to see the Goddess in the mirror rather than someone else's shallow ideal or criticisms? What if we raised our sons to honor the value of the earth and women?

We can study the hard-earned wisdom of saints and sages, but the journey is ours alone to take. The path of the mystic is a solitary one, and there are still shreds of belief that it must be a tortuous one—that only self-sacrifice, asceticism, celibacy, or severe consciousness can earn God's blessings, forgiveness, and a place in a heavenly afterlife. The Hindu mystic endured years of self-deprivation while the Christian mystic lashed the body into agony. St. Catherine of Siena, one example—despite profound mystical experiences—whipped herself three times daily to earn her visions.

Even though we no longer live in such brutally religious times here in the Western world, the human psyche, particularly the female psyche, is still haunted with inhibition, guilt, and fear of pleasure. Yet in early childhood, we knew the rapture of our ancestors who entered trance or looked to the stars to know the divine. The natural instincts of the child are also the same longings of the mystic—to experience Deity in the manifested world directly through our physical and spiritual senses. The entire concept of mysticism—the goal to know Deity directly—has been achieved by both sexes throughout history, but when most of us think of mystics, we immediately envision medieval monastics, physically deformed ascetics, or tribal Medicine Men uttering the language of the spirits. Though some of these images are rooted in fact, the most common mystic is the one who fits into society without speculation and without dramatics. Save for a few female Hindu, Sufi, and Christian saints, the female visionary has been lost beneath the dusts of history. Due to the patriarchal ravages of the Spanish Inquisition and subsequent witch hunts, female spirituality came to be associated with evil. In later times, during the surge of occult interest in the nineteenth century, many women came into view as powerful mediums, but it was short-lived. Many were proved to be hoaxes, and no matter how convincing or genuine the "table tapping", female mystics lost credibility and fell into the hollow confines of entertainment. Despite the current commercial flurry of psychic hotlines, reality show mediums, and blockbuster books, the mainstream stereotype of women's spirituality is a shadow of its reality and deepest potential.

Female and male are two halves of the divine whole; life could not exist without these two equally powerful forces. The Ultimate Deity is genderless as is the individual soul, but in order to know our true selves, we must find the taproot of our spirits. This taproot is often found by discovering the spiritual power of our own gender. In order to do this, we must sift through ages of preconceived ideas about feminine spirituality and reclaim the uniqueness of our visions. We do not need churches, temples, sacred ground, elaborate and complex ritual, or magical invocations to experience Deity or to remember our mystical birthright. We only need to know ourselves beneath centuries of cultural dogma. In our modern, youth-obsessed world, we often forget the value of maturity. Earth is a beautiful role model; the fruit would never exist if not for the withering of the blossom. Many of us are taught to believe that youth or the ways of seduction are the essence of feminine power, but in ancient matriarchal societies, a woman who healed, created art, or bridged the worlds was the most respected among her gender but considered unfit to be a spiritual teacher until she reached a certain age. The essence and cultivation of Goddess consciousness is to *understand* our unique power and grow into it joyfully.

Many of us come to know the Goddess without ever putting a label on our experiences. When I was ten years old I had a secret ritual that I shared with no one. Whenever I was outside at sundown, I stopped whatever I was doing to watch the day descend into dusk. I imagined the last rays of the sun as the outstretched arms of a shining goddess. As the sun's amber light pierced through the web of branches behind my swing set, I felt blessed by this goddess that seemed more real to me than anything else. Ten years later, through books and women's spiritual circles, I discovered the world of the Sacred Feminine and the history of Goddess-centered cultures. I knew then that the feminine presence I felt at sunset during my childhood was not fantasy. I studied, prayed, and invoked Her for a decade, but these years of quiet yet sometimes profound spiritual communion did not prepare me for the moment when She would literally change my consciousness.

One summer morning at dawn, I was startled out of deep sleep. There had been no noise or other intrusion, yet I had been awakened suddenly. I was alert but could not find it in my power to move my body. Beginning at my feet, accompanied by a diffused light, energy began to move through me. I knew this soft light was not coming from the window—the curtains were closed; the sun had not yet broken through the haze. As this energy ascended toward my head, every cell of my physical body became conscious almost to the point of pain. I had never felt more alive, awake, or aware. Even more profound was the overwhelming feminine Presence at the heart of this energy. I felt so deeply embraced, so nurtured, I was dissolved to tears. There was a complete loss of identity, and only my bare essence and this Presence existed. I heard a female voice echo as the energy reached my head, an exquisite singing voice that was also the collective voices of flutes, humming bees, wind, and breaking surf set to a steady heartbeat. Within seconds, the primal self deep in the wilderness of my own spirit recognized this voice. I knew it was Her, and that we are all part of Her vastness. Deep, earthy scents of forests and flowers both familiar and unknown to me filled my nostrils as the energy reached the rim of my skull. For an infinite few moments, I drifted into the deepest peace I had ever hoped to know.

Then without warning, as quickly as it had begun, the energy left my body and all went still, dark, and silent. What felt like an eternity had only been a few minutes. The Goddess Force had shifted my consciousness and was gone. Immediately, almost with desperation, I struggled to call Her back, to be within Her heartbeat once again, but all efforts failed. I sobbed and finally understood mystics through the ages who described feeling deep grief after immersion in the Infinite. The separation and return to the finite self was almost intolerable. I likened it to the sadness and confusion a newborn infant must feel when propelled from the mother's womb into a world of blinding light and noise, the cosmic umbilical cord severed. No wonder Sufis believe that babies cry when they are born because of this separation from the Source.

My sadness eventually settled into deep, multilayered self-awareness in the subsequent days, weeks, months, even years following this extraordinary experience. I knew the possibility of my own being and consequently, saw life through different eyes. I also knew that communion with Spirit was not intended to be weighted with struggle, sacrifice, or manmade creed but imbued with joy. The Goddess energy, in our deepest and most challenging darkness whispers, "Come live with me. My name is Joy, and my face is yours."

I hope you enjoy the journey of this book that celebrates the Goddess in every corner of life—from self-empowerment to divination and prayer; spiritual medicine in the kitchen to sacred sexuality in the bedroom; the ancient, mystical uses of cosmetics to finding yourself in the four elements. This work is a culmination of twenty-five years of passionate study and dedication to the Sacred Feminine inspired by multicultural sources and based upon material I've created for circles and retreats. It is also infused with priceless wisdom from Spirit Elders who graced me with their knowledge. In short, it is a love song to the Goddess and Her power manifested in each of us.

Before you begin, take a moment to remember if you've ever heard a stone whisper a secret to you or if the thunder has ever beckoned you to dance. Remember the last time you made love and tasted fire. You are already a mystic; you only have to remember. No matter your age, vocation, income, or political inclination, I invite you to preserve one of the world's most endangered resources— your own feminine being with all of its beauty, scars, and perfect imperfection. I invite you to join me in a renaissance of personal sacredness that nourishes your body's magical and spiritual origins. I invite you to breathe in a new day, to relinquish the burden of existing and embrace the deliciousness of living; to betray what you've always done and how you've always done it with something designed with more of your happiness in mind. It does not require pain, sacrifice, praying a certain way, being loved by a particular person or living a certain lifestyle. You are invited to come home to your true self. You are female, a spiritual being and powerful beyond measure.

# 1

# *The Flower's Thunder: Woman's Sacred Energy*

Many references to female influence run through our common language: *A woman's intuition. A woman's touch. A woman scorned.* Positive or negative, truth or myth, women's power has been revered, suppressed, feared, and misunderstood. We have been attributed to possessing both the Evil Eye and the healing touch. Our hair has been seen as our crowning glory and personal power but also something that attracted demons, and if loosened and combed, could conjure wild storms and changes in the weather. Our pointed fingers supposedly had the power to bless or curse according to will. Our menstrual blood has been regarded as both life-giving and demonic. The vagina or *yoni* has been perceived as the sacred gateway of life or the man-eating, toothed *vagina dentata*. Caught within this religious and cultural dichotomy, we have learned to doubt, fear, or disregard our own gifts. All human beings have innate spiritual potential, but as women, we hold unique energy. Human beings are beautiful, divine mysteries; as women, we are keepers of these Mysteries.

Whether or not we conceive and give birth, our capacity and design to bring forth and nurture the next generation is a power that holds much significance and transcends the physical. The creative capability within our bodies is also within our spiritual selves. This *birthing energy* is our greatest resource which can be accessed for strength and spiritual advancement.

The navel has been considered a center of power for centuries. It is the place where the umbilical cord connected us to our physical birth mother. On the spiritual level, it is the place where our spirits connect to the Cosmic Mother, the divine creative force of the Ultimate Deity. In Eastern religions, this special area of the body corresponds to the second chakra which influences creativity and sexual energy. For women, this is also the place of the womb. It is interesting to note that the navel is the physical body's point of balance. It is natural to conclude that both physical and spiritual balance are connected and share this power center.

Despite our many differences as human beings, we have mothers in common. We were all carried in a woman's body. Because of this soul-to-soul, pre-birth arrangement, the spiritual significance of mother and child is profound, especially when the child is a daughter. It is common metaphysical belief that we choose our lives before birth; family, friends, physical and emotional characteristics, career, lovers, challenges, and victories are all predestined by our own souls. If this is indeed true, it is no wonder why the mother-daughter relationship provides the most intense karmic lessons of our lives. Even when our relationships with our mothers (or lack of them) are extremely negative and challenged, we often learn the most about ourselves through them. The spiritual bonds between mothers and daughters go very deep, and these connections also link us to the Divine Mother. Somewhere in the deepest recesses of our psyches, we first remember the Goddess through our physical mothers.

A woman with a growing life inside her is part of the universal creative rhythm, and for reasons beyond the physical, her spiritual power often strengthens during gestation; many pregnant women experience heightened senses which can almost seem supernatural. This sharp sensory awareness often includes second sight and can result in vivid psychic dreams, spirit communication, or deep meditative states. Gestation can be a spiritual bridge from one way of life to another and a form of powerful initiation. The Goddess energy is at its peak during this time in a woman's life, and spiritual birth—or rebirth—transpires via the changing female body and delivering a baby. This force is still concentrated in a woman's body for months afterward, especially if the mother nurses the child.

Adoptive mothers, stepmothers, co-mothers—women who are not physical birth mothers—are also vessels of the Goddess Force, godmothers in the purest sense of the word. Women who create and nurture life come in many packages. Some give birth; others raise children birthed by other women. Some nurture animals while others create life through art, music, writing, and other forms of soul-expression. Creative women are mothers, conceiving ideas and nurturing them to fruition. When this art is infused with global, social, or spiritual consciousness, its creator works as co-creator with the Goddess Force and becomes an open channel to be an instrument for positive change.

As the babies are born, the children are raised, and the art is produced, our planet is protected, preserved, and healed by activists, many of whom are women. These tireless and fearless individuals are mothers of the earth, caretakers of the planet when she is spent, abused, polluted, and raped by ignorance and greed. As mothers and creators risk their lives for their children or their art, earth mothers risk their lives for the wellbeing of the earth and unborn generations.

Looking at these powerful feminine roles, we conclude that our essence and greatest areas of potential are creativity, positive justice, vision, healing, and the powers of rejuvenation and destruction that prepares for new growth and life. To be female is a spiritual gift. We are both flower and thunder; the energy within us—if utilized with wise and conscious intention—is akin to the explosion that unearths the gold.

### Accessing Your Birthing Energy

Most of us long to have more energy and to feel more centered. Spending time in nature, maintaining a yoga or fitness practice, and meditating can help immensely, but regularly tapping into our innate feminine power can be profound. And the best part is that it only takes a few minutes. *Note: Being post-menopausal or having had a hysterectomy does not diminish your innate Birthing Energy.*

Here are a few simple visualizations to help stir your Birthing Energy and to connect to the Goddess self within and the Goddess Force in general. I have presented four meditations that correspond to a different element— Earth, Air, Fire, and Water. You may wish to use the one that you are drawn to most or use each of them at different times. You may also consider using all of the meditations during a single session. Accessing your Birthing Energy can be used as a simple meditation tool or a more practical way of increasing energy when you get a slump during the work day. It can also be employed before making love to experience more pleasure. Getting in touch with your Birthing Energy is simple and empowering, and if practiced over time, can strengthen the physical body and accelerate spiritual growth. When you are pressed for time or in a situation where meditation isn't possible, simply placing your hands over your womb and connecting to your Birthing Energy for a few moments will give you similar benefits.

### *Birthing Energy Meditation: Earth*
*(for more physical energy or to regain emotional stability)*

Find a quiet place and lie on your back, outdoors if you wish. Rub the palms of your hands together vigorously until you feel the burn and immediately place them over your navel. Breathe deeply and consciously, feeling your belly rise and fall beneath your hands.

When you reach a relaxed breathing state, imagine your body sinking into fragrant grasses. *Feel* yourself becoming one with the soil as if rooted. Once you feel part of the earth, focus your consciousness on your navel. Continue to be aware of the rising and falling of your breath until you can imagine that you are breathing with your belly instead of your lungs. Focus all thought, concentration, and emotion into the area of your womb. Know this is the center of your being, the center of your universe, the center from which you respond to all outside influences.

Now imagine that your navel is a beautiful river rock positioned in perfect stillness, and the waters undulate around this rock, flowing around its curves. You can see this river as the outward distractions of your life and then see that the rock—your ultimate center—is totally unaffected by the waters. Become one with this rock and know you are inviolate and grounded.

Do this meditation as long as you wish until you feel an anchored security in your navel. You are safe, in control. Try to memorize this feeling so you can call upon it later in the day when you need strength or balance.

Give yourself time to come back to full alertness. Claim your path as Seeker, Priestess, and Creator. In this moment, take back any power you have relinquished, denied, or feared. From this moment on, you are vital and awake, a woman co-creating with the Cosmic Creative Force. Be free.

### Birthing Energy Meditation: Fire
*(for more physical energy, creativity, or heightened sexuality; also for protection)*

Find a quiet place and lie on your back, even better if you can lie in a path of sunlight streaming into the room or somewhere outside. Rub the palms of your hands together vigorously until you feel the burn and immediately place them over your navel. Breathe deeply and consciously, feeling your belly rise and fall beneath your hands.

When you reach a relaxed breathing state, imagine your entire body cocooned in warm sunlight, be it sunrise, sunset, or the heat of noon. Bask in this nurturing light; let it envelop you and sink into every pore. Once you feel part of the sun's energy, focus your consciousness on your navel. Continue to be aware of the rising and falling of your breath until you can imagine that you are breathing with your belly instead of your lungs. Focus all thought, concentration, and emotion into the area of your womb. Know this is the center of your being, the center of your universe, the center from which you respond to all outside influences.

Imagine that your navel houses a single, burning flame. Visualize its heat reaching into your hands, your fingers, your palms. Breathe with the flame as it wavers, imagine it dancing and moving with each inhalation and exhalation. Now imagine this flame growing in height until your navel is a contained, beautiful fire. See its amber light in your mind's eye, *feel* the heat. Become one with the flames, knowing that nothing can trespass this psychic energy field within your womb. Feel powerful, alive, and protected.

Continue this meditation until you feel pleasant warmth in your physical being and allow the energy that has been awakened to disperse throughout your body. Welcome the energy and try to memorize the feeling so you can call upon it later in the day should you need strength, energy, or a brighter outlook.

Give yourself time to come back to full alertness. Claim your path as Seeker, Priestess, and Creator. In this moment, take back any power you have relinquished, denied, or feared. From this moment on, you are vital and awake, a woman co-creating with the Cosmic Creative Force. Be free.

### *Birthing Energy Meditation: Water*
*(to feel more relaxed, to reconnect with your emotions, or to tap into deep inspiration)*

Find a quiet place and lie on your back, outdoors on a beach or by a body of water if you wish. Rub the palms of your hands together vigorously until you feel the burn and immediately place them over bare navel. Breathe deeply and consciously, feeling your belly rise and fall beneath your hands.

When you reach a relaxed breathing state, imagine you are floating in warm waters, buoyant upon the blue. Feel free and safe; become one with the sea, pool, or river of your imaginings. Feel that you are becoming more pliant with each breath, until you can envision your body as a wave rising and falling with each inhalation and exhalation.

Once you feel the waters inside your being, focus your consciousness on your navel. Continue to rise and fall with your breath until you feel that you are breathing with your belly and not your lungs. Focus all thought, concentration, and emotion into the area of your womb. Know this is the center of your being, the center of your universe, the center from which you respond to all outside influences.

When you feel conscious at the womb level, imagine that your navel is a soundless whirlpool of energy moving clockwise, drawing all healing and strength of the universe into your flesh and spirit. See this force funneling all that you need and hunger for into your life.

Continue this meditation as long as you wish until you feel empowered, and try to memorize the feeling so you can call upon it later in the day should you need strength or renewal.

Give yourself time to come back to full alertness. Claim your path as Seeker, Priestess, and Creator. In this moment, take back any power you have relinquished, denied, or feared. From this moment on, you are vital and awake, a woman co-creating with the Cosmic Creative Force. Be free.

### *Birthing Energy Meditation: Air*
*(to feel invigorated, more connected to Spirit or mentally stimulated, or during times of menstrual cramps or hormonal fluctuations)*

Find a quiet place and lie on your back, outdoors if you wish. Rub the palms of your hands together vigorously until you feel the burn and immediately place them over your navel. Breathe deeply and consciously, feeling your belly rise and fall beneath your hands.

When you feel in a relaxed breathing state, imagine you are drifting upon the winds. Feel leaf-like, weightless, with no limitations. Visualize floating on twilight breezes or exhilarating storm winds. Once you feel part of the heavens, focus your consciousness on your navel. Continue to rise and fall with your breath until you can imagine that you are breathing with your belly, not your lungs. Focus all thought, concentration, and emotion into the area of your womb. Know this is the center of your being, the center of your universe, the center from which you respond to all outside influences.

When you feel that you are conscious at the womb level, imagine the winds blowing away all problems and concerns right through your hands. Now envision your navel as a portion of sky the color of cobalt flame. Daydream about flying into the heavens' blue infinity where nothing can touch you.

Continue this meditation as long as you wish until you feel a sense of lightness in your being and try to memorize the feeling so you can call upon it later in the day should you need strength or renewal.

Give yourself time to come back to full alertness. Claim

your path as Seeker, Priestess, and Creator. In this moment, take back any power you have relinquished, denied, or feared. From this moment on, you are vital and awake, a woman co-creating with the Cosmic Creative Force. Be free.

2

# Goddess Rising:
# Visualizations & Self-Blessings

Visualization is a popular practice and a powerful tool that connects us with self and Spirit and also has physical benefits similar to meditation. If done consistently, visualization can untangle us from negative habitual patterns, boost immunity, and literally influence every cell in our bodies. It is used by those in need of more abundance, students who want better grades, and cancer patients who strive for increased immune response to fight the disease. Visualization, in simple terms, is daydreaming with intention. We inadvertently and negatively use the power of visualization every time we worry and imagine worst-case scenarios or rehash past traumas and arguments; all of these can weaken the body's natural defenses, dull creative impulse, and compromise the effect of the brain's feel-good neurotransmitters. On the other hand, positive imagery can stimulate physical healing, soothe over-wrought nervous systems and psyches, and invoke the Goddess within so we can make better life choices based on self-empowerment rather than fear.

We women are busy creatures, and maintaining a meditation or visualization practice is often challenging. The good news is that we do not need to do a hundred recitations or sit in a lotus position for hours. The soul is unhindered, therefore true spirituality does not need elaborate, time-consuming rituals. Here you will find visualizations that take under five minutes yet can be adapted for longer periods of stillness if you wish to put the time in. You can do them lying in bed before going to sleep or upon awakening, and the positive results increase the more you incorporate them into your daily life.

Here you will also find self-blessings that can be done while you are getting ready for the day. Self-blessings help us take back our power, connect us to Her, and nourish the body with much-needed self-love that has nothing to do with vanity and everything to do with accepting ourselves with joy and grace.

Feel free to add your own elements or make changes to the following visualizations and blessings, and consider passing them along to your mothers and sisters, daughters and granddaughters, nieces and friends. May we pass the empowering light of the Goddess from one woman to another and create a sisterhood of self-love and acceptance.

## *Goddess Rising, Goddess Descending*
### A Self-Blessing

This mini ritual/active meditation invokes the Goddess within (rising) and the Goddess without (descending). Both energies intersect and unite the forces of the earth and the heavens.

1.  To begin, stand with both feet together with your arms raised at chest level, elbows bent and close to the breasts with your palms facing outward. Your hands will be positioned as if you are pressing them against a wall, fingers together (See illustration on page 33.) *This ancient Goddess stance was the position used by women when communing with Deity. It was both an invocation of reverence as well as a symbol of the priestess' power to bestow blessings. This pose is commonly seen in ancient art including temple sculptures and icons depicting the Divine Feminine*

*Principle—from the Blessed Mother to the paradoxical Lilith. This women's ancient prayer pose awakens the Goddess within and links us to our rich matriarchal past.*

WOMEN'S ANCIENT PRAYER POSE

2. As you stand in this pose, envision pinpoints of light emanating from your palms, illuminating your fingertips. Now see light blooming from your heart radiating outward, petal by petal into crystalline

streams of energy. Know you are created in Her image—healthy, whole, beautiful. Perfect.

3.  Now part your feet until they form a wide but comfortable triangle and raise your arms to form a mirror image of the same. *With arms and legs forming a V, your physical body serves as an energetic bridge that connects heaven and earth, male and female, yin and yang. This traditional Goddess position invokes the Divine Mother of the universe.*

4.  While greeting Her with raised open arms, visualize Her energy streaming downward, pouring a rain of blessings over your body. Cup your hands as if to net the energy and then close them tightly to hold in the healing light. Lower your arms and touch your face as if rinsing your skin with sparkling, cool water, eventually working your way down along the entire length of your body—along your arms, breasts, trunk, legs, feet, calves, hips, back, neck and back up to your head.

5.  Cross your hands over your heart and say aloud or silently, "Great Mother, I am Your instrument on this earth. Bless me with Your presence and enable me to do Your work. I walk in Your name."

# *Goddess Consciousness* ★

## *Embodying the Milky Way*
### *Evening/Bedtime Visualization*

Many ancient cultures saw the Goddess manifested in the heavens, namely, the great band of starry filament we call the Milky Way. Early peoples envisioned their life-giving creator as the Mother of the Cosmos, Her breasts spilling milky streams of stars from which all living beings are nourished.

This following visualization is a wonderful meditative tool to use before sleep while you are lying in bed or when you are feeling disempowered and need to mother yourself. Practiced regularly, this visualization may stimulate dormant creative energy and nourish the pineal gland in the brain which has great influence on psychic ability.

1.  Lie in any comfortable position, preferably on your back. If you are alone and have room in bed, stretch out your arms to your sides and part your legs. If not, rest your hands gently on your navel.

2.  Take slow, easy breaths, imagining a silver stream of light entering your nostrils. This light softly makes its way into your sinuses, into your brain, down your spine, into your spinal cord, illuminating each vertebra as it passes through to your hips and then down your legs.

3.  See your cells glowing, millions of them glistening like

stars.

4.  Now visualize your body at the center of our spiral galaxy; your being is iridescent, immense, and untouchable. Your long, silver hair blows in the cosmic winds, brushing by planets and wrapping around suns, tresses flaming white with energy. See streams of stars spewing from your full, life-giving breasts, your belly glowing with Earth's full, fertile moon. The power to create is alive and pulsating at your fingertips, inside your heartbeat and Hers.

5.  Allow yourself to drift into sleep or deep meditative rest, knowing you are both the Goddess and a child of the Goddess.

## Birthing the Sun
### Wake-Up Morning Visualization

In most ancient cultures around the globe, the moon was seen as feminine while the sun was regarded as masculine. One of the few exceptions is Amaterasu, the Japanese Shinto Goddess of the sun and the universe. She symbolized laughter and bright benevolence. In Greek myth and spiritual belief, the sun god was also the god of healing and the arts.

The following visualization invokes the sun's blazing hope and inspiration as well as its energetic healing forces. You may wish to use it in the morning before you get out of bed, when you are sunbathing, or sitting in front of a sunny window. It is also ideal to use on days when you feel tired, drained, or have a case of the winter blues.

1. Lie in any comfortable position, preferably on your back. If you are alone and have room in bed, stretch out your arms to your sides and part your legs. If not, rest your hands gently on your navel.

2. Take intentional breaths, deep and easy, feeling your inhalation reach into your lungs. When you feel peaceful, imagine the sky before dawn, that magical pause between night and day when the gray curtain opens to a mural of rose-pink and orange-gold. Hues of salmon, tangerine, and lavender intensify, permeating the ether and gilding the clouds. Imagine lying back on the billowing silk of the heavens, your body completely supported by gentle, unseen hands; the Goddess, will not let you fall.

3. Breathe in the vibrant color until it enters your nostrils, filling every pore with dawn as it passes through to your face, neck, shoulders, arms and hands until are iridescent. See this radiance become brighter as it reaches your breasts and pours into your belly, spilling over your hips in a waterfall of color. Visualize parting your legs to make a sacred passage for the sun.

4. Inhale deeply. When you exhale, see the sun emerge from your yoni, the most sacred part of your body—

the gateway of life. Give birth to the morning and know there is no pain, only exquisite joy as the light emanates from your core, illuminating the heavens in which you are suspended.

5. Give the sun a name—something you wish to manifest at this moment in your life—*peace, love, health, joy*; the choice is yours. Birth the sunrise, your limbs streaming light and your hair blazing and woven with tangerine and yellow fire-ribbons. You are the youthful, ever-new, powerful, life-giving day. Breathe in the power. Burn away all that is no longer needed in your life, heart, and psyche.

6. When you are ready, come back to reality with a few easy breaths, retaining the vivid memory of light inside your body, filling your soul with everything you need.

## Mirror of the Goddess
### A Self-Blessing

As women, we can experience much distress in our bodies; sometimes the challenges are physical while others emotional. Many of us grapple with self-image, and loving ourselves can be a life-long, agonizing quest. The following self-blessing is a deeply sacred exercise, one that is a beautiful invitation to take back your power, to rise above cultural whims, deep-seated self-consciousness, and shame. It is a visualization that may take time to ease into but one that is well worth the effort. You may wish to buy a beautiful bath towel and reserve it for this self-blessing.

1. When you step from the shower or bath, take a few moments to take a few easy breaths before you reach for a towel. Imagine that the towel of your choice has been placed there by the Divine Mother and holds her unconditional love within its threads.

2. As you dry yourself with the towel, visualize this universal love inside the fibers. As you dry your hair, say aloud or silently, "In Her image, I am perfect." Now do the same as you dry your shoulders, arms, breasts, and belly. Do this until every part of you has been dried and blessed.

3. Now look into the mirror and say, "_____, (insert your name) you are beautiful. Beautiful at every age, every season, beautiful during health and during illness, during joy and during distress, beautiful even when you feel it least. You are a mirror of the Goddess— provided for, celebrated, and unique. You are the only one of your kind, and I am here to take care of you as I would take care of anyone I love. Unlike times in the past, you can depend upon me to shield you from anything and anyone that is not compatible with your highest good. You are precious. You are loved."

4. Dip your index finger into rose water, a favorite perfume, or plain tap water and touch the area

between your brows (the third eye), between your breasts, your navel, and the palms of your hands while saying, "I am Goddess."

II

# Feminine Spirit

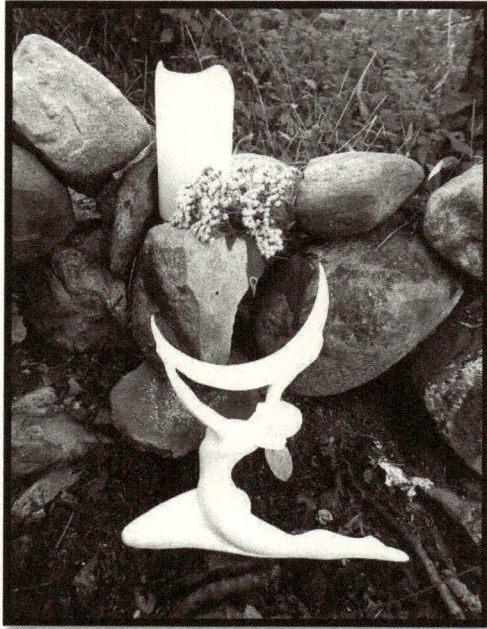

*3*

# A Corner of the Universe: Goddess Altars & Sacred Space

Sacred space is wherever we honor Deity, a revered person, or an event with devotion or remembrance. Places of worship, both traditional and secular, are as diverse as human beings. Be it the home shrine of a practicing Hindu or a nightstand where Catholic rosary beads and a Bible are placed between times of prayer, a Wiccan circle drawn in the sand beside a lake or a Native American Medicine Wheel, wherever intention meets Spirit a connection to the Divine is made. Even little children have their own versions of sacred space—secret hideaways, treasure boxes, and imaginary places. National tragedies inspire space that could be seen as hallowed in the most tactile sense; Holocaust museums and the 9/11 Memorial in New York City are prime examples. Many highways and back roads of America are dotted with makeshift memorials to loved ones lost to tragic accidents, places marked with flowers, stuffed animals, and religious symbols that catch our eye as we zoom by on the way to somewhere else.

Every religion and faith around the world since the beginning of time has sacred ground in common. In ancient Greece, spiritual communion and celebration culminated at the city of Eleusis, a religious center known for its public and private Mystery Schools. The Eleusinian Mysteries are still shrouded in history, but we do know that they involved complex initiation rites, worship of the Goddess Demeter (Lady of the Grain), and rituals focusing on the soul's journey through the Underworld. A cave called the Plutonian at the heart of this ancient center housed a stone thought to be able to harness the divine energies of both the Underworld and the world of mortals.

Even today, within the grand Ise Shrines of Japan's Shinto religion, the inner sanctum is sacred to Amaterasu, the eternal Lady of the Sun. The Ise shrines are rebuilt every twenty years. Not a single nail is ever used, and the 1,300-year-old design is preserved. The tori or sacred gateway precedes all Shinto shrines, and visitors are required to wash the hands and mouth before entering. Worship of kami also takes place in nature, particularly near waterfalls. Spiritual society was ruled by female shamans who came from a long line of spiritual leaders.

Like Shinto philosophy, many cultures including Tribal Nations have always regarded the natural world as sacred space. Canyons, mountains, prairies, deserts, and beaches are all living altars. Arizona's Superstition Mountains are sacred to the Apache where it is believed that a cave leads to the heart of the sacred earth. The Native Medicine Wheel is also example of holy space and balance.

Tibet's Mount Kailas is seen as a direct link to the divine. Countless Buddhists and Hindus journey to its windswept heights to erase their sins. The mountain itself is seen as a sacred and capable of purification. For this reason, many visitors change their clothes on the mountain and leave their old garments behind as a metaphor for shedding the past and changing consciousness.

Spirit houses or *san phra phum* of Southeast Asia are miniature temples set in the corners of homes and businesses to ensure good fortune and health. Here, offerings are made to appease the spirits and invite benevolence. In our modern western world, we often do not see cemeteries or burial spaces as sacred, save for personal sentiment and Native American reverence for the final resting place of ancestors. However, in the Middle East, a tomb can be the highest place of holiness. The *dargah* or burial place of a saint is seen as sacred space where the *barakka* or grace

# *Eleusis*

*The Eleusinian Mystery schools of the ancient world were prime example of ceremonial complexity. This great religious center of ancient Greece was centered upon the worship of Demeter, the Mother of the Grain, and her daughter Kore, Mistress of the Underworld and renewal. These esoteric rites are often a footnote in history books and are seen as by-products of a mere fertility cult; however, despite the fact that we know very little of the actual rites, we do know for certain that Eleusis was an elaborate, multidimensional spiritual center. Eleusis—meaning advent—was named for the birth of the Holy Child, often represented by an earth deity such as Dionysos in his title of Iacchus. In essence, the Holy Child was the light-bearing divinity of salvation and symbolic of the awakened spiritual self in each initiate. Part of the rites included eating bread made from the last or first sheaves of the harvest, an act seen to represent gaining immortality after death. Initiates partook of the holy "body of the earth", thus receiving blessings and the eternal embrace of the Goddess. The religious activity of Eleusis lasted for almost two thousand years and lived up to the meaning of the word mystery. Mystery, from the Greek musterion meaning "reserved for initiates only", was the beating heart of this ancient center. The Mysteries were divided into Lesser and Greater, the latter being the most secret. The Greater Mysteries, if divulged, were punishable by death.*

of the deceased holy person can be absorbed and retained by devotees.

Of course, these are only a few cultural examples of sacred space. On the personal level, it is instinctual to have a corner in our lives that is for us alone, and that corner is even more magical if we can reserve it for spiritual work and connection. Some women are fortunate to have an extra room to designate as their private sanctuary, but a lot of space is not necessary to have a temple of one's own. A shrine by the bedside, an inconspicuous altar in the kitchen, a corner in the garden or on a work desk, or the hollow of a tree are all beautiful ways to commune with a higher power. An altar is a psychic vessel and bridge to divine, subtle energies.

The energy, power, and intent you bring to your altar are absorbed right into its fibers. These unseen vibrations build with time, which in turn, feed your spiritual work. Because of this absorption of energy, it is advised to never set up or change your altar when you are in a state of anger, agitation, or emotional upset. The initial creation of a new altar or the changing of an established one requires peace and positivity in order to harmonize with the universal energies. Here are a few suggestions:

-Play beautiful or uplifting music while you create your altar.

-Be sure the surrounding space is clean and uncluttered so the energy is unhindered.

-Burn incense or smudge the space before you create your altar. For information on consecrating your space with essential oils and customized room spritzers, see page 218.

-Clean, wash, or polish the altar itself before setting up.

-Do not allow anyone else to handle objects on your altar so your personal energy will not be diluted.

There are many books available about creating altars and sacred space if you need inspiration. The suggestions in this chapter are designed to give you a template of ideas to create your own unique space where your soul can feel at home. Altars or sacred spaces, like other things in our lives, tend to change as we grow, outgrow, learn, and simply change our minds. Our altars can go through several incarnations until they feel "right" or change with the ebb and flow of our needs and passions.

If having a sacred corner of the world is new to you, you may be wondering what exactly is accomplished by having an altar. Having such a place provides a focal point where you can pray, practice visualizations, meditate, commune with Deity, do creative work, chant, deep breathe, come back to yourself and de-stress, honor seasonal shifts or sacred days, use affirmations, contemplate, daydream, and whatever your soul is in need of. If you are well-versed in creating altars and sacred space, perhaps the following ideas can inspire something you may not have tried before.

If you choose an outdoor altar space, it can provide opportunity to commune with the Goddess Force within the earth. My favorite places for spiritual work have been the hollows of trees during all seasons, times of day, and weather. Inviting the elements into your sacred time can amplify your experiences, so don't hesitate to use your outdoor altar space during snow storms, on rainy days, or daily transitions such as sundown, twilight, midnight, or dawn. Follow your bliss!

Before moving onto suggested themes for altar and sacred space, here are a few tips and ideas to keep in mind:

-If you have a loved one's ashes (four-legged ones included), you may wish to place them on your altar. My mother's fabric-draped box of ashes provides a beautiful and purposeful dais to uphold an image of Deity or an incense bowl. Not only does this honor your loved ones but it also strengthens the altar space with ancestral energies.

-Candles can be substituted with clear or colored holiday lights. This type of altar illumination is especially beautiful when interwoven with faux leaves, fruit, greenery, or flowers.

-Consider having a wall altar. For example, take an unframed print, painting, drawing, or plaque and hang it above a shelf or a chest of drawers. Add faux leaves, greenery, branches, flowers, fruit, or garlands by inserting push pins into the leaves or stems to partially or completely frame the image. This way you can have more working space on your altar (shelf, table or chest of drawers). If you wish to have even more space or to leave the area entirely free, consider hanging sconces on either side of your image on the wall. According to preference, this can add an ancient, Gothic, or Victorian mood to your sacred space.

-If you want to add an image of the moon to your altar, you can purchase one at a nature, science, or toy store. Planets and stars are also available. Let your imagination play!

-Altars are traditionally positioned North which is ruled by the Earth element. However, if you are a woman of fire and passion, consider setting your South which is governed by Fire. If you are creative, practice healing arts, or are drawn to water, position your sacred space West which is ruled by that element. If you are a woman of deep intellectual or cosmic thought, or simply love the air and the winds, set your sacred space facing East which is ruled by Air.

-Consider placing your altar out of reach of pets and children. If you have a cat that is fond of jumping, perhaps a wall altar would be more practical.

-Look for items in craft and art stores, flea markets, thrift or vintage stores, toy stores, online marketplaces, and of course, nature. Consider creating your own items as well. You may also consider choosing heavy-weight fabrics, for lighter materials can easily catch fire if you use real candles.

-If you suffer with allergies and tend to avoid incense, you may consider essential oils, natural room spritzers, or a beautiful, natural potpourri on or near your sacred space. See page 227.

-If you choose to find your materials in the wild (mosses, fruits, barks, stones, etc.) please harvest responsibly and take only what is needed.

-To include traditional Goddess symbols in your sacred space, see textbox on page 80.

## Aromatics in Sacred Space

Plants, barks, roots, flowers, and resins have a long history in sacred space. Here's a brief list of the most common:

**African Violet:** used for protection and has affinity to the moon

**Benzoin/Styrax:** used to purify surroundings, increase prosperity, and for an incense base. Invokes the ancient lineage of Priestesses; used by shamans in Mali for shape-shifting; included in Taoist elixirs for longevity

**Cedar, Atlas:** dispels evil influences, opens the psychic eye, and prevents nightmares; symbolizes eternity

**Cinnamon:** ingredient in ancient anointing oils used by the Hebrews. Wreaths of cinnamon leaves adorned Roman temples.

**Copal:** purifying resin incense used widely in Mexico; dispels negative entities, thoughtforms, and energies

**Frankincense:** used in ancient Egypt and offered to the sun god; also burned in Christian churches and used for exorcisms

**Gardenia:** attracts angels and carries feminine lunar energy

**Henna Flower:** used in Middle Eastern countries to attract love, good health, and to ward off the Evil Eye

**Jasmine:** used to induce prophetic dreams and peaceful sleep; sacred to the Goddess and attuned to the moon; connects to the angelic realm and inspires joy

**Juniper:** traditionally used to chase ghosts, protect people and places, open the psychic eye, and dispel bad energy; ancient Nordic peoples buried their dead with juniper branches for an easy passage into the next world

**Lavender:** used to attract peace, prevent the Evil Eye, and in baths for spiritual purification; grown in monasteries

**Lily:** Sacred to Kuan Yin, goddess of compassion and

Mother of the World; Attracts higher energies including angels

**Linden:** traditionally used for all manners of love and protection

**Mint:** used for purification and cleansing of evil influences; also used to attract abundance and prosperity

**Myrrh:** burned in honor of the goddess Isis and sacred to Ra, the Egyptian sun god in ancient Egypt; used to consecrate amulets/talismans; induces deep meditative states and raises vibrational level of people and places

**Myrtle:** sacred to goddesses Venus/Aphrodite, Artemis, and Astarte; used to attract peace, love, and money and considered doubly potent if a woman plants it; one of the sacred plants chosen for the evening Sabbath by ancient Israelites

**Palo Santo:** used by shamans to purify spaces and lift the vibrational level of a person

**Pine:** sacred to earth deities and used in exorcism, healing rites, and to increase prosperity and physical strength; encourages endurance

**Rose:** sacred to the Goddess, the Blessed Mother, and Mary Magdalen; attracts higher energies including angels and used to open or heal the heart chakra

**Sage:** used to purify spaces; different varieties used in various way including divination and ceremony; most often used in sacred smoke clearing (smudging)

**Sandalwood:** used to honor the moon, ward off evil, and induce deep, meditative states

**Spikenard/Nard:** used for anointing and initiation in the ancient world; invites higher energies; the oil Mary Magdalen used to anoint the Christed Yeshua

**Thyme:** burned in ancient Greek temples and to clear a person from sorrow or sins

**Sweetgrass:** used traditionally to clear sacred space before ceremony; used in sweat lodges

**White Sage:** used to drive away evil spirits from places and to clean a person's energy field

## Elemental Altar Themes and Ideas

Elemental energies surround us from birth until death, sustain life, and are mirrored in our unique personalities. Building sacred space around the elements Earth, Fire, Water, and Air—and the seasons—Spring, Summer, Autumn, and Winter—can nourish the Goddess self and help us see magic in the mundane. For more on the four elements, please see Chapter 12: *Elemental Identity: Finding Yourself in Earth, Air, Fire, and Water*

## THE EARTH ALTAR

Creating an Earth altar is a beautiful way to feel more grounded, invite healing and mending to any area of body and soul, or to simply celebrate the turning of seasons. Earth cradles us, feeds us, and provides for all of our needs when we observe Her subtle yet profound ways. Earth altars are especially helpful during times of transition, during and after major change—loss of a loved one, relocating, career fluctuations, divorce/break-ups, illness, pregnancy, and menopause.

Honoring the element of Earth is a fun and meaningful focus for sacred space because the choices are plentiful and varied. The foundation for an Earth altar begins with choosing one that is made of real wood rather than plastic, metal, or simulated wood. The very heart of the earth's energy is concentrated in the life force of trees. When you use wood, you are honoring the tree that sacrificed its life as well as working in harmony with the tree's particular energetic imprint. Altars made of unfinished wood offer a greater abundance of Earth energies/qualities and can be made glamorous by simply adding beautiful cloth.

## Spiritual Significance of Trees and Types of Wood

**Oak:** The oak, sacred to the Druids, is known for its long life and hard wood as well as its magical lore of offering protection and good fortune. Oak has the most sacred history of all trees; ancient Druids revered the oak so highly that they did not hold ceremonies where this tree was absent. It is sacred to many deities including the goddesses Rhea, Cybele, Diana, and Hekate as well as the gods Pan, Zeus, Herne, and Thor.

**Pine and Cedar:** Pine holds concentrated energy due to its resinous quality. Resin is the blood of the evergreen and highly charged. It was once a Japanese custom to hang pine over an entrance to preserve joy within the home. Cedar, sacred to many Tribal Nations, is used for purification, exorcism, and cleansing in the form of smudging and sweat lodges. In general, evergreens invoke the Earth Mother, especially Artemis as well as the masculine Earth energies such as Pan and Dionysos.

**Maple:** Maple, known for its sap tuned into sweet syrup, is associated with love and longevity.

**Walnut:** Walnut is a beautiful tree with a mystical reputation for granting wishes and bestowing good health.

**Ebony:** Ebony is valued for its powers of protection.

### Adorning your altar

Earth-appropriate fabrics range from natural and organic (cotton, wool, flax) to elaborate faux animal prints such as tiger, snake, leopard, zebra, or giraffe. Prints can include leaves, flowers, trees/branches, animals, or fruit. You may wish to paint your own cloth with a chosen design or tribal pattern. You may also wish to coordinate your altar cloth with the changing of the seasons.

Anyone can create an attractive yet functional incense burner by simply filling a bowl with pebbles, crystals, river stones, sand, fresh soil, rice or another grain, colorful legumes (red lentils are beautiful), or salt (pink is especially pretty and good energetically). Be sure the bowl is at least three inches deep so it will support inserted incense sticks. You may also consider using a thick, flat or hollowed rock upon which to burn sage leaves.

Fresh flowers and/or beautiful plants including bonsai trees on your Earth altar add a beautiful touch to any sacred space. When flowers wane, you may consider scattering the petals over your altar as an offering before prayer or other spiritual work. You can do the same with silk flowers by snipping off the petals and sprinkling them around for lasting beauty and color.

You may wish to choose an Earth-ruled musical instrument to place on or near your altar. Designating an instrument brings something special to your sacred space and can be used to clear the area of accumulated energies. Your chosen instrument can be anything percussive, including a hand drum, rattle, or something simple like two rocks or sticks that can be struck together.

## Colors

all shades of brown—from espresso brown to sandy tan, terra cotta/clay to autumnal russets; all shades of green including chartreuse, emerald, olive, sage, moss; neutrals such as gray, white, and black; all flower colors

## Fabrics/Prints

all natural fabrics including cotton, wool, silk (optional); animal patterns such as snake, zebra, tiger, leopard, cheetah, giraffe, jaguar, all floral and leaf patterns; representations of animals, birds, and reptiles; tribal designs, tweeds, leather (optional)

## Earth Deities/Energies

**Archangels Gabriel and Uriel**: Angels of Earth

**Artemis:** Goddess of the Wilderness, Animals, and Women

**Astarte:** Lady of the Beasts and Goddess of Fertility

**Baba Yaga:** Goddess of the Forest and Magic

**Bast:** Goddess of Cats, Protection, and Celebration

**Ceres:** Goddess of Grain

**Cernunnos:** God of the Wilds; the Horned God

**Corn Mother:** Mother or Maiden of the Corn and Plenty

**Demeter:** Goddess of the Earth's Abundance

**Dionysos:** God of Wine, the Arts, Creative Ecstasy, and Rebirth

**Durga:** Mother of the Universe

**Fairies, Elves, Gnomes, and Nature Devas:** Keepers of the Land and Guardians of All Plant Life

**Gaia:** Feminine Embodiment of our planet Earth

**Ganapati/Lord Ganesha:** Remover of Obstacles; God of Good Fortune and Higher Learning

**Green Man:** Quintessence of Vegetative Life Force

**Herne:** Similar to Cernunnos (see above)

**Kokopelli:** Deity of Plant Growth, Spring, Reproduction, and Music

**Kuan Yin:** Mother of the World and Compassion

**Mother Kali:** Goddess of Rejuvenation and Mother of Time

**Pan:** jovial, goat-footed God of the Woodland

**Persephone:** Goddess of the Underworld, springtime, and Psychic Arts

**Rhiannon:** Goddess of the Earth, Fertility, and Animals (horse and birds)

**Tammuz:** God of Spring Renewal and Agriculture

**White Buffalo Calf Woman:** Mother of Life, Peace, and Harmony

### Stones/Minerals

wood, petrified wood, fossils, bones and animal antlers, clay, pine cones and resin, stones and rocks of all kinds, all gemstones and semi-precious stones (especially moss agate, green calcite, cat's eye, jasper, malachite, peridot, smoky quartz, smoky topaz, and turquoise), coal, salt, amber (especially green), diamond, metals

## Places and Seasonal Times of Power

*Direction:* North; *Seasons:* winter (traditional), summer (peak life force); *Places:* gardens, farmlands, mountains, meadows, forests, deserts, beaches

## Incense and Fragrances

pine and all evergreens including piñon, cedar, palo santo, patchouli, vetiver, sage, sandalwood, resins (frankincense, myrrh, copaiba, and copal), sweetgrass, sweet flower scents (especially ylang ylang), vanilla, cypress

## Earth Altar Themes/Templates

*Mother Earth Theme:* green cloth or a large cluster of mosses (found in the wild or craft stores); faux or real leaves; found branches, twigs, bark, pine cones; faux or dried grapes or whole dried pomegranates; incense bowl filled with small stones, dried grains, legumes, or sand; images of the Goddess, any Earth deity, the Blessed

Mother/Lady Guadalupe, or photographs of a cherished female role model (mother, grandmother, etc.) or your children; green or brown candles (spring green, moss green, and forest green are lovely choice); cornucopia

**Shamanic Theme:** animal-printed cloth (snake or jaguar), images or representations of Corn Mother; photos or ashes of loved ones/ancestors; totem/power animals such as bear, jaguar, wolf, serpent, birds of prey; Kokopelli; rattle, rains stick and/or drums; Kachina dolls; smudging wands (sage, sweetgrass, or cedar); found snake skins; bones, feathers, antlers; fossils

**Artemis/Diana Theme:** any earth-tone cloth; image or representation of Artemis, Mistress of Animals and Goddess of the Wilds; representation of bear, bee, rabbit/hare, or deer/stag; crescent moon; bow and arrow; faux greenery

**Desert Theme:** terra cotta or sand-colored cloth; pottery incense bowl filled with sand; images or representations of Lady Guadalupe or Mary Magdalen, Egyptian, Middle Eastern, Aboriginal, or Native American deities; Moroccan or Arabian-style oil lamps; serpents/rattlesnakes, lizards, cacti (living or decorative)

**Spring Theme:** spring green cloth; image of Persephone or other earth goddesses; pussy willows (fresh, dried, or decorative), faux flowers such as daffodils, lilac blooms, crocus, and forsythia; nests, eggs (wooden or plastic), craft birds

*Summer Theme:* emerald or forest green cloth; bowl of faux fruit and/or vegetables; faux or real flowers and silk flower garlands; image of Mother Earth, Aphrodite/Venus; festive candles/candle holders

*Autumn Theme:* golden-yellow, orange, red, russet, or brown cloth; leaf or mum printed cloth; faux leaf, fall flower, or grape garlands; image of harvest deities such as Dionysos; cornucopia, faux or dried grapes, pomegranates, berries, rowan, faux apples and pears; gourds; acorns

*Winter Theme:* white, pale blue, royal blue, midnight blue, silver, or black cloth (velvet is especially beautiful); image of the Snow Queen as Goddess; branches or twigs painted white; faux evergreen; representations of snowflakes; white candles; white birch bark or twigs

*General Earth Theme:* cloth and colors of choice; found stones, feathers, and bones; green candles; faux leaves or garland; bowl or cornucopia of decorative fruits to represent abundance

## Sounds/Instruments

Any drum or percussive instrument of choice; sound recordings of birdsong howling wolves or spring peepers

## Earth Symbols

trees, leaves, all flowers, and buds; all animals, insects, arachnids; cornucopia, fruit/vegetables; fairies, elves, gnomes, devas; unicorn

## THE FIRE ALTAR

The Fire altar is a place to honor our passions—creative, sensual, spiritual, and intellectual. Fire is the force of lovers as well as the highest enlightenment. Its energy is transforming, life-sustaining, and intense. Fire is permeated with *eros,* the very *life force* of the universe. Creating a Fire altar is a wonderful way to connect us to creative inspiration, cosmic consciousness, deep and sacred sexuality, and physical vitality.

It is traditional to place an altar North, but you may consider placing yours South if you create a Fire altar. In occult lore, South rules Fire, creativity, sexuality, and passion for life. If you use a wooden altar, you may consider choosing a wood from a tree that is ruled by Fire such as cedar, pine, or walnut. Fabrics for Fire altars can be bold, brilliant, or exotic as you dare and all shades of red, orange, and yellow. If you prefer cooler colors, by all means consider choosing blue, the color of gas flame. This color is the shade of blue that can be seen closest to the wick and right before a candle blows out. All metallic colors such as gold, bronze, copper, and rose gold are also ideal for Fire altars. If you choose metallic fabrics, choose a heavier fabric; most metallic material is light and can catch on fire easily if you use real candles. Metallics work well as accent cloths with a solid— for example, gold draped over a corner of solid red.

The main focus of energy on a Fire altar is that of light source, the focus being the primal energy of the living flame. Candles or any other fire source are essential. You can choose multi-wick candles for more light and to save space. You might consider a more exotic source of light and choose Moroccan hanging candle lamps, Arabian oil lamps, or Hindu/Jain ghee lamps. Antique oil lamps are also a beautiful option. If you choose an outdoor Fire altar, fir pits, bonfires, and tiki lights are all ideal. The presence of incense also invokes the energy of Fire, and choosing Fire-ruled spices such as cinnamon and herbs like rosemary harmonize beautifully with the Fire altar's unique energy. Wood or even a small piece of bark from any tree that has been struck by lightning is naturally charged with Fire and is a good addition to any Fire altar.

If you wish to include an image of deity, there are many Goddesses to choose from—from the powerful Celtic Brigid, lady of arts and healing—to Pele, Hawaii's fierce and sensual embodiment of the volcano. Be sure to check the subsequent references to get some ideas.

If you have a hearth or fire place in your home, you might want to place your altar there. In ancient Greece, the central home fire was considered the spiritual heart of the home and sacred to Hestia, Goddess of the flame and familial harmony. To ensure Hestia's blessings, it was custom for a young woman to take embers from her family's hearth to her new home. Similarly, in ancient Rome, the city's central fire was tended by priestesses who vowed loyalty not only to Rome but to keeping its flames perpetually lit.

All stringed instruments are ruled by Fire, including piano, dulcimer, and table harp. If you are a pianist at any level of ability, you might consider creating your Fire altar near or on top of the piano itself.

### Colors

all shades of red—from ruby to scarlet; all oranges from tangerine to persimmon; all shades of yellow excluding yellow-green; all warm metallics from gold to copper; gas flame blue; warm white; charcoal gray or black; smoky blue-gray; accents of burgundy/wine and russet.

### Fabrics/Prints

any fabric of choice; beaded, sequined, metallic

### Fire Deities/Energies

**Agni:** God of Fire, Lightning, and the Spark of Life

**Amaterasu:** Goddess of the Sun and the Universe

**Aphrodite:** Goddess of Sexual Love and Beauty

**Apollo:** God of the Sun, the Arts, and Healing

**Archangels Michael and Ariel:** Angels of Fire

**Brigid:** Goddess of Inspiration, Healing, and Fire

**Dragon:** Fiery Symbol of Primordial Power and Master of the Elements

**Hephaestus:** God of Fire, Volcanoes, Blacksmiths and Craftsman

**Hestia:** Goddess of Home and Hearth

**Kiskililla/Lilith:** Demon Goddess of Sexuality, Storms, and the Night

**Maya:** Goddess of Creativity

**Pele:** Hawaiian Lady of the Volcano and Goddess of Creation and Destruction

**Phoenix:** Symbolic Bird of Transformation and Rising From the Ashes

**Ra:** God of the Sun and Rebirth

**Salamanders:** Elemental Energies of Fire

**Sekhmet:** Goddess of the Scorching Sun and Transformation

**Shakti:** Goddess of the Life Force and Cosmic Energy

**Thunderbird:** Sacred Native American Creature of Storms,

Power, and Strength

**Vesta:** Goddess of the Hearth and Family

## Stones/Minerals

lava rocks, gold, pyrite sunstone, opal, fire opal, citrine, topaz (yellow and blue), tiger eye, amber (golden amber), flint, copper, garnet, ruby, carnelian, diamond/yellow diamond, black sand (volcanic sand), bentonite (volcanic ash)

## Places and Seasonal Times of Power

*Direction*: south; *Season*: summer *Places*: deserts, anywhere candlelit or fire-lit

## Incense and Fragrance

cinnamon, cassia, ginger, orange, blood orange, tangerine, lime, allspice, mint, lemongrass, lemon verbena, orange blossom, clove, juniper, pine, rosemary, nutmeg, cedar, coriander, basil, copal, frankincense, fennel, dragon's blood, mints, marigold, carnation, liquidamber, tea

## Fire Altar Themes/Templates

**Pele Theme:** three cloths of harmonious colors; image of Pele (as beautiful young woman, old woman, or the volcano itself); red candles; faux flower lei draped around a Goddess image; faux hibiscus blooms sprinkled over the altar (or a live hibiscus plant); gleaming brass or copper bowl/goblet filled with sand or grain for incense; offering of brandy (traditional offering to Pele)

**Hestia Theme:** white cloth; central multi-wick candle (number of wicks matching number of household members if possible); framed photos or treasured items of family/ancestors or loved ones' ashes

**Sun Goddess Theme:** golden cloth; image of Amaterasu (Japanese Sun Goddess) and/or Apollo (Greek God of the Sun); mirror (resting flat or hanging over altar space); crystal prisms; any image or engraving of the sun with extended rays

**Egyptian Sun God Theme:** flame-blue cloth accented with gold or copper fabric; image of Ra, the Egyptian God of the Sun; scarabs; cobras; myrrh incense

**Brigid Theme:** red cloth; cross of Brigid or image of Brigid as Saint or Goddess; a scroll of poetry; any representation of a swan; a small bowl of water changed daily (represents her sacred well)

**General Fire Theme:** colorful cloth and colors of choice; exotic light source such as Moroccan candle lamps or Arabian oil lamps

## Sounds/Instruments

all stringed instruments including the piano; sound recordings of crackling fire and thunderstorms

## Fire Symbols

dragon, phoenix, the sun, flames, torches, thunderbird, lightning bolt, volcanoes

# THE WATER ALTAR

From amniotic fluid to ancient oceans, Water holds powerful feminine energy. Life begins and is sustained by this element and in esoteric traditions, governs the realm of emotions. Some of our most powerful Goddess images are associated with the element of Water. Aphrodite, the Greeks' embodiment of beauty and sensuality, sprang from sea foam. An image of the goddess was ritually bathed in the surf and anointed with costly perfumes and garlanded with fragrant flowers.

Timeless tales of mythology are infused with the siren's song. If we look below the treacherous surface of the un-dine's lure, the mermaid archetype personifies the paradoxical nature of the Goddess, creative yet destructive; metaphorically, her song and beauty breaks down human defenses and drowns the negative ego so we can transform consciousness.

a Water altar

Creating a Water altar induces peace, connects us to healing energies, and helps us to clarify our personal, emotional truths. A Water altar is ideal for the bedside, as it connects us to the subconscious and the world of dreams.

Driftwood tables make beautiful Water altars. The cloth you choose for a Water altar can greatly enhance the mood of your sacred space. For example, a heavy satin fabric can evoke a lake's reflective stillness while a sparingly sequined cloth can suggest sun or moonlight flickering across the waves.

Water's place in religion is ancient and worldwide. Christian baptism and anointing, Hindu ritual bathing, and Islam's cleansing with rose water are only a few. To incorporate sacred use of water in your spiritual space, select a goblet, votive candle cup, or small bowl and fill it with equal amounts of distilled water and a flower water of choice. Rose, orange, or jasmine flower water contributes a delicate scent as well as an energetic component to the water. Fragrance has long been used to invite benevolent spirits and is a lovely addition to any altar, especially one dedicated to Water. (Flower waters can be purchased from health food or culinary stores, Middle Eastern markets, aromatherapy shops, and online.) Your sacred water can be used to anoint the forehead, heart, and palms of the hands prior to meditation, prayer, ceremony, or sleep. Anointing these points on the body is also an uplifting way to begin the day.

# *Goddess Consciousness*

The sound of water is one of nature's most beautiful songs, and you may consider placing a small, table-top fountain on your altar or in the same room. These tiny fountains are valued by Fen Shui practitioners and range in price to fit any budget. Outdoor Water altars are ideal near backyard fountains, swimming pools, water gardens, ponds, lakes, rivers, streams, old water pumps, and of course, beaches.

## Colors

all shades of blue from powder blue to midnight blue and indigo; all shades of blue-green including Caribbean aqua; all shades of green; all shades of gray from pewter to blue-gray; all cool metallics including silver

## Fabrics/Prints

any fabric of choice including satin, silk, sequins

## Water Deities/Energies

**Anuket:** Goddess of the Nile River

**Aphrodite:** Goddess of Beauty and Sensuality

**Archangel Raphael:** Angel of Water and Moving Waters

**Kuan Yin:** Goddess of Healing Waters and Mercy

**Mari:** Ancient Goddess of the Sea

**Oshun:** Mermaid Goddess of Sweet Waters and Healing

**Osiris:** God of Water

**Poseidon:** God of the Sea and Earthquakes

**Sulis:** Goddess of Healing Waters and Thermal Springs

**Tiamat:** Primordial Goddess of the Ocean

**Undines:** Elemental Spirits of Water

**Yemaya:** Queen of the Waters (especially the oceans and seas) and Mother Goddess and Protectress of Women

## Stones/Minerals

all shells and corals, aquamarine, emerald, green and blue tourmaline, blue sapphire, blue/green fluorite, pearl, blue calcite, rose and clear quartz, jade, moonstone, rhodochrosite, blue lace agate, lapis lazuli, amethyst, silver, genuine sea glass, found river stones, salt

## Places and Seasonal Times of Power

*Direction*: West; *Season*: Autumn; *Places:* beaches, riverbanks, lakes and ponds, waterfalls,

## Incense and Fragrances

African violet, orris root, rose, gardenia, jasmine, lemon, myrrh, sandalwood, thyme, vanilla, eucalyptus

## Water Altar Themes/Templates

*Aphrodite Theme:* cloth of choice, any shade of blue; image or sculpture of Aphrodite; roses (faux or fresh); conch shell or any other shell of choice; bowl or scallop shell filled with sand to hold incense

*Mermaid/Water Spirit Theme:* green or blue cloth of choice; fish net for accent cloth; image or sculpture of a mermaid or siren; shells of any size; conch shell; photo/print/poster of the ocean or waves behind the altar as a backdrop; incense bowl filled with sand or evaporated sea salt

*Kuan Yin Theme:* solid white or off white cloth, preferably velvet or anything luxurious to the touch; image or sculpture of Kuan Yin; decorative jar to symbolize Her healing waters; white floating candles and water bowl; faux lotus or water lilies; colors white and gold

*Yemaya Theme:* sky blue cloth; an image of Yemaya; cowrie shells; representation of an anchor

*General Water Theme:* blue, green, or aqua cloth; aqua candle on a dais or raised platform (a couple of books stacked beneath the cloth serve this purpose very well);

medium-large decorative glass or metal bowl filled with water placed beneath the candle to serve as a reflection pool; faux water lilies; craft items such as realistic frogs, turtles, dragonflies, or water birds; driftwood

### Sounds/Instruments

all bells including Tibetan singing bowls, crystal singing bowls, tingshaws and other hand cymbals, meditation bells; rain sticks; sound recordings of waves, rivers, streams, rain, and frogs

### Water Symbols

shells, coral, fish, dolphin, mermaid, mirror, raindrop, anchor, cup, frog, turtle, water lily, lotus, whirlpool

## THE AIR ALTAR

Air is the element that signifies intellect and spirit, as well as the cleansing energy needed for progress and change. Respiration, seed dispersion, and weather patterns have this element in common, and it is no wonder that the word *inspiration* has both creative and physiological definitions. In terms of breath, there is no life without inspiration, and there is no quality to that life without inspiration in terms of incentive. This dynamic is mirrored most profoundly in the movement of the winds—literally and metaphorically—as they sweep away what is no longer needed or spur us to new heights during our spirit-

an Air altar

tual work. Air altars can be set up on the corner of a desk, in an office, or outdoors where sacred space can include a wind garden of various chimes hanging from a breezy tree. This kind of altar is also best if you include healing breathwork, chant, and mantra in your spiritual practice. Air is aligned with our breath, and it is our most direct connection to this life-giving, inspiring energy.

Because of Air's intangible nature, the Air altar is composed of metaphorical correspondences; birds and feathers represent Air as well as images of the heavens. You may wish to place your altar facing East, its power direction, and even do spiritual work at sunrise to utilize the energies at their peak. If you wish, choose Air-governed pine or wood for an altar.

### Colors

white, black, all shades of blue, all shades of gray, all lighter shades of violet and lavender, silver and other pale metallics

### Fabrics/Prints

any fabric of choice; prints of birds, winged insects, clouds, rainbows, or stars

### Air Deities/Energies

**Aeolus:** God of the Four Winds

# *Goddess Consciousness* ★

**Angels and Archangels:** all

**Athena:** Virgin Goddess of Wisdom and Intellectual Prowess

**Aurai:** Nymphs of the Breezes

**Fujin:** God of Wind

**Hermes/Mercury:** Winged Messenger of the Gods, God of Travel and Trade

**Iris:** Goddess of the Rainbow and the Sky

**Njord:** God of the Wind

**Nut:** Star-clad Goddess of the Sky and Mother of the Gods

**Shu:** Primordial God of the Air and Wind

**Stribog:** God of the Winds and Directions

**Thoth:** God of Intellectual Arts and Knowledge

**Urania:** Muse of Astronomy

**Winged Isis:** Goddess of Rebirth and Mistress of Magic

**Zeus:** Father of the Gods and God of Fate, Justice, and the Sky

## Stones/Minerals Ruled by Air

clear quartz, Austrian crystal, celestite, meteorite, platinum, white gold, hematite, blue topaz, amethyst, mica, lapis lazuli, turquoise, phantom quartz, angelite

*Goddess Consciousness*

## Places and Seasonal Times of Power

**Direction**: East; **Seasons**: Spring; **Places**: hills or mountain crests, windy fields and beaches

## Incense/Fragrances

frankincense, rosemary, lavender, pine, lemon verbena, almond, benzoin, sage, mint, star anise

## Air Altar Themes/Templates

**Heaven and Earth Theme:** sky blue cloth; a large branch or small decorative tree in the corner or behind the altar space; craft birds of all colors to nestle in the branches; representation of a dragonfly to honor the totem of Air; tealights in blue glass

**Goddess of the Sky Theme:** blue or violet cloth with gold or silver accent cloth; image of the Egyptian sky goddess Nut; stars (stick-on or confetti) sprinkled over cloth to reflect the candlelight; blue bowl filled with salt to hold incense; blue, black, or lavender candles

**Angelic Theme:** lavender cloth; image(s) or sculpture of winged angels; silver candle holders with white candles; flower petals scattered over cloth; celestite or angelite

**Goddess of the Rainbow Theme:** rainbow-colored or solid black cloth; various colored glass candle holders; faux irises; crystal prisms on altar or hanging above it near a window

*Goddess of Higher Thought Theme:* charcoal gray cloth sprinkled with silver stars (stick-on or confetti); silver accent cloth; image/sculpture of Athena, Greek Goddess of Learning and Justice; representation of an owl; large feather of choice for fanning incense; white or silver candles

*General Air Theme:* cloth of choice; various feathers; representation of an eagle; smudging bowl with sage

## Sounds/Instruments

any wind instrument—from flutes to didgeridoo; the human voice; wind chimes; sound recordings of wind

## Symbols

birds and all winged creatures; clouds, stars, Milky Way, rainbow, feather

# *Goddess Symbols through the Ages*

crescent moon and moon phases

the spiral

5-petaled flowers

the rose

the pomegranate and the fig

almond-shaped yoni

upside down triangle (Yoni Yantra)

the chalice

the circle or ring

the numbers 3, 5, 8, 13, 28

the labyrinth

the labrys or double-headed axe

the serpent

the owl and the dove

the bee and the cicada

the hare, deer, and bear

the Milky Way

cowrie shells, shells

# 4

## *Woman in the Moon: Goddess Ceremony*

If we parted the curtains of ages gone by, we would see women uttering sacred words as they work the soil, bless newborn babies, call the winds to bring needed rain, and heal the sick using medicinal herbs from the Great Mother's apothecary of field and forest. We would see women together, gathered around one of their sisters giving birth, easing the passage with sacred dance and song.

Ceremony of any kind changes our consciousness. In essence, this is the reason why human beings have created ceremony throughout time. Birth, death, marriage, holy days/holidays, and annual birthday celebrations are observed with ritual, whether or not we label it as such. Ritual is the first thread in the immense tapestry of cultural and religious life. Whether we light a prayer candle in a church or call down the moon in a moon-dappled glade, ceremony is a bridge that lessens the chasm between the mundane and divine. Ceremony for the sake of breaking through walls of illusion and elevating consciousness can be a sacred tool; such intention can be a beautiful and fulfilling avenue to discovering the Goddess self.

This chapter offers ceremonial templates that can be used alone or with other women of like-mind. You will find Goddess-centered rituals designed to honor your wild spirit and working with the moon's healing energy. You will also find Goddess prayers, ancient mantras and chants rooted in the Sacred Feminine, and an introduction to the healing powers of toning. All or any can be used at your altar/sacred space or adapted for group ritual.

# Rites of Transition

Life is a journey of change, and by ceremonially acknowledging these transitions and shifts, we can better navigate human experience—joyous or painful—with spiritual meaning. I hope the following rites inspire you to celebrate yourself, find closure, offer new points of beginning, and prompt you to create other rituals tailored to your own individual passages.

## Birthday Renewal Rite

Celebrating your birthday with a personal spiritual rite can invite a new year of possibility and meaning. It is a conscious message to the universe that we are willing to value ourselves and our place in the world, a spiritual New Year of sorts, one of private reverence and resolution.

The Birthday Renewal Rite is deeply personal and individual, one that can include elements not listed here, so please add your own items of meaning. To this, you may consider adding a small birthday cake or cupcake, for this annual custom has roots in ancient Goddess worship. Round cakes or breads were baked in honor of the Greek goddess Artemis in her lunar aspect. Ancient worshipers included candlelight on these baked offerings to emulate and honor the radiant moon.

### *What You Will Need:*

*your *favorite* fresh flowers or greenery*

*2 white candles—pillars, votives, tapers, or tea lights*

*newly-bought piece of jewelry—ring, bracelet, or
necklace*

*cupcake or cake and birthday candles*

*culinary or cosmetic rose or orange blossom water
in a small bowl*

1.  To begin, place your favorite flowers or greenery on
    your altar along with your cake, jewelry you have
    purchased for your special day, and the flower water.
    Leave the candles unlit for now.

2.  Draw a bath or step into the shower. Ceremonial
    bathing is traditional before any sacred rite involving
    personal initiation or new beginning. As you bathe,
    take a moment to close your eyes and visualize being
    in the womb of the Goddess, the water the amniotic
    fluid from which you will emerge anew. Take a
    moment to be in a space of stillness—that suspended
    brief time before the child enters the world or the seed
    breaks through dark soil and into the light. Then
    silently or aloud, announce your rebirth, saying, "I am
    the dawn breaking, the river thawing, the seed
    returning; I am Goddess birthing, unearthing a new
    self." After this affirmation, extend your arms and

declare, "I am reborn!" Leave your bath knowing that the past will wash down the drain.

3. Adorn and celebrate your Goddess self by putting flowers in your hair or donning a beautiful robe, dress, or kimono. Do anything that makes you feel beautiful.

4. Go to your sacred space and light your candles.

5. Dip your index finger (power finger) into the flower water and anoint your forehead, palms of your hands, navel, and pubic bone.

6. Invoke the Goddess by standing with your feet apart and arms raised in a V. In this traditional Goddess position, greet the Divine Mother and your own Goddess Force within. Invoke Her by saying, "Great Mother of the Universe, Mother of my Soul, I stand before you born anew. Bless this day and the woman I strive to be."

7. If you have a "new year" birthday resolution, voice it aloud or silently and say, "I dedicate each day to nurturing my spirit. It is done."

8. Put on any jewelry you have selected to represent your commitment or to celebrate your new year

9. Find a comfortable spot and light your birthday candles. Make a great wish and then eat your Goddess

cake, putting a portion aside to put outdoors later as an offering to the spirits. Happy birthday, sweet woman! Be free!

...

## Uncoupling Rite

Regardless of circumstances, when a relationship ends, we are left changed, and sometimes it takes quite a while before we feel whole again. Divorce, break-ups, and death all change our consciousness, sometimes with the deepest pain we can experience in a lifetime. Seeking completeness through Goddess work can provide healing and solace, and help us to connect to a cosmic source of strength.

### *What You Will Need:*

### *scraps of paper and a pen

### *one red rose

1. To begin, find a quiet place where you can write on a firm surface...table, desk, floor, or anywhere with a lapdesk

2. Take scraps of paper one at a time and write something on each that you feel you need to take back. Here are a few examples: *I take back my power. I take back my body and my pleasure. I take back my*

*trust. I take back my sense of self.* If you've been separated from your loved one through death, your affirmation might be: *Despite my grief, I take back my willingness to be happy and whole.*

3. When you are finished writing, mix up the papers and put them into a pile in front of you.

4. Now pluck petals from the rose until you have a nice handful to place in another small pile next to your affirmation papers.

5. Take a few moments to breathe freely, allowing yourself to just be. When you feel ready, take a paper and read it aloud and then read it again. Affirm each time, "I take back my _____." Do this until you go through each paper.

6. Take a deep breath and conclude, "My heart is mine, and it is eternal. My love is infinite, and I give it to myself first."

7. Now choose rose petals, one at a time, and state something you want in your life. Here are a few examples: *I want peace. I want contentment. I want better health. I want closure. I want a partner with a heart like mine*

8. When you are finished, scatter the rose petals outside as an offering or sprinkle them onto your altar if you

have one. You may wish to dry them and put them in potpourri or your bath.

9.  Collect your papers and discard them any way you like, concluding the rite with a statement of self-affirmation, "In the name of the Goddess, it is done."

...

## Healing the Past Rite

Healing the past can mean very different things to each of us, and we can probably agree that it is an ongoing process as we go through life. The following rite is a simple but powerful way to reconnect with who we once were at a particular time in the past. This rite can be done more than once and may even develop into a journal if you feel so inclined.

### *What You Will Need:*

**\*paper and a pen or your computer**

1.  Choose a particular time in your life you'd like to focus on. See your younger self clearly; feel her emotions. Be willing to feel vulnerable and know you are safe in the presence of the Goddess.

2.  Write a letter to your younger self as if she is a separate person and address yourself by name as if you are communicating with a dear friend. If you feel

negative emotions toward your younger self and do not feel you are able to be loving, try to be neutral.

3. Write stream of consciousness, not worrying about creating a work of art or saying the "right thing". Be honest, angry, sad, whatever emotions come up for you and allow them to have a voice as you speak to this younger self.

4. When you are finished, sit with your letter in hand (print it out if you wrote it on your computer) and allow yourself to fully feel any emotions left over. The act of writing a letter regarding the past can be emotionally intense, so be gentle with yourself.

5. When you are ready, put the letter in a safe place where only you can find it or discard it by ripping, shredding, or burning it to release the past. It is your decision.

6. Addressing your younger self may take a series of letters or even a journal dedicated to her. If you are writing to your child-self, you may wish to shower her with a beautiful scrapbook with your letters. Healing can be creative and fun, too.

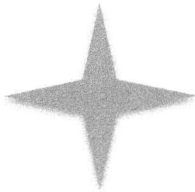

# *Rites of the Feminine Body*

## *Rite of the Ruby Nectar*
### (monthly menstruation rite)

In the distant past, women usually menstruated at the same time due to the moon's effect on their hormonal rhythms. Because of this, women gathered together during their "moontime" for support, community, and magic. Women knew they were especially open psychically and spiritually during the moontime and shared their visions with each other as well as the community. They also allowed their blood to seep into the earth to ensure fertility of the crops and a good harvest.

Electricity and enclosed indoor lifestyles have changed our bodily rhythms, and the moon no longer has such influence on our menses. Attitudes have also changed, and the life-affirming spiritual power of the menstruating woman has been all but forgotten. For some of us, our moontimes are riddled with inconvenience, pain, and even sickness. It is easy to turn against our own bodies and forget our power each month when the blood flows. The following ritual is designed to take back your power during your moontime, make peace with your body, celebrate your womanhood, and most of all, welcome your thoughts, dreams, and visions. You can also give voice to any negative emotions that may come up during hormonal swings. Hormones are teachers if we see them as such;

many times emotions and moods associated with moontime are blamed on "PMS", but in most instances, these emotions peak with our hormones for a reason and subside once they are taken out of the shadows and acknowledged. For this purpose, you might consider keeping a journal during your moontimes.

### *What You Will Need:*

**\*a libation of juice from pomegranate, cranberry, cherry, or red grape OR red wine or red herbal tea made from hibiscus and rose hips (i.e. Red Zinger by Celestial Seasonings is  nice choice) Whatever you choose, pour your libation into a beautiful glass. If you wish to have hot tea, pour it into a white mug so you can enjoy its lovely color.**

**\*red cloth or a shawl, pillows and anything luxurious and soft to the touch (blankets included)**

**\*1 red candle and 1 white candle**

**\*pen and paper or journal (optional)**

1. On the first day of your period or during the heaviest flow, choose a spot where you can sit or recline comfortably.

2. Light a red candle to represent your body's crimson flow. Light a white candle to honor the purity of your

spiritual gifts at this time.

3. Wrap your chosen red cloth or shawl around your shoulders and welcome the shift in consciousness it may bring. Be aware that you are now stepping into the realm of the Goddess where you are welcomed with loving care.

4. Take a sip of your ruby nectar and feel it nourishing your body, mingling with the crimson light emanating from your yoni, the sacred gateway of life.

5. Breathe deeply into your own power, and even if it's difficult, bless your own body with gentle understanding, respect, and gratitude.

6. When you feel ready, speak aloud or silently, "I am in my time of Power. I am a woman of vision. I am of the Goddess."

7. Allow yourself to go into a place of stillness. If you long for rest, allow your body to do just that. Your moontime is not only a time of physical cleansing when the body sheds the lining of the uterus but a time of emotional cleansing. Acknowledge this by visualizing all the emotional baggage of the past month being released with your blood flow.

8. Close your eyes; notice any images that float on the screen of your closed eyelids or be aware of any

sensations in your body. Acknowledge emotions that surface and allow them to *be* without self-monitoring or self-judgment.

9. If you wish, write down everything you see or feel during this time or use a divination tool, perhaps one from Chapter 6.

10. Place your hands over your navel and invoke your Birthing Energy (see Chapter Two). Honor your body's innate healing capacity and call it forth if you have pain or unpleasant symptoms.

11. Remain in this space for as long as you like. Upon conclusion of the rite, thank the Goddess for witnessing your innermost thoughts, emotions, and visions. Drink as much as you want from your libation, and if you have access to an outdoor space with a tree or a garden, pour out the remainder as an offering.

## *Bridge to Midlife*
### (perimenopause rite)

Much is written and spoken about these days about menopause, but perimenopause—the period of transition before our periods stop—isn't always addressed and can be the most challenging time of a woman's life. Physically and emotionally we may feel as if we are suddenly living on a swinging bridge with little stability. We may experience digestive and intestinal disturbances, hot or cold flashes, severe anxiety or panic attacks, headaches, muscle pain, unpredictable periods, depression, and intense emotional swings that make those of our teenage years pale in comparison. This wild walk on the swinging bridge is not what we ever expect to experience in midlife. Sometimes it comes as the shadow side of finally feeling more comfortable in our own skins and knowing ourselves more completely. Sharing our stories with one another can be a great comfort, and most of all, allowing ourselves non-judgmental, gentle self-care.

Aside from nourishing our bodies more than ever with healthy food and doing what we can spiritually to transition to the next phase, the following rite may be a wonderful addition.

### *What You Will Need:*

**\*a small serving of your favorite sweet treat**

**\*rosewater, an anointing oil, or your favorite perfume (see Chapter 9)**

1. To begin, you may wish to light candles or burn some incense on your altar/sacred space, or put on some beautiful music

2. Breathe deeply and allow yourself to just to be

3. Aloud or silently, acknowledge whatever you may be struggling with physically and emotionally. Name each challenge and follow it with, "but I love myself anyway." For example:

   *"I no longer feel like myself, but I love myself anyway."*
   *"I feel nervous all the time, but I love myself anyway."*
   *"I am depressed, but I love myself anyway."*
   *"I feel hormonal, but I love myself anyway."*

4. Now dip your finger into the rosewater, anointing oil, or your fragrance of choice and anoint your forehead, heart, navel, pubic bone, and wrists, saying each time, "I bless my body always and in all ways."

5. Take a bite of your sweet treat and say, "Dear Goddess, I ask that you help me to see the sweetness in this time of life, even during the difficult days. Help me to see the sweetness of my own Being and remind me that all that I struggle with is temporary."

6. Sit with yourself with full acceptance and any emotions that may surface. Have a good cry; breathe deeply; express what you need.

## Celebrating the Wise Woman
**(menopause/post menopause rite)**

### *What You Will Need:*

# *Goddess Consciousness*

**\*three white candles**

**\*three photographs of yourself, if possible-
one from your youth, one from your 30s or 40s, and one
from present time. If you do not have photos, choose an
object, no matter how small, to represent these three
phases of your life**

**\*a beautiful robe, shawl, or scarf, preferably
purple or maroon**

**\* a bowl of water with fresh flowers and/or greenery
floating within it**

**\*an anointing oil or fragrance of choice**

1. To begin, light your three candles, preferably on your altar/sacred space and place a photo or object by each one to represent your three selves and the triple aspect of the Goddess (Maiden, Mother, and Crone)

2. Breathe deeply and find your inner stillness before you put a drop of fragrant oil in your hand.

3. Dip the index finger (the finger of power) of your other hand into the oil and touch the first candle with the fragrance while saying, "(insert your name), I honor your love for life, your dreams and ideals, and your determination. I honor the times your heart was broken and the times you were not heard. I honor

everything I did not honor back then. I honor the Maiden who will always live within my heart."

4. Now anoint the second candle saying, "(insert your name), I honor your accomplishments and the people you nurtured. I honor your disappointments and victories, and the struggles you never shared with anyone. I honor the Mother who will always live within my heart."

5. Anoint the third candle saying, "(insert your name), I honor your arrival, blessed Wise Woman. I honor the countless miles and choices that brought you to this moment in time. I honor your survival and this glorious new Self. I celebrate your age of Power and your unique visions. I, (insert your name), celebrate the woman I am...

I am a woman
Who has birthed my own suns
Danced my own dreams
Conquered my own abyss
I am a woman who has tasted life
The salt of blood and loss
And the bitter honey of unanswered prayer
I am a woman who owns her soul...lock and key

Her body...breast and bone
Her mind...thought and vision
I am a woman who has tamed the shadow
Invented a new self times uncounted

Woven a tapestry of memory
I am a woman only beginning
Having ended so many times
I am a woman who has been here
And there is a scar
Where my fire has been

6. Sit with any emotions that may have been stirred and when you feel ready, put on your beautiful robe, shawl, or scarf, saying, "I have arrived. Blessed Be."

7. When you extinguish your candles, make a wish with each one.

## Post Miscarriage Rite

Losing an unborn child can be a deeply painful experience, a passage rarely marked with ceremony. This rite is designed to give your body and heart space to express grief, anger, and feelings of loss as well as give you a chance to honor the soul of the child and your body's wisdom.

### What You Will Need:

**\*a flower of your choice—a rose, daisy, wildflower, etc. or a freshly-picked or found leaf**

**\*a candle and a stick of incense to burn**

# *Goddess Consciousness*

**\*a heavy book**

1. To begin, light your candle on your altar or anywhere you feel safe and peaceful.

2. Breathe deeply as you sit or lie down with your hands gently resting over your womb. Connect with your body's sacred creative space and aloud or silently say, "Dear Goddess, I bring my loss to you and ask you to fill the void that is left in my body and my heart."

3. Acknowledge any emotions that arise, even rage if it comes up. Cry, scream, do whatever you need to do to express your feelings.

4. When you feel ready, speak to the soul of your child and tell him or her everything you would like to say. There is no right or wrong way to do this, but you may say something like, "Precious soul, I was your mother for a brief time. Though you and I did not have the life I thought we would have, you *happened*. And I love you. You were love inside of me and now you are a spark of love that exists beyond my womb, and I honor you." At this time, you may consider choosing a name for this special soul.

5. When you feel ready, light your incense as an offering and say, "I also honor my body and trust its reasons for not fulfilling this dream at this time, even though I do not understand these reasons."

6. As the incense burns, pick up your flower or leaf and hold it in the palms of your hands. Close your eyes and imagine enclosing the flower or leaf with love for the soul you are honoring today.

7. Place the flower or leaf inside the book and allow it to remain pressed for a week or more.

8. When the incense is burned to ashes, breathe deeply, and upon exhaling, reach your arms in a V toward the heavens and say, "In the name of the Goddess, I release my pain as best as I can and release the spirit of the child who chose me for a time, however brief." Cross your arms over your heart and conclude, "I am strong even when I feel vulnerable. I am worthy even when I am angry. I am beautiful always and in all ways."

9. After your flower or leaf is pressed and dry (after a week or so), you may wish to place it in a frame with beautiful stationery paper behind it as a backdrop. You might consider writing something or including an image of something inspiring or of significance. If it gives you comfort, hang the framed flower or leaf in a special spot.

*Variation: *This rite can also be adapted for pregnancy termination. Such a passage is deeply personal for whatever reason a woman chooses and deserves equal closure.*

# Sacred Self Rites

The following ceremonies invoke the wild self that is dormant in most of us unless we make a conscious effort to nourish her. These are ways that can help us honor the wilderness within, stoke the creative fires, and use healing lunar energies.

## Woman of the Wilds Rite

This rite invokes wilderness consciousness sacred to the goddess Artemis, protectress of women, forests, and animals. The ancient Greeks saw her as the many-breasted Mother who nourished all creatures or as the virgin huntress who protected life or took it away painlessly with her silver-tipped arrows. Artemis represents the inviolate feminine self that remains untouched, unconquered, and most of all, self-possessed and beholden to no one. White sage or any incense can be substituted for the suggestions below, but if you'd like to use the listed herbs sacred to Artemis, please refer to Resources as the back of this book.

### *What You Will Need:*

**\*charcoal for burning incense and a fireproof container (a simple heatproof bowl filled with sea salt)**

**\*white willow bark, dried cedar tips, or white sage**

1. To begin, light your incense on the hot charcoal and let it fume. As the scented smoke rises, stand with your feet together with arms raised at breast level, palms facing outward. Assuming this ancient women's prayer pose (see page 33) invokes the Goddess within.

2. Envision and feel light-energy emanating from your palms, fingertips and heart. Imagine forest green light pouring forth from your heart center, filling the room with vibrant life force.

3. Call the Wild Self to rise by making a sound called *zaghareet*, a bird-like trill that is found in many cultures to express joy, celebration, or farewell (see page 105 for history). Simply rest your tongue behind your front teeth and open your mouth just enough so you can flick your tongue up and down rapidly as if saying LaLaLaLa...When your tongue finds a very quick rhythm, voice a high-pitched note and continue to move your tongue against your teeth. Zaghareet can put you into a deep communion with Goddess energy. As you trill, feel the energy rising from your heart, into your throat, and out of your mouth. Close your eyes and feel the vibration of sound inside your body.

4. Invoke the Goddess of the Wilds by envisioning a forest filled with primordial trees—fragrant pine, towering redwood, and dense live oak. In your mind,

inhale the deep, earthen scent of soil and moss, lichen and leaves. Visualize clear brooks singing over rocks in crystalline tones. Choose the season and see the landscape.

5. Once you have a clear image of this untouched wilderness, call on the Artemisian Force with the following words, "Artemis, Goddess of Earth, the moon, and women, I call on you from the wild depths of my soul. The Wild Self within remembers and seeks your solace. Great sculptress of seasons, I bow to your altars of green. Haunting composer, I sing with your choirs of wind, wave, and field. Eternal Goddess, I thank you for your sustenance and protection."

6. Remain standing or sit to meditate for a few minutes. Allow the energy of the wilderness to enter your body, filling you with vitality as you breathe in the healing scents of the forest.

7. Before concluding the ceremony, if you are so inclined, you may wish to make or renew a commitment to honoring the earth in whatever way you can.

*Deep places in the wilderness
and the feminine spirit
are represented by the fiercely beautiful
and inviolate spirit of Artemis*

# Zaghareet

This ancient ululation made by women in Middle Eastern and African countries is a bird-like trill that expresses celebration, joy, mourning, or farewell. It is also heard in South Asia and Mexico, and similar calls can be found among Tribal Nations and Gypsies. Zaghareet is also used during birth and death ceremonies as well as rites of healing and exorcism. It is often used to invoke good spirits, express joy or sorrow, bid farewell to a loved one's soul at its time of passing, or to welcome someone home from a long journey. Belly dancers often incorporate zaghareet into their routines. Ululation in ancient times accompanied rituals, and as today, was primarily expressed by women. When performed correctly, its intense vibration of sound can be felt in one's very bones; this reverberation can stimulate psychic awareness by fortifying the pineal and pituitary glands which play in an important physiological role in mystical experience.

# *Rite of Creative Fires*

This ceremony honors and celebrates women's creative fire and enlightenment. It is a beautiful rite to use when you need to stand in your power, bless your sexuality, or awaken creativity.

### *What You Will Need:*

**\*one red candle**

**\*1 stick of incense and incense holder**

**\*cosmetic or culinary rosewater**

1.  Before you begin, anoint your forehead, heart, navel, and pubic bone with rosewater, honoring each point on your body with intention.

2.  Light your red candle and stand with your feet together with arms raised at breast level, palms facing outward. Assuming this ancient women's prayer pose invokes the Goddess within (see page 33.)

3.  In this Priestess prayer pose, open yourself to the Divine Mother saying aloud or silently, "In the name of the Goddess, I am Shakti, animating creative force of the universe. Divine Mother, I come home to you."

◆

4.  When you feel energy rise within you, place both hands over your navel. Invoke your Birthing Energy by visualizing a blue flame beneath your hands. See your navel as the center of the world, the birthing place of all things, a womb from which the Goddess in you is reborn.

5.  Imagine this flame warming your entire body and extending in height until it travels like a serpent upward toward your head. When this light reaches your forehead, place both hands over your closed eyes and say, "From this moment on, I burn all that is not needed in my life." After this spoken affirmation, hold the stick of incense and visualize any unwanted emotion, obstacle, or fear that you wish to discard from your consciousness, anything that you feel is keeping you stuck.

6.  Light the incense and place it in its holder. See what you wish to burn from your life rising and dissolving with the sweet smoke.

7.  When you feel you are cleared from all psychic hindrances, announce, "I am co-creator with the Goddess, a living channel of the Creative Force."

8.  Breathe deeply and raise your hands saying, "Great Mother, bless my hands so they may do your work. Bless my voice so I may speak your truth. Bless my

heart so I may be inspired to stand in my power, not to have power *over* but to kindle the dark."

9. Conclude the ceremony by folding your hands over your heart and saying, "It is done."

## Breath of the Moon Rite

### What You Will Need

**\*a white shawl, scarf, cape, or robe**

**\*1 stick of African violet, frankincense or myrrh incense**

**\*a cigarette lighter or matches to light the incense**

# *Goddess Consciousness*

1. On the first or second night of the full moon, choose a place indoors, and if possible, where you can see the moon; if not, light a white candle. You can also choose a place outside where you will be safe but have the privacy to commune with the moon's light. If the sky is cloudy or the weather calls for rain, the rite is still powerful and can be done inside.

2. Wrap yourself in your chosen article of white and step into your sacred space. Light your incense; if you are outside, place the incense stick into the ground where there are no dry leaves.

3. Inhale deeply and look at the moon if she is visible to you; if not, close your eyes and imagine her light flooding the landscape and illuminating the clouds.

4. As you inhale, stand with your arms raised in a V and your feet hip-width apart. This traditional Goddess pose honors the Sacred Feminine and prepares you for spiritual communion.

5. As you stand in this pose, breathe in and envision a gossamer stream of moonlight entering your nostrils, filling your head, your brain, spilling down your brain stem and into your spinal cord.

6. Relax your arms and let them rest by your side as you

continue to breathe even deeper and slower, imagining the silver river of moonlight illuminating each vertebra in your spine, lighting up all the nerves that extend from your spinal cord outward to your organs.

7. See the cells of your body ignite with platinum energy as the moonlight passes through into your arms and downward into your hands, into your hips and downward into your legs, pouring out of your feet and onto the ground like silver water. Breathe in the beauty and the healing peace of the moon's spiritual energy. See your body aglow in shades of sapphire, violet, and silver, vibrating with joy and serenity.

8. Aloud or silently say, "I am whole in the name of the Goddess and every part of my being is blessed and renewed. I am pure and filled with peace."

9. Remain in your sacred spot until the incense is burned down or crush out the stick before leaving and say, "It is done. Blessed Be."

# The Triple Goddess

*Many goddesses of antiquity were believed to have three-fold natures; in our modern age, the Goddess is often seen as and represented by the phases of the moon—waxing, full, and waning. When she is personified, She can be referred to as the Maiden (waxing moon), the Mother (full moon), and the Crone (waning and dark moon,) and springing from the work of Robert Graves, called The Triple Goddess. The Triple Goddess also refers to the phases of a woman's life but is considered to simultaneously exist within her as well. Depending upon tradition, the Crone aspect officially awakens within a woman with the appearance of gray hair (if it's not prematurely gray) or upon the onset of menopause (one year without a menstrual period). Unlike conventional collective thoughts of modern culture, the Crone or Wise Woman in Goddess spirituality receives significant reverence. Many women welcome their Wise Woman years by holding special ceremonies that celebrate coming into full spiritual power.*

*...the Crone aspect of the Goddess*
*symbolized by the waning moon,*
*eclipses, and the cycle of death and rebirth*

5

*Earth Psalms:*
*Goddess Prayers, Chant,*
*and Sacred Sound*

In our modern times, most of us associate prayer with religion and petitions to Deity in times of need. In essence, prayer in the truest sense and purest form is communion with our Higher Power. There is no right or wrong way to pray, and only a forthright heart is required for the full effect. Reverence, quietude, and grace are beautiful offerings we can bring into prayer. Prayer as communion can help us find the stillpoint in the chaotic whirlwind of our lives and bring clarity where there is uncertainty. The following Goddess prayers can bring you more in touch with the Compassionate Mother and the sacredness of the earth.

You may wish to place a beautiful scarf or shawl over your head or shoulders as you pray. This simple act can have a profound effect on your ability to shut out the rest of the world and honor your body with beautiful colors, textures, and patterns. Storing a prayer shawl in a box with incense adds a beautiful touch of fragrance

### *Prayer to the Earth Mother*

*We call on you, Ancient One of the Green,*
*Divine Mother of leaf and dale,*
*Heart of the mountains*
*And nectar of the blushing grape...*
*We call on you, Ancient One of the Wilds,*
*Goddess of moss and fern*
*And the wet hollow*
*Where the waters pool in the shadow...*
*We honor you, Queen of Rejuvenation*
*And seasons of the sacred wheel.*
*Touch us with your wild soul*
*And help us to remember ours.*
*Enfold us in your robes of leaf and light-*
*Chartreuse, emerald, olive, and sage,*

Teal, verdigris, and robin's egg;
We drink each mood of green
Until we, too, pulse with Life in Gaia's hand.

...

## One of Ten-Thousand Names

Goddess, speak to me
In the voice of the wind
So I may learn a different song.

Goddess, gaze at me
Through the eyes of the moon,
And remind me of my own beauty.

Goddess, touch me
With hands of twilight rain
Until I am healed.

Goddess, find me
On the battlefield of broken dreams
And hold me in Your arms of peace.

...

## Ode to Persephone, Goddess of Spring

Your smile is carved from sunlight
As you happen to pass through my darkness.
You are a butterfly streaming light,
Yet you brave my heart's net of shadows.

# Goddess Consciousness

Bright Goddess, before you depart on the wind,
Teach me about transience;
Speak of wings;
Remind me
I, too, am a child of the cocoon.

...

## Summer's Birth

Leaf, blade and blossom
Bearing no scars of snow
Earth giving birth
To green
O, Mother Eternal
You offer your breasts of rain
Tree, flower, and grain
Bearing no scars of snow,
Mother Earth giving birth
To Herself

...

## Samhain Prayer
## (Celtic New Year October 31)

Time of the dark moon and final harvest,
I bring my full self to this sacred place.
As the ghost of summer dances by us,
I look toward the wisdom of shorter days
And the wild darkness
That has much to teach.

Today, I name my fear and release it

# Goddess Consciousness

To you, Mother of the Heavens.
Here, in Your presence,
I take back my power.

On this night, Autumn awakens
In a whisper of embers;
Soon the hills will catch fire and burn
In tongues speaking topaz and cinnabar.
Goddess of gold wind and days winding
Down to cold stillness,
Hear my prayer
As I stand in the threshold of what the ancients
Called the Dark Time.
In the name of all that is sacred,
It is done. Blessed Be.

...

## Winter Faith

Alone, I take the old road.
The path is covered; leaves turn in their sleep.
December is an old woman,
And she passes me with gray eyes.

Where do they go, the hours we hold in vain?
Where do we go,
The selves that dissolve in dark water?

Winter's heart is an old woman,
And she whispers in the dusk.

The snows cover all of us

*And the fires within, the fires no one knows.*
*The forest takes us in*
*Without tears or regret.*
*New dreams will take root from the old;*
*Faith is an old woman, and she knows the way.*

...

### Prayer for Times of Loss

*I bury tired dreams*
*As the sun shuts its eyes*
*Over the mountain's breast.*
*Though, sun, you were brief*
*And dreams, you were few,*
*You will forget me in your timeless rest,*
*But I will remember you.*
*Night folds Her sapphire arms*
*Across the day;*
*I sit beneath the stars,*
*Wise, brokenhearted but free.*
*Dreams, I watch you dance away.*
*O, sweet Goddess, comfort me. Comfort me.*

...

# Mantra and Goddess Chants

**Divine Harmony, Music of the Earth, and Soul Sounds**

# ☽ *Goddess Consciousness* ★

Many religious creation stories around the globe share a common thread: God uttered a word and all of life was sparked into being from holy sound and breath. Hindus in India revere the Goddess of the spoken word named *Voc*. The words *vocal, voice*, and *invoke* all come from this Queen of all deities who is attributed to speaking Om and igniting the creative spark that birthed worlds into being.

The great mathematician and mystic Pythagoras speak of *musica universalis* or Music of the Spheres in which the heavenly bodies, possessing vibrational energy, emit their own unique hum which is beyond the human ear. All of life and the quality of it is upheld by this inaudible harmony of the cosmos.

Our beautiful planet Earth sings in many languages—from the wolf's haunting plainchant to the purr of the beloved house cat; from the wind blowing through a weak tree limb to the murmur of flowing water, nature brings us healing music if we have ears to listen. It is believed that listening to natural sounds such as breaking surf, running waters, peaceful winds, songbirds, or rain for two hours a day strengthens the immune system and quells the autonomic response of fight or flight. Earth's magnificent vocal expression is embodied in the enigmatic desert phenomenon coined "singing sands." Dunes of deserts and beaches around the world emit mysterious drones when the wind or human movement shifts tiny grains of silica-rich sand against one another. It is a wonder not yet fully understood, but once heard, it is never forgotten.

Nomadic tribes throughout the ages who have spent countless nights beneath starlit deserts have been witness to one of Earth's most haunting soul-sounds.

Tuning into the inaudible Symphony of Being means tuning out the noise of humanity—the noise of everyday life and the noise of our own thoughts. One of the most powerful ways to do this is to embrace mantra, chant, or toning. As Pythagoras and Plato, mystics throughout the ages have referred to the harmony of existence as well as soul sounds. Each of us possesses frequency, and within the inner planes of being, this frequency manifests as the song of each individual soul. Individuals exquisitely tuned can hear the music of all life, including that of humans, animals, plants, oceans, colors, even sunlight filtering through the trees. When we intentionally use the power of sound and our own voice, we can manifest the highest good in our lives, raise our vibrational frequency at the cellular and atomic level, spark deep healing, and commune with the Infinite. In essence—sound, breath, and harmony create, sustain, and honor life—the divine Creative Force.

## Mantra and Chant

Mantra—a sacred syllable or word, contrary to common assumption, is intended to be spoken silently. The word *mantra* literally means thought form. Mantras are seen as transmitters of power. In Hinduism, mantras are passed from guru to disciple and are usually highly secret. The sacred word is seen as a spiritual key that unlocks the door to superconsciousness and has the power to manifest the unseen and intangible. Ultimately, mantras are believed to be the manifested energy of the Supreme Being. Many times mantras are used by midwives during the birth of a child. Some mantras must be repeated a thousand times or more before their powers can be activated.

A *chant*, on the other hand, is an intoned sacred word or phrase. A chant can create vibration that stimulates higher consciousness and strengthens an individual's magnetic field. Chanting for a few minutes in the morning can set the day on a positive note, while a mantra before sleep can help you to connect to your Goddess self during the dream state.

Affirmation, a close cousin to mantra and chant, is conscious positive thinking. Affirmation can change negative subconscious patterns over a period of time. It can be combined with chant and mantra for maximum benefit. This positive self-talk can be applied to issues of self-esteem and body image, habits you wish to break, and connecting with the Goddess within.

The following sacred words/phrases can be used as chants or mantras. For best results, reserve at least ten minutes a day to sacred sound. You can recite mantras silently in your own thoughts on the way to work or as you do the dishes. You may wish to sit comfortably in a sunny spot and take a few moments to chant aloud and meditate. Sun meditations can be deep and powerful due to the spiritual energy and life force of sunlight. Chanting in the shower can also be a wonderful way to begin or end the day. There are countless mantras and chants, most ancient and used with reverence. Here are a few that you may wish to use, some of which are dedicated to the Sacred Feminine and Shakti energy.

## Om Mani Padme Hum
### (pronounced **om-mah-pahd-may-hoom**)

This chant is sacred to the Goddess in her aspect of Kuan Yin, Chinese Goddess of mercy, women, and children. Many use this chant to invoke protection, healing, and help even in desperate situations. Translated as *jewel in the lotus*, it is also The Holy Phrase of Tantrism and symbolizes the union of feminine birth-energy and fiery masculine vitality that sparks new life into being.

## Ma
### (pronounced **Maaah**)

Ma is the universal syllable meaning *mother*. It can be chanted, holding the tone as long as possible. While doing so, open your mouth as if singing "laaaaa" and allow your heart and throat chakras to blossom and expand. Breathe into the chant and allow this holy sound to envelop your energy field. Use it to connect to the Goddess, the ancient lineage of mothers and grandmothers, your own inner

Goddess, or when you need to be nurtured and protected. It is a wonderful and beautifully simple chant to use during lunar rites.

## *Namo Arihantanam*
### (pronounced **nahm-o-ahree-hahn-tah-nahm**)

This Jain chant is a supreme sound vibration and can be used for healing. Jain master Acharya Sushil Kumar stated that it is a pain killer equal to any analgesic drug. When Kumar was just a boy, he used the chant to heal a girl stung by a very poisonous black scorpion. A blue line extended from the girl's foot to her thigh, and it was obvious that the girl was in great danger. Kumar applied the chant, and right before his eyes, the poison retreated down to the girl's ankle. The following morning, Kumar applied the chant again, and the poison left the girl's body completely. The profound effects of sacred sound worked despite the fact that Kumar knew very little about spiritual healing or vibrational science at the time. The incident, coupled with many years of study with his spiritual teacher led Kumar to a lifetime commitment to the power of sound and syllable.

## *Om*
### (pronounced **awh-oom**, emphasis on 'm')

This familiar Hindu and Tibetan chant is considered to be the sound of the universe and to hold the spark of creation. When chanted, Om possesses 432 Hz, the frequency found most often throughout the natural world. All planes of consciousness and energies are within the Om. Its syllables, when broken down are: "awh"= the energy of creation; "ooh"= preservation; "mmm"= destruction. When combined, these sacred sounds stimulate the premier spiritual center in the body known as the crown chakra. When this charka is awakened, enlightenment and God/dess consciousness can result.

### Hu
### (pronounced **hoo**)

This Sufi word and chant is an ancient name for the divine energy of the universe, particularly in its masculine form as the Heavenly Father and translates as "he." In other traditions, Hu is the cosmic sound of the spheres. Hu is a wonderful chant to use and alternate with Ma, creating a balance of yin/yang, feminine/masculine.

### Om Dum Durgayei Namaha
### (pronounced **ome-doom-door-ga-yay-nar-mar-har**)

This mantra invokes the Great Goddess known to Hindus as Durga. It resonates with the Mother Goddess and is used for protection for yourself or others.

### Om Bhoginyei Namaha
### (pronounced ome-bow-gin-yay-nar-mar-har)

This is wonderful chant/mantra to dispel negative, melancholy, or depressed thoughts and invokes Shakti within the body by rousing kundalini energy at the base of the spine.

### Amen
### (pronounced **ah-men**)

This sacred word is the most recognized as the conclusion of Christian prayers. In Hebrew tradition, the word means *let it be*. In ancient Egyptian religion, it corresponded to the god Amen-Ra. Amen the word and the chant is a balance of female and male energies and represents the Father/Mother principle.

### Om Shrim Maha Lakshmiyei Swaha
### (pronounced **ome-shreem-mar-har-luck-shmee-yay-swar-har**)

This mantra is sacred to the beautiful Hindu and Jain goddess Lakshmi, the deity of good fortune, wealth, and abundance in all forms. It is believed to bring new opportunities and good luck.

## Toning

In her groundbreaking book, *Toning: The Creative Power of the Voice*, author Laurel Elizabeth Keyes speaks of the profound effects of sounds and vibration. Among its many cases of validity, toning has been associated with documented cases of tumor shrinkage and cancer remission. The principle of toning involves the chanting of vowel sounds that resonate with and correspond to specific areas of the physical body.

The following tones can foster stress reduction, increase energy, release emotional blockages in the energy field and the body's tissues, and most of all, balance both hemispheres of the brain. Incorporating toning into your spiritual practice can be a beautiful tool for wellbeing.

### *Tone: A* (as in *say*, *sat*, and *saw*)

The **long "A" sound** corresponds to the heart, chest, lungs, and circulatory system. On a spiritual and emotional level, this tone stimulates balance and love. Use the long "A" tone to open the heart chakra, resolve anger, and access soul memories.

The **short "A" sound** corresponds to the throat and mouth. Spiritually, it encourages clairaudience and creativity by stimulating the throat chakra.

The **"Aw" sound** relates to the stomach, intestines, and functions of the left side of the brain. Spiritually, it fosters inspiration and multisensory psychic ability by stimulating the solar plexus chakra (the source of that "gut instinct" and intuition).

### *Tone: I* (as in *kite* and *it*)

The *long "I" sound* stimulates brain function and balances both hemispheres. It also activates the brain stem which is considered a spiritual portal.

The *short "I" sound*, like the short "A" sound, affects the throat, throat chakra, speech, and creativity associated with the human voice.

### *Tone: E* (as in *eat* and *get*)

The *long "E" sound* corresponds to the pituitary, pineal, and other glands of the body. These glands play an important role in spiritual and psychic development, and enlightenment. The long "E" sound stimulates the crown and brow chakras and is the sound of cosmic consciousness.

The *short "E" sound* relates to the throat chakra (like the short "A" and short "I" sounds) and encourages clairaudience.

### *Tone: O* (as in *low* and *knot*)

The *long "O" sound* directly affects the navel area, reproduction, and the muscular system as a whole. Energetically, it awakens the belly chakra and encourages higher emotions, inspiration, and physical energy.

The *short "O" sound*, like the short "A", affects the left side of the brain, stomach, intestines, and the process of digestion. Energetically, it relates to the solar plexus chakra and stimulates "gut feelings", awareness, personal power, and creative ideas.

## *Tone: U* (as in *muse* and *nut*)

The **long "U" sound** corresponds to the genitals, circulation, and lower parts of the body in general. It is also the spiritual sound of the kundalini and the essence of spiritual life force.

The **short "U" sound**, like the short "E", "A", and "I" sounds, relates to the throat, speech, expression, and psychic ability.

6

# Whispers of the Goddess: Second Sight & Creative Divination

Beneath a tree sacred to the goddess Diana, thirteen-year-old Joan of Arc heard spirit voices for the first time. The young mystic continued to hear the voices of saints for the remainder of her brief life. Sometimes the other-worldly messages were accompanied by light, and other times they woke her from sleep, barely comprehensible. The purpose of these voices would later change the course of history. But being a willful woman and mystic in the fifteenth century—despite political victory—would only

129

prove to be disastrous.

It is difficult to believe that women were burned alive for having visions and wearing men's clothes when we don a favorite pair of jeans or see yet another psychic advisor advertised. Despite centuries of persecution, psychic ability is now accepted to the point of exploitation. However, the reality of both extremes does not define the existence and purpose of second sight.

Psychic ability *is* a sixth sense, a sense every human being and many animals are born with but is rarely used. Like any other sense, second sight can be sharper in one individual than in another. For this reason alone, ability of this nature, no matter how impressive, does not automatically make an individual spiritual. If the psychic sense was like the sense of smell, anyone with an acute nose would be qualified to be a spiritual advisor. Because psychic ability is so often misunderstood, over-glorified, and misused, those who develop the sixth sense and use it with intention often find themselves caught in a battle between keeping it sacred and offering it to others who can benefit by it. Being a mystic in our modern times does not invite torture or death, but it does invite conflict.

As women, we hold the jewel in our spiritual DNA. Second sight is often passed from one generation to another. My maternal great grandmother was a very spiritual woman with psychic abilities she rarely spoke of. My mother followed in her footsteps, and second sight saved her life more than once, led to a diagnosis of an unidentified illness, and came in handy in everyday living. Her second sight became apparent after a shamanic period of illness when she experienced a profound spiritual awakening. From this, she also acquired the ability to travel in the soul body and create deeply inspired music and poetry. On the mundane level, she would walk over to the phone before it rang and rest her hand on the receiver knowing who would be on the line before she answered it. The practicality of her second sight helped her to find her diamond ring after it flew off her hand into a two-foot-deep snowfall. Not knowing where it landed and not knowing where to even begin searching, my mother closed her eyes, opened her spiritual eye, and followed where the mental image drew her. She walked about twelve feet and found a miniscule hole in the snow, reached down into the white, and picked up her treasured ring.

Ancient people easily walked between worlds due to their constant interaction and immersion in nature. As humankind progressed, the sixth sense became less and less developed. Most children come into the world with psychic awareness until they grow older and become distracted by the fullness of their lives or others make it painfully clear that such abilities are not to be trusted. The third eye closes until an event, trauma, or conscious effort reopens it. Due to mountainous obligation in our adult lives, many of us have little time to dedicate ourselves to spiritual quests. However, purposely prompting psychic sight can help to unlock the door. The Tarot and other oracles can be wonderful tools to open the psychic eye. But sometimes tools can limit our abilities once we expand our awareness. Like training wheels, oracles enable us to break through, yet our true spiritual potential far outreaches the scope they provide. The greatest psychics and mediums in the world rely on their own developed gifts. Oracles are wise teachers, but like all teachers, they can be outgrown as they are meant to be. Biblical prophets as well as more recent seers such as the renowned Edgar Cayce looked to the Source within. Oracles help us find answers like road maps, but if the uncharted path is to be taken, they can only get us so far.

Just as psychic ability is a rarely-used sense, it is also a gift. Sometimes this gift is apparent in a child born with open consciousness, and other times, it is seen in a seeker who has invested many years of effort into its development. Second sight is a jewel waiting to be polished by each of us, but in order to benefit by it, we have to keep it sacred and not compromise its brilliance by confining it to one-dimensional use. Psychic ability and the gift of its full development is a multidimensional, spiritual art form. Its purpose, like ritual and ceremony, is to give the soul an open door into its own unlimited possibility. When we wear this valuable jewel as an egotistic ornament or place it in the hands of those who will abuse its purity, the door is slammed shut and the soul cannot claim its rightful fruits of Goddess Consciousness. With higher purpose in mind, the sixth sense moves beyond entertainment, curiosity, and the thirst for power. Psychic arts are often pursued out of desire for personal power, but true power is gained only after spiritual refinement. When the kingdom within is sought, all else is given. After the soul seeks its origins and finds its self-contained universe, psychic ability and other powers are acquired naturally. In the ancient Mystery schools, magic and the psychic arts were taught to initiates only *after* the spiritual foundation was given. Spiritual teachings and psychic arts were rarely separated, and the knowledge itself was so sacred that some Mystery schools went to the extremes of punishing those who mishandled or squandered the information.

In the past, shamanic training—now available in watered-down courses—was not a six month or two year undertaking, but rather, a vocation that involved many years of arduous study of the mystical arts with an elder, either living or in the spirit world. Only the strongest in body and spirit survived shamanic initiation. Though individuals who expressed earnest desire to become shamans were accepted for training, those who were "called" by the spirits had the gift of open consciousness and were considered more powerful. Refinement of spirit, tenacity of character, and worthiness of power molded the student like gold in the harsh reality of the fire. After all, the physical health and spiritual consciousness of the entire tribal community were dependent upon the Medicine Man or Woman.

As modern women, we do not have the opportunity to refine our spirits in such concentrated intensity, but many of us are still called. Some of us use spiritual abilities to promote healing, inspire, teach, or guide. We may not wander in the wilderness on the verge of death from starvation or exposure to the elements searching for visions, but our karmic experience gives us the opportunity to turn pain into gold, a spiritual alchemy that transforms the neophyte into a shaman in her own right and in her own environment. Suffering is not necessary to develop Goddess Consciousness, but it often is a bridge between the complacent unawakened self and the conscious realized Self. Not all women are shamans, but all women possess inherent second sight and the potential of spiritual development.

When psychic ability is approached intellectually, the desire or need for evidence often arises. Time, money, and effort are spent every day by skeptics and believers alike, all trying to disprove or prove psychic reality. The truth is that no one can accomplish either, yet individuals who have parted the veil between worlds do not need proof in the conventional sense. Experience itself is validation, and it is the only thing we need once we penetrate one reality to access another. There is no mystery involved if we realize that *reality is consciousness and consciousness is reality.* Consciousness is Spirit. Once Spirit breaks through the concrete wall of the lower limited self, physical reality is seen for what it really is—merely *one* facet of the multidimensional prism of existence.

# Hildegard von Bingen

German abbess, visionary, author, poet, playwright, composer, artist, and herbalist Hildegard von Bingen stands out among accomplished individuals of the medieval world. In a time when women were considered soulless, Hildegard corresponded with the political brass of the day and even advised members of the clergy including the Pope. Unlike many of her contemporaries, she focused on the Sacred Feminine within Christianity, composing much of her angelic music in honor of the Blessed Mother and penning accounts of her visions which often included a cosmic feminine being birthing peoples and prophets of the world. Her philosophy of health addressed the elements Earth, Air, Fire, and Water within human constitution and emphasized the *veriditas* or "greening power" of God which permeated all life, especially through the restorative forces of plants and the natural world. Hildegard, also known as the Sybil of the Rhine, suffered from periods of intense physical distress and exhaustion, most likely from migraine headaches which accompanied her most powerful visions. Today, recording artists have preserved her musical legacy, and her Latin plainchant composed for women's voices reaches across the centuries with its exquisite, other-worldly peace. Her art and writings are also available in print and speak to us today as profoundly as they did in the 12th century.

When we are touched by the Infinite, we receive infinite vision. This is the true mystic's way of life. Study, practice, and applications are companions on the path, but not the path itself. Ancient Delphic priestesses chewed laurel leaves and inhaled vapors to induce expanded consciousness, but these trance mediums were first filled with divine inspiration from the God. Ancient Irish mystics observed cloud formation and the flights of birds to divine the future, but they were first awakened spiritually. Tribal shamans traveled between worlds, healed the sick, and controlled weather with the power of thought only after the Great Spirit called them. Without love for Deity, we are only going through the motions, and our powers are hollow imitation compared to the good that can be accomplished when spiritual development accompanies psychic ability.

To open your second sight or add some freshness to an old approach, the following oracles can be fun, personal, and creative. Before beginning, here are a few suggestions as well as ways to protect yourself energetically. Protection exercises help link our consciousness to higher realms, lessening the risk of receiving answers from less desired sources. The spirit world, like the physical world, has beings with good intentions and beings with negative intentions. Opening psychically also opens the door to both influences. Time and experience teaches us how to handle all situations and how to discern between positive and negative energies, but this subject could be a separate book. For now, here are some guidelines to ensure positive and beautiful experiences before you use the oracles found later in this chapter.

## Tips and Suggestions

It is not advisable to do psychic work when you are under the influence of alcohol or recreational drugs, for it can weaken the aura's protective shield. Shamans throughout time have included ceremonial intoxicants in their training to part the veil between worlds. However, the primary foundation of the shaman's spiritual training is the ability to break through without the use of hallucinogens. When peyote or other consciousness expanders are used by shamans, it is in a sacred environment.

What must be considered here is the thorough training a shaman undergoes. Shamans begin training in early childhood and learn how to access inborn spiritual powers through a number of ways. When hallucinogens are used, the knowledge of their effects and the intricacies of their volatile nature are part of the teachings of an elder or spirit teacher. No matter how dedicated we are to our spiritual training and evolvement, our lives differ from that of the shaman's because most of us deal with the outside world constantly. This means we are always surrounded by the negativities of society and we are forever in process of shielding the purity of our spiritual quests from these influences. The shaman, on the other hand is continually surrounded by like-minded people who encourage, support, revere, and nurture his/her vocation and special abilities. Over a period of challenging years, the shaman learns his trade, so to speak, and is prepared to use hallucinogens as a sacred practice. Since we work and raise families in our modern world, I believe very few of us can live a sheltered shaman's life, no matter how we think we are succeeding. We may try recreational drugs in a very inspired moment and have a beautiful and shimmering mystical experience but, after these first few times, the drugs begin to puncture that taut psychic resistance of the aura until it becomes so slack that lower vibrational forces flow into our space with unchallenged ease. Our drug use, no matter how ceremonial, does not contain the preparation, positive environment, and spiritual power of the shaman's. Lastly, when we use drugs to aid our spiritual or psychic work, we become accustomed to relying on substances and not our own inborn potential. We are independent women, and being independent Priestesses can be just as vital to our wellbeing.

Playing beautiful music, sound healing recordings, or nature CDs can enhance your psychic work or prepare the space where you will be divining. Gregorian chant, Tibetan bells, ceremonial music, or soothing classical recordings are all good choices. Hildegard von Bingen's ethereal vocal music, preserved by today's musicians, channels the Sacred Feminine and female voices dominate her chants. Many of her compositions are devoted to the Blessed Mother.

Prior to doing psychic work, consider using a protection

technique provided here or one of your own. Attempt psychic work and the use of oracles at an appropriate time. If your child is running around the room, the dog is barking, or you have an appointment in an hour, do not expect great results or profound answers. Choose a quiet time when you are not compelled to adhere to a schedule.

Lastly, oracles of any kind can be reliable, provided we are attuned, and our second sight is stimulated. For the best results, practice and trust that even when we do not receive answers, we are answered. Sometimes no answer is telling us that we have to see the situation at hand to the end. Sometimes the good spirits test our ability to have blind faith. This is difficult, but once accomplished it can bring us to resolution and open consciousness. Once we learn to let go, we can fly.

**Protection Techniques and Exercises**

## Goddess Protection

Light a candle and assume the ancient women's prayer pose (page 33) and address the Cosmic Mother saying, "Divine Mother, Creatress, Protectress, please bless my work and the answers I receive in Your name." Create a circle with your arms by touching the fingertips of both hands over your head with your elbows bent. Stand strong and erect, envisioning the moon within the circle of your arms. Conclude the prayer by saying, "Only spirits of light are permitted here. No darkness can enter. This is Goddess space." Proceed with your psychic work.

## Light Protection

Light a candle and hold both hands at a comfortable distance in front of the flames, palms facing outward. Begin moving your hands in circles in opposite directions (left hand circling to the left, right hand circling to the right.) Feel the energy in your fingertips and the palms of your hands; imagine light radiating outward as you increase the speed of your circles. Say aloud or silently, "Only light can enter here. All inner negativity is cleared; all outer negativity cannot gain access. This is sacred space, and my work is sacred. The light is my Source." Raise your arms as if spreading wings, adding, "I seek light. I receive light. I am light." Imagine a prismatic beam raining down upon you and becoming silver-white as it washes over you. Imagine soaking up the protective energy like a plant takes in rain through the soil. Proceed with your psychic work.

## Sound Protection

Choose a drum, rattle, tambourine, bell, or rain stick and begin sounding your instrument in a slow rhythm. Close your eyes and allow your consciousness to become part of the sound. When you feel at one with the instrument, invoke protection by saying, "Darkness cannot live where there is music. Music is the heartbeat of the Mother. My hands and my rhythm call forth only spirits of light. I am protected. It is done." Increase your rhythm until you cannot go any faster and then stop to allow the energy to seep into the silence and your sacred space. Proceed with your psychic work.

## Oracles

...

# *Wisdom of the Stones Oracle*

### *what you will need*

**\*20 small stones (found in nature or craft stores) or 20 pieces of glass, wood, or plastic with a flat surface suitable to write on with a permanent marker)**

**\*2 cloth or leather drawstring bags, pouches, or boxes (found at craft stores)**

**\*1 or 2 metallic markers (gold, silver, or both) or black markers that will write on glass or plastic (found in craft stores)**

### *How to make your oracle*

1.  Obtain 20 small stones; real stones are preferred for their Earth energies, but if you cannot find them, you can also use any craft material (glass, wood, plastic) with a surface suitable for writing with a marker or metallic paint marker. If you are an artist, consider using a brush and acrylics.

2.  Divide the stones into two sets of ten, reserving one half for your Question stones and the other for your

Wisdom stones.

3. With pen or brush, apply the following symbols, one
   per **Question stone**:

♡ your emotional life (romance, loved ones, or family)

⌂ your physical security (physical environment)

$ your finances

W your work/professional life

● your past

☀ your future

☆ your spiritual life

◊ your sexuality

⚥ your health

? open question- "what do I need to know at this time?"

**SYMBOLS FOR QUESTION STONES**

4. Take pen or brush and apply the following symbols, one per **Wisdom stone**:

| | |
|---|---|
| **!** | caution, have restraint, or think twice |
| ⬦ | something needs to be cleansed and healed, cry, or let it go |
| ▽ | yield, pause, or give someone or something the benefit of the doubt |
| (☥) | protect yourself or you must come first now |
| (♥) | keep it to yourself, keep it sacred, keep it confidential, or protect what is important |
| (⏱) | in time or give it time |
| N | be in the moment, now, or it is time |
| H | someone needs your help or help yourself |
| ☺ | you made the right decision, joy is on the way, or all will be well |
| ⊘ | wrong direction, find another way, or trust the obstacles that appear |

**SYMBOLS FOR WISDOM STONES**

5. Select two large pouches, boxes, or bags in which to store your oracle stones. Be sure to keep the **Question** and **Wisdom** stones separate.

### *How to use your oracle*

1. Choose a **Question** stone that best represents your area of concern. Hold the stone in your hand. Meditate and think about the need, desire, or problem. Ask the spirits to give you an answer that will help you with the question at hand.

2. Take your bag or pouch of **Wisdom** stones and shake them gently. If you keep your stones in a box, move and rearrange them with your fingers without looking at them. Ask your question once again, and then close your eyes. Select one stone from the Wisdom batch. Sometimes the answer requires a little contemplation before it is understood. What might seem inappropriate may make sense a few days or weeks later. Trust the wisdom of the stones and your Goddess Self to guide you to a particular answer.

# *Fire Art Divination*

Finding answers and faces in fire art can be a fun and easy project. Imprinting images onto paper with the smoke of a lit candle can produce intricate patterns and you can look at for days and see something you might not have before. *Note: Due to the smoke that can accumulate in a small space you may wish to use this oracle out of doors or by an open window. Use with caution if you have allergies or asthma.

### *What you will need*

**\*heavy art paper with texture such as watercolor paper preferably 5x7 or letter size (8.5 x 11.5)**

**\*1 taper candle**

**\*newspaper or old cloth to catch any wax that may fall**

### What to do

1. Light your candle.

2. Meditate or say a prayer as you hold a piece of paper in your hands. If you want a question answered, think of your question, repeating it aloud or silently. If you'd like to see spirit faces in your fire art, ask your spirit helpers or the Fire beings themselves to imprint their energy onto the paper.

3. When you are ready, hold the paper in one hand and the lit candle in the other hand. Make sure you hold the candle on an angle as you pass the surface of the paper over and into the candle flame with quick movements. Vary the distance between flame and

paper, anywhere from 1/4 inch away to actually touching the flame for a second or two. If your paper catches fire, blow it out quickly. Scorched paper adds a nice touch to the finished product and can be happy accidents or deliberate.

4. Continue to move the paper over the flame in all directions as well as circular motions. Try to remain in a meditative state and try not to peek at the smoke patterns.

5. Inspect your results only when your paper is full of smoke art but not covered completely; make sure you have plenty of bare spots between the smoke stains and burns or your answers and designs will not be noticeable. *Do not touch the smoke patterns on the surface of the paper or they will be disturbed, altered, or lightened. If you'd like to keep your fire art, place it in a large manila envelope or a picture frame under glass where it will be protected. Framed fire art is a lovely addition to any altar, especially a Fire Altar.

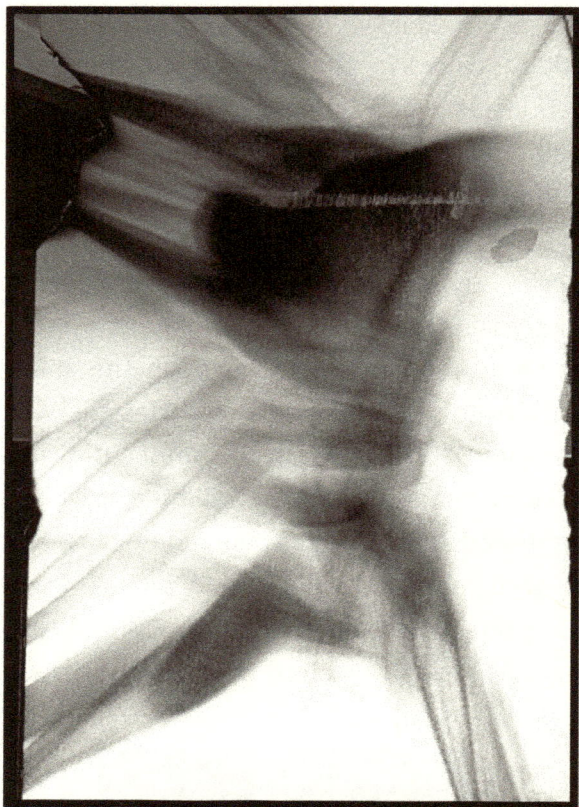

**Fire art divination**

# Water Gazing and Wax Oracle

Dripping hot wax from a candle into cold water can produce amazing tiny "sculptures" that can hold messages or answers to our questions. *Note: This oracle is best used in a dark or dimly-lit room.

### What you will need:

**\*dark color glass bowl filled with cold water**

**\*2 taper candles**

### What to do

1. Light your candles and place your bowl on a table or desk.

2. Sit down, breathe deeply, and find peace within yourself.

3. Hold both sides of the bowl and look into its depths. Notice reflections in the water—the candle flame and your own face.

4. Now gently squint, as if the sun is in your eyes but try to relax your facial muscles at the same time. *This*

*blurred focus is the "between vision" that dulls physical sight so the second sight can be dominant.*

5. Allow yourself to go into a light trance by looking at the fire on the water with *between vision*. Allow yourself to be lulled.

6. Ask your spirit helpers to show you an answer to a question or simply to show themselves. With practice, your consciousness will shift at this point and you will see moving pictures in the water.

7. To add possibilities to your oracle, after you ask a question, take a candle and tilt it over the water and drop hot wax into the cold water. *Be sure to hold the candle in a still, horizontal position in order for a copious amount of melted wax to drip into the bowl.

8. When the wax cools and hardens, remove it from the water gently. Study the wax forms carefully for answers in symbols, faces, and forms.

# *Ink Blot Divination*

Ink blots can be fun artistic projects as well as divination tools. Paper dabbed with paint or ink and then folded can produce amazing effects and provide a lot of wisdom when we need answers most.

### *What you will need:*

**\*any kind of heavy textured paper such as watercolor paper or card stock used for printing—white is best.**

**\*various colored inks or water-based paints, a medium-sized brush or two, and a jar of clean water to rinse your brushes**

151

**\*newspaper to protect table surface**

### *What to do*

1. Place your piece of paper on top of newspaper so your table surface won't be soiled from ink or paint. Say a prayer aloud or silently or ask for assistance from your spirit helpers. If you have a problem, question, or area of concern, place it in their hands and ask them to bless you with a visual answer.

2. Take your brush and dip it into a single color ink or paint and dab the *middle of the paper* with the brush with thick applications of color. Rinse your brush quickly when you are finished with that color.

3. Repeat #2 with another color of choice and then again with another color in rapid succession. You can use up to 4 colors—any more than that will produce a muddy effect.

4. Now again, concentrate on your question or areas of concern as you fold the paper length-wise, pressing down with a quick, firm hand. Make sure you put even pressure all the way across. Do not do this excessively, once is enough. Don't be concerned if some paint or ink slips out from the paper.

5. *Slowly* open the paper and make sure it dries flat. Your will have an intricate ink blot design—so intricate, it

may take you a long time to notice everything in the piece. Many times the answer is very clear and very detailed, as if someone had painted it with deliberate intention (see image on page 143.) Consider framing your ink blot and hanging it in your sacred space or somewhere you will be reminded of your message when you need it. If there is nothing profound in your ink blot, you might simply love how it looks and hang it anyway!

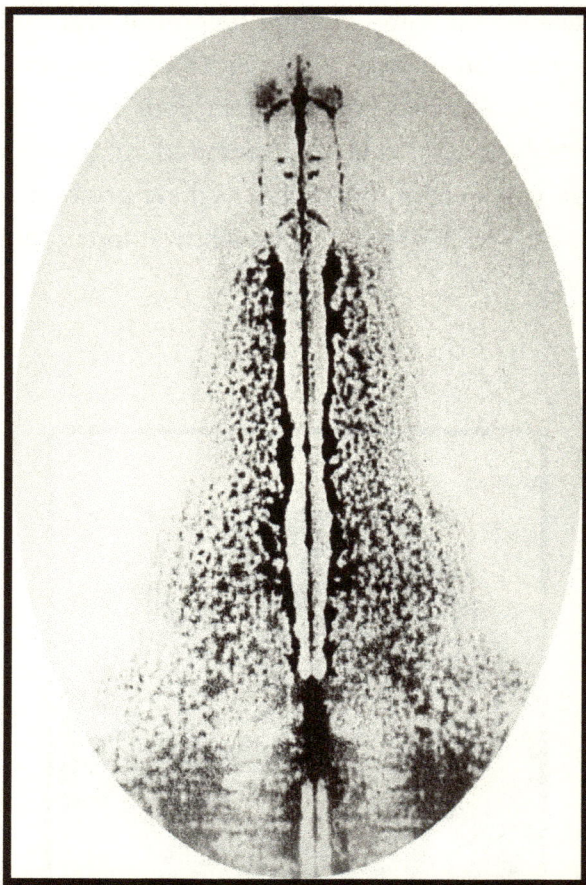

*my mother's ink blot divination*
*after she requested to see her spirit helper*

7

# *Women's Wings:*
# *Dreams and Spirit Journeys*

The *American Heritage* dictionary on my desk defines the word *soul* as "the animating and vital principle often conceived as an immaterial entity that survives death." If we look at this definition through purely intellectual eyes, we are given the impression that the soul is unseen, unheard, and unfelt—therefore, in the category of all fanciful facts that can only be useful to poets and visionaries. Yet even before there was what we could call language, there was a universal belief in the human soul. There is not a single known religion, ancient or modern, that does not take into account this very essence of an individual. For something that cannot be perceived with the five physical senses, it certainly has been an unavoidable object of wonder, religious debate, and hope since time began. As invisible and vital as the air we breathe, the soul, by definition, gives life to the flesh.

Throughout the ancient world, the soul received as much attention, validation, and reverence as the body itself. In our modern world, the soul is often seen as no more than poetic theory, yet those who have experienced enlightenment, trauma, illness, or who have come back from clinical death describe what it is like to be in the soul body, separated from the physical body. Many report the out-of-body experience as a journey to other realms of existence—an afterlife that not only waits beyond our physical world but one that parallels it.

Ancient cultures not only believed in this human soul and its capabilities but also in the souls of animals, plants, trees, elements, and minerals. The ancient Greeks honored the soul of every living being. The spirit of the smallest pebble to the most majestic of mountains was accounted for in daily life as well as in ritual and sacred festivals. The Greeks' timeless mythology is brightly colored with spirits, gods, goddesses, demigods, and fantastic creatures. The physical world and spirit realms were intricately interwoven and never divided.

Ancient Egyptians portrayed the life and activities of the *ba*, or soul, on the walls of their temples and tombs. As part of their spiritual belief system, ancient Egyptians supposed that each woman and man not only had one soul, but seven.

Most ancient cultures' words for the soul were feminine. Many believed that every person, whether male or female, had a feminine essence inherited from the Great Mother Goddess through the physical birth mother.

Though the projected human soul is most often invisible to the physical eye, it is sometimes seen by the living as if it is the actual physical person. The human double or specter of a living person that is seen still lingers in our cultural language in terms such as the German *doppelgängar* ("double walker"), the English/Irish *fetch*, and the Swedish *vardoger*. Within superstitious and occult beliefs, you will soon die if you should see your own double. English poet Percy Bysshe Shelley saw double not long before his tragic drowning at age thirty.

Soul travel is as natural to our spiritual selves as breathing is to our physical selves. Contrary to common belief and fear, it is not a by-product or symptom of mental illness, hallucination, nor is it only reserved for ecstatic saints or very enlightened masters. Death does not have to occur in order to have access to invisible realms of being, those inner planes of existence commonly called astral planes. Soul travelers know that "dying" is a spiritual art that can be learned while living. Projection of the soul, most often associated with death, need not be an inevitable fear; it may instead be cultivated as a sacred practice for spiritual growth. No matter who you are, where you live, how old or young you are, which lifestyle you choose, or which religion you practice, you are already a soul traveler. You share a common experience with all human beings: astral travel during sleep, whether you remember your journeys or not. Those who experience, without trauma, unplanned projection during waking hours most often leave the body during deep meditation, lovemaking (at or near the moment of orgasm), the twilight state just before sleep, or through the use of recreational drugs.

Sleep is a sweet gift, a pause in the dance of life when the body finds solace and the soul steals into other worlds. Each of us, regardless of personal beliefs experiences nocturnal spirit journeys. When the soul leaves the body during sleep, the sojourn is sometimes remembered through a vivid dream, but most of the time, it dissolves into the mists of forgetfulness. Working with our dreams, spiritually preparing for sleep, and using the techniques of conscious regression can bring us knowledge of the soul's activities and fast-forward our progress as mystics and Priestesses.

It is a common belief that the soul is one-dimensional consciousness contained within the physical body. In metaphysical reality, the soul itself is composed of many bodies. Each component of the soul exists and functions on a different plane of being and consciousness. In other words, as our physical selves go about our daily business, our soul bodies go about their business in the invisible realms that parallel the physical dimension. The higher we go on the spiritual ladder, the more we become aware of our other selves. Fully realized individuals are aware of their soul fragments and are not only able to fully comprehend their activities but are also are able to be fully conscious in each soul body simultaneously. This may be very difficult, if not impossible to grasp when trying to get to work on time with three kids and a non-stop merry-go-round of daily obligations. Most of us never reach such a state of awareness, nor is it necessary in order to be spiritually accomplished. However, to be aware of the soul and its possibilities gives us a wilderness within to explore. It also provides us with a conscious link to deceased loved ones, inner teachings, and helps us understand the reality of physical death.

Consciously leaving the body can be learned or comes naturally in certain individuals. Due to limited space, I chose not to discuss this aspect, for it is far too broad of a subject to confine to a single chapter. Rather, I chose to discuss a much more useful avenue almost anyone can apply to her daily routine.

I had my first conscious (waking) out-of-body experience

at age fifteen, and after many years of knowing the joys and pitfalls of this spiritual art, I have come to realize that if one learns to remember his or her nocturnal spirit journeys, the same amount of knowledge can be gained. It also can offer invaluable insight into the nature of consciousness. Part of this knowledge of consciousness is the comprehension of death. Once we consciously know that dying is simply walking through another door, we can live fully. From my own travels, I have learned that the physical world is only a tiny atom within an infinite network of existence; just as the physical body is a small part of the whole, so too the physical world. Dying is a passport to the uncharted territory beyond the tactile plane. In essence, when we leave the body during the dream or waking states, we visit these far territories. At death, we simply relocate.

In the physical world, when someone moves to another city or country, it is easy to lose contact with them. The same thing happens when a loved one passes from this plane to another, but it does not have to be this way. The soul always knows where another soul is; there is constant, unspoken, invisible contact. We only have to remember it. This is where sacred sleep, dreams, and personal regression come in.

The first step on the journey to remembrance is perceiving the soul in a different light. The soul is not a nebulous substance or notion. It is the vital part of our beings that is beyond our most fantastic faculties, including the brain. It is where the heart beats and the blood flows. The body and soul are so close, the two are intertwined. Like actors who "get into character" to bring a role to life, all we have to do is move into the soul's all-encompassing space. We begin by knowing that we are *not* the body; we *are* the soul. We live through the consciousness of our souls when we love deeply, create from inspiration, and follow our callings.

Dreams are a bridge between the soul and other worlds. If we are lucky, soul memories slip through the sieve of subconscious images and we get a glimpse of a spirit journey. Though most times, the true soul memory gets lost in the strange blizzard of our dreams, if we remember them at all. On the following pages, you will find a simple and enjoyable plan to stimulate and retain spiritual dreams, as well as safe personal regression techniques to access deep soul memories. Here are a few suggestions before you get started:

1. Try not to go to bed on sweets, including hot chocolate, sweetened tea, or cereal. Sugar consumption before sleep may lower blood sugar levels which can cause nightmares, insomnia, and poor dream recollection. If you snack before bed, be sure it is rich in protein and low in carbohydrate.

2. Stay hydrated, as water is a conductor of energy.

3. Give yourself at least half an hour at night and in the morning to devote time to the plan. If it means going to bed and waking a bit earlier, it is worth it.

4. If you use an abrasive alarm clock, try to find a quieter one or set it to the radio (classical or soft music). Nothing inhibits soul memories like being jarred awake. For best results until you are proficient, use the plan on your days off.

5.  Keep a pad of paper or journal by your bedside so you can record dreams, memories, visions, or experiences. It is best to keep an active diary so you can study patterns in your psychic experiences.

6. Be sure the room you sleep in is not too warm or too cool. Temperature can affect your quality of sleep.

7. Be sure not to watch or read any horror, homicide, or other negative material before going to sleep.

8. Make the plan a way of life rather than sporadic practice. The most reliable and fulfilling results are gained over a long period of time.

9. Know that the worlds are divided only by thought and belief is the passage through.

**Spiritual Preparation for Sleep**

Ten to twenty minutes of spiritual work can go a long way concerning the quality of your sleep, dreams, and ability to recall spirit journeys in the morning.

To begin, lie in bed or light a candle in your sacred space and ask your helping spirits and the Goddess to visit you in the dream state. If there is anyone on the other side whom you wish to contact or visit, speak to them as if they are with you in the room. Ask them to meet you between worlds. Blow out the candle and affirm, "In the morning, I will remember my dreams and my spirit journeys." If you wish, sprinkle a few drops of lavender essential oil on your pillow or sheets.

As you retire for the night, try to let go of the day and its events. If you have difficulty doing this, imagine your stresses dissolving into the ground, burning up like paper in the flames, washing away with the rain, or blowing away on the winds. When you feel detached from the day, repeat to yourself where you wish to direct your spirit by naming a place or a person you would like to see. See it as making travel plans that you will definitely carry out. Don't fight sleep; if you doze off before your get this far, don't worry. Your soul knows where it needs to be. Making "plans" to yourself only helps you to make a conscious connection.

If you wake in the middle of the night and have memories of any kind, even if you think you may be imagining them, quickly write them down so you can look at them in the morning. Sometimes memories come as feelings and emotions, so be sure to include them. If you wake and feel that you've been gone for a very long time, a spirit journey is bubbling to the surface of your memory. It's a good sign.

If you are lucky, you will have a vivid dream. Sometimes the clarity can be astounding. However, most often, we get bits and pieces of the actual journey mixed in with subconscious imagery like a strange and confusing brew. Isolating the reality of the soul journey requires a simple technique and a little time in the morning before you get out of bed.

### Personal Regression*

*Note: in this instance, the term "regression" has nothing to do with clinical hypnosis or self-hypnosis. Doing the following exercise does not "put you under" and there is no danger in not being in control. Your conscious self is fully awake, alert, and responsive. You are simply accessing your spirit journeys in the gentlest way possible.*

Regularly using this technique enables you to record times with loved ones, bring back spiritual teachings, and help you to form a conscious one-to-one relationship with soul guides and helpers. The latter is very important if you find it difficult to contact them or interact with them in the waking state. It also exercises your second sight, which in turn, helps you to connect in the conscious state. If you practice this often, you will probably notice greater results

164

when using oracles or your own psychic aptitude.

1.  In the morning, take at least ten minutes to "go over" the night. When you are still under the spell of sleep and not fully awake, silently ask yourself, "Where did I go last night? Where has my soul been?" Ask yourself these questions three times and then allow yourself to settle into a dreamy stillness by allowing any thoughts and images to float by. Don't hold onto any of them. When a soul memory emerges, it can be vivid or hazy, depending upon your receptivity. Soul memories *always* repeat, so if you see an image or vision that will not go away or keeps returning, you are remembering a journey.

2.  Once you get to this point, drift into the images and do not control them. "Pushing" the memory can cause you to create a vivid daydream that has nothing to do with the actual sojourn. If you have difficulty holding onto soul memories once they surface, ask yourself the above questions again until are you again in a state of stillness. It may take some practice maintaining the "relaxed concentration" needed to fully recall soul journeys, but once it is accomplished, anything is possible.

3.  Once you are proficient, you can reach the level of ability where you can see a continuous stream of images. As you see these images, you actually can

relive them. When you get to this point, notice the time on the clock before you regress and again after you come out of it. It is an accurate way of knowing the actual length of your spirit journey.

4. With dedication and progress, you may get to the point where you will remember your soul's nocturnal journeys without regression.

...

You will probably notice that your receptivity varies; on some days you may seem "open" and others you may feel you don't have the ability at all. This is normal. Blocks can be caused by fatigue, stress, or the simple fact that your body needs more electrolytes. Increasing potassium-rich foods can put you back on track, for the body's electrical connections play a vital role in psychic ability.

May you have beautiful journeys and exciting discoveries!

## 8

# Shadow of the Sword: Calling the Dark Mother

Times come when we encounter a menacing outside influence from which we need strong protection. Be it physical or psychic, bad things sometimes happen to all of us, and our wellbeing or our very lives are threatened.

People of the ancient world as well as our current time have honored what we call Dark Goddesses. Kali, Hekate, Eresh-Kigal, Lilith, and Morgana, just to name a few, are from various cultures but share many common grounds. All are fierce, associated with death and transformation, and Crone-like in wisdom. These archetypes reach deeply into our psyches from the collective unconscious, sometimes as frightening demons and other times as symbols of the soul's cycle through time. Many individuals who walk paths that embrace the Sacred Feminine acknowledge and work with these energies. Some use the rede *"Do what you will, so long as it harms none"* while others choose a more aggressive path. The latter is sometimes justified by the idea that psychic acts of revenge mirror the necessary and sometimes-brutal ways of nature. But, nature, in essence, does not destroy to hurt, seek revenge, gain personal power, or degrade life. Nature's fury is not personal.

Using one's powers to bend the will of another, bring revenge upon someone, or gain material possessions defaces the light within. This is not the power of what my Spirit Elders call The Dark Mother. In this role as cosmic guardian, this avatar of the Goddess is the sword of truth, karmic justice, protection, and the all-knowing "eye" that can pierce through the illusion of self-righteousness and see into the soul. The Dark Mother is often invoked for powerful protection, to apprehend a known violent criminal, or to banish negativity. This is a healthy practice for those who choose it, and Her power can be called upon in times of desperate need, but if our intentions do not resonate with Her universal laws, we not only invite disaster upon ourselves but also our spirituality. Her aid is sometimes invoked for revenge, and when these powers are called upon with gratifying results, it is not The Dark Mother's work at hand, but rather the work of energies waiting for an opportunity to oppose the positive force. The power of The Dark Mother and the word *dark* does not connote "evil" or vengeance, therefore cannot and should not be used without spiritual integrity to back it up. Like an explosive, Her power must be handled with knowledge and caution. The negative result from misusing it is the simple but merciless law of cause and effect. When we assume the role of cosmic vigilantes, we are psychic suicide bombers. Universal karmic law guarantees it. No matter how justified we feel in any given situation, we do not have the spiritual right or authority to take matters into our own hands. The positive and negative forces of the universe oppose yet attract each other in a purposeful karmic dance. However, just because the negative is part of the scheme of things does not mean we should aid, glorify, or surrender to it. Nothing comes from negativity but negativity.

This being said, calling The Dark Mother should be reserved only for times of great need when life or wellbeing are threatened or when your soul has been violated. Soul-violation does not mean the result of a cheating lover or the loss of a job. All of the above means that the power of The Dark Mother is called upon only when our bodies and spirits are at risk for injury. During these times, She knows our position at hand and knows better than we how to handle the situation.

Invoking The Dark Mother has been handed down to me from Spirit Elders, and the few times I have requested Her aid, I followed their instructions to the letter. Each time, I called upon Her presence, explained my problem, and asked Her to remove it from my life. I saw profound results every time and within a period of thirteen days. To request Her intervention, you do not need to do rituals or burn foul-smelling incense. The Dark Mother is a not a dramatist but a realist who has a soft heart for justice and a sincere request for help that does not include begging. From personal experience I can say that begging definitely falls on deaf ears. I have not been in the position to need Her help immediately, but judging from the undiluted power, I would definitely request Her aid while exercising every effort to resolve the situation.

If you should call upon Her with a sincere heart but do not receive Her help, most likely your problem is not serious enough for the concentration of Her power. If this is the case, try to find resolution through Her guidance, rather than direct intervention. Again, I cannot stress enough the importance of spiritual responsibility. Even the most virtuous of mystics and seekers are challenged to the point of ethical weakness. To *want* to lash out, seek revenge, and call upon The Dark Mother for personal justice is only human; *surrendering* to this natural impulse is satiating the lower forces and the lower self. When I have been tempted, I have remembered my love for the Goddess within who wants only my greatest potential to be realized. When we choose the other path, the Goddess within is betrayed and soiled, communion is no longer possible, and we become imitators. Free will is a gift and a test, both equally sacred.

# III

# Feminine Arts

# 9

# Sacred Beauty: Ancient Mysticism of Cosmetics and Adornment

As women in the modern Western world, we are admired for and judged on our accomplishments, fashion sense, or sexual appeal—in other words, what we do and how we look. But in ancient times, women were respected for simply being women during a time when God was Goddess, and the cosmos itself was the divine product of the Great Mother. Our ancient sisters were considered vessels of bliss and the female body a healing instrument, each part linked to the higher power of the universe. Adornment in ancient times began with worship of Deity before spilling out into the everyday. And cosmetics— including make-up—had mystical intentions long before it became a template for superficial beauty. People in ancient times saw Deity mirrored in the beauty of the earth, and from this strong belief in feminine connection to natural and supernatural forces, superstitions ran deep in many cultures.

### The Magic in Her Hair...

The belief that women's hair attracted spirits or demons was a common one. Early Christian custom, enforced by Paul of the New Testament, required women to enter church with covered heads so rebellious spirits would not enter with them. Witches were thought to gain power through their hair and were magically impotent without it. Common folk believed that women could unleash storms by the simple act of unbinding their hair, and those with male relatives at sea refrained from combing their hair until they returned safely. Vestal virgins of Rome entered their temple careers with ritually-shaven heads while Christian nuns as well as Jewish brides were required to shave off their hair to deter demons, yet a woman who sheared her own locks was condemned. Joan of Arc's act of cutting her own hair was considered a serious crime that was a significant factor in her torture and death. Today, Buddhist nuns shave their heads as an act of mindfulness and renunciation.

According to old gypsy lore, hair that waved like rippling water was indicative of witches, and Gypsy and Hindu women braided their hair for the same effect. However, Gypsy women never kept their hair braided or in a bun during childbirth for fear of binding the energy, thus restricting the birthing process. Midwives in Europe used braided hair as amulets to bring good luck and health to babies and those who took care of them.

Hair was thought to hold a portion of the person's soul, thus the sentimental custom of lovers exchanging locks of hair for safekeeping. Because of this life force accounted for within the tresses, it was also believed that anyone with ill intention could gain control of another person simply by possessing even a miniscule amount of that individual's hair. Widows in ancient Egypt buried a lock of their hair with their husbands to safeguard them in the next world.

Belief that a menstruating witch's hair would spring to life as snakes if put into soil or water has its origins in the myth of the serpent-haired Medusa. In classical mythology, Medusa was seen as a gorgon—part woman, part monster—who could turn a man to stone with a mere glance. But Medusa's origins are much more ancient and most likely from the Libyan Amazonian goddess who embodied feminine wisdom. Medusa can also be traced to North Africa under her name Ath-enna. Through the ages, hair has been associated with wisdom, especially gray or white hair which comes with age and hard-earned insight, and it is interesting to note that Athena, the Greek goddess of wisdom, was depicted wearing a breastplate sporting an image of the snake-haired Medusa. Most of all, Medusa was once a goddess of protection and women's mysteries, especially magic practices involving menstruation. Centuries later, these ancient ties to Medusa lingered in cultures where menstruating women were isolated during their menses because of the persistent belief that eye contact with a bleeding woman could be fatal to a man.

Hair color was also significant; blonde appeared other-worldly; fair-haired women were seen as having mystical powers. Those with shades of red, including copper and auburn, were considered to possess supernatural powers. During the Inquisition, women with red hair were especially feared, believed to cavort with the Devil, and consequently labeled as witches. In the Middle East, Africa, and India, coloring the hair red with dye from the henna plant was believed to ward off evil, bad spirits, and ill fortune. Tantric beliefs included the idea that binding or loosening a woman's hair set forces in motion that could create or destroy in the great cosmic sense.

Today, thanks to the extensive work of theologian Margaret Starbird, Mary Magdalen is seen more than Christianity's redeemed prostitute. Magdalen—more than any other figure in history—is linked to her hair in both Scripture and popular myth, and considered to be the woman who dried the feet of Christ with her long tresses.

Many modern scholars support the theory that Mary was not a harlot but a Priestess of the Goddess who anointed the historical Jesus (Yeshua) to commemorate His Christed status. If this is indeed true, the Magdalenian association with hair reaches even a deeper level.

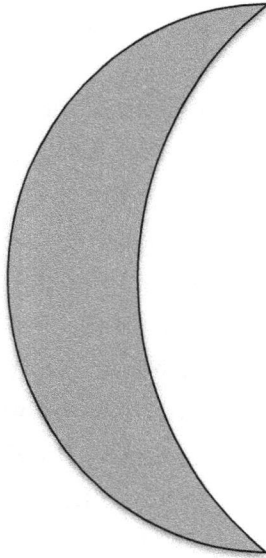

# Henna

Henna and the art of *mehndi* have permeated North African, Middle Eastern, and Indian cultures for centuries. Dye from the henna plant has been used by women to color hair, stain finger and toenails, and to stencil and protect the skin. The orange-red dye is used to decorate women's hands and feet before special occasions including marriage and birth to invite good fortune and to chase away bad spirits. Hennaing before a marriage goes back to the Bronze Age in the Eastern Mediterranean. Pre-modern Muslim countries adopted Semitic menstrual taboos and believed that women attracted malicious *jinn* or spirits during their periods. Henna was the antidote, so to speak, and was included in post-menstrual bath routines. Henna was also used in rituals of exorcism. Today, the use of henna usually does not include these old ways and is secondary to modern hair dyes and nail polish, but as in the past, henna designs on the skin are a visual marker indicating strength of body and spirit and an invitation to good fortune. In general, henna rites are believed to repel the Evil Eye and are joyous gatherings for women. Henna is a wonderful alternative to chemical hair dyes and can be mixed with other plant dyes such as indigo and marigold for a variety of colors. *Note: For serious health concerns, henna should never be applied to children under the age of six.*

### The Power of Her Glance...

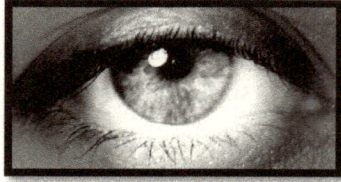

Maat, the ancient Egyptian goddess of truth, was the all-seeing eye; the hieroglyph for the universal syllable *Maa* was an eye. The feminine eye was believed to have power to judge souls as well as send ill fortune. The concept of the Evil Eye persists to this day around the world, especially in Middle Eastern and Mediterranean cultures. The belief that jealousy or envy-based energy travels through a mere glance is ancient and attributed to women, especially those in post-menopausal years. In patriarchal cultures around the globe, it was custom for respectable women to keep their eyes lowered when in male company. During the Inquisition, men protected themselves from the dreaded Evil Eye by ordering alleged witches to walk into court backward so women could not have the upper hand and cast their glance first.

It is believed that the Evil Eye is most often sent unintentionally, and this is why it has been feared throughout the ages. Compliments, hidden envy between friends and relatives, or outright jealousy lurking behind smiling neighbors are seen as culprits. Women's eyes, especially blue, were believed to be magical and capable of sending ill fortune with a single glance. The Evil Eye was so embedded in tradition that it is still significant in many parts of the world, and pieces of jewelry are crafted as amulets against the effects of the envious glance.

In the ancient world, fear of the Evil Eye gave birth to the custom of both women and men wearing cosmetics, namely eye make-up. In ancient Egypt, this meant lining the eyes with kohl, a blue-black substance made from the ash of frankincense resin and minerals. Applying the dark liner was believed to not only protect the eyes from the desert sun but one's entire person from the Evil Eye. Along with kohl, pulverized minerals such as intensely green malachite were worn as eye make-up for the same purpose. Painting the eyes was also seen as an offering to the Gods when approaching the altar or entering sacred space.

### Her Lips Like Rubies...

Some sources say that the first use of lip color can be traced to the ancient Sumerians who used often toxic minerals to accentuate the mouth as far back as 5,000 B.C. Egyptians followed suit and used similar minerals that accumulated in the body over time and led to illness and fatalities. Painting the mouth mimicked the flush of the vagina during sexual arousal. Taking this association even further in patriarchal Islamic cultures, Muslim men required women to cover their mouths with veils to erase any visual connection to the feared vagina dentata, the ludicrous mythical toothed vagina found in various cultures.

### Lady Fingers...

Each finger on the female (and male hand) related to a specific planet, but the index finger was considered feminine; therefore, women were capable of blessing as well as cursing with what was often referred to as the poison finger. Jewish brides wore a ring on the right index finger to temper so-called negative powers associated with it. Rudeness related to pointing the finger at someone is a direct link to this ancient belief.

The left hand, especially in the eyes of the Catholic Church, was the hand of the Devil, and witches were considered to be left-handed. In ancient esoteric philosophy, the left side of anything, particularly the body, was considered to be ruled by the feminine. Through the ages, being left-handed was considered demonic, and up until well into the twentieth century, left-handed children were taught how to be right-handed in an attempt to assure that their souls would go to Heaven after death.

As far back as antiquity, painting the fingernails was a symbol of status and once reserved for royalty and the upper class. Dye from the henna plant was the first nail "polish" and reportedly used by Cleopatra. During the Middle Ages, hennaed nails were considered to be a telltale practice of witches.

Throughout many cultures, the hand in general has been seen as protective and replicas of it worn as jewelry are believed to ward off the Evil Eye. Sacred hand gestures in Hindu and Buddhist culture called *mudras* are used to stimulate the body's prana or energy and are used in yogic practices as well as Classical Indian dance. The word *mudra* means "seal" in Sanskrit, and the belief that sacred hand gestures can also bestow blessings are most often evident in Indian iconography where deities are portrayed using them. The hand gesture called "the horns", usually used to propel back bad energy to the sender, was once symbolic of the Goddess. In India, the gesture of "the horns" is a mudra sacred to Jagadamba, the Mother of the World.

## The Dancer and Her Sacred Navel...

Oriental dance or belly dance as it has come to be known, originated exclusively as a woman's dance for Deity and other women. Unlike its modern association with men's entertainment, in ancient times, the dance was strictly forbidden to men's eyes. Women faced the altar to dance for the gods or danced with other women during times of transition including birth and death. The dance helped to strengthen a woman during pregnancy and prepared her for birth. It was also employed during the birthing process by female members of the family and community who danced around a woman in labor to help bring the baby into the world. Old and young alike, women's belly dance celebrated the power of the female body and its link to the primal forces of nature. The navel was the sacred symbol of regeneration, reproduction, and the dance of life.

## Earth Beneath Her Feet...

Ancient cultures including the Egyptians and Babylonians believed in stepping onto sacred ground with bare feet in order for worshippers to absorb the earth's maternal and sacred energy. Roman female magicians performed ceremonially with bare feet.

## Jewels of Her Spirit

Adorning the body with semi-precious stones and metals began as an offering to the gods and protection against negative influences. Amulets and talismans were ancient ornaments to ward off the Evil Eye, ensure fertility and good health, or bring prosperity. In any culture, the office of Priestess was marked by distinctive jewelry, especially serpent designs that wrapped around the fingers, wrists, or arms. Anklets, headdresses, and girdles (waist bands usually made of beads) kept evil spirits at bay, especially when made of tinkling bells or shells. Priestesses of ancient Greece were buried with their possessions, including jewelry that signified their holy office. Placing an article of jewelry on the body for ritual or spiritual work was an act of power and protected the physical and spiritual bodies.

Catholic rosary beads and mala or japa beads in Eastern religions were (and still are) used for prayer, the latter for recitation of sacred mantras. Originally, the Catholic rosary was pre-Christian and reserved for Goddess prayers. When established religion stamped out early faiths, the rosary was dedicated to Christianity with an emphasis on Mary, the Blessed Mother. 108-bead malas of Eastern religions often were fashioned from fine scented woods like sandalwood as well as precious stones, and like the rosary, from "dough" made of rose petals.

Gold was considered sacred to the gods and symbolized immortality due to its inability to tarnish, but silver was and is still considered the precious metal of the Goddess- the color of moonlight and attuned to divine feminine energy. Stones and minerals possess frequency that resonates with our energy fields; the ancients knew of these connections and fashioned their jewelry accordingly. All gems have a rich history of lore, but the following list is specific to Goddess energy.

### Significant Goddess Stones, Minerals and Metals

**Amazonite:** carries the energy and wisdom of the Sacred Feminine; promotes trust in one's visions, intuition, and psychic impressions

**Amber:** ancient Earth energy; a Priestess stone; fossilized resin holds a spark of life force and aids in healing; brings light, hope, and warmth to the energy field; ideal stone to wear when recovering from illness

**Amethyst:** protection; aids meditation and psychic abilities; sacred to Artemis; connects to the energy of St.

Germaine and the Violet Ray; protects against psychic attack

**Angelite:** attuned to higher energies, peace, and the angelic realm; aids communication with loved ones on the other side; invites divine intervention when needed

**Aquamarine:** attuned to the Mother and healing oceans; connects us to our origins; aids psychic ability; sacred to Aphrodite; opens a passage to communion and communication with the Goddess

**Celestite:** connects to angelic realms; invokes peace; opens the third eye

**Clear Quartz:** attuned to Goddess energy and higher energies; speeds healing; clears energy field

**Copper:** attuned to universal and personal love; sacred to Aphrodite/Venus; opens psychic channels

**Chrysocolla:** inspires creativity and communication; attuned to the Goddess within

**Diamond:** channels spiritual purity and connects to higher realms

**Fossils:** carries the energetic imprint of ancient Earth/Gaia

**Garnet (almandine):** attuned to women's reproductive

energy; invokes passion, strength; wakes the kundalini energy; helps to bring dreams and plans into physical manifestation

**Holey Stones:** believed to carry healing energy; brings luck

**Jade (green):** carries energy of the heart center; sacred to Kuan Yin; invokes compassion, luck, and healing; increases life force or chi in the body; resonates with prosperity and heals the fear of lack

**Jet:** Priestess stone; invokes grounding Earth energy; lifts negative energies/entities from one's energy field; supports the energy of Shakti

**Larimar:** connects to higher realms; carries Goddess energy and invokes the Goddess within; tames menopausal symptoms including hot flashes

**Moonstone:** attuned to the moon and the Goddess in her lunar aspects; a Priestess stone; resonates with the female reproductive/hormonal system; helps one to access soul memories; good for past life regression; promotes emotional balance

**Moss Agate:** attuned to the energies of Earth and plant devas; carries Goddess energy; inspires persistence

**Pearl:** sacred to Kuan Yin, Aphrodite; carries energies of the ocean and the Mother of the Seas

**Petrified Wood:** carries the energetic imprint of ancient Earth/Gaia; inspires patience

**Picture Jasper:** carries energies of the Goddess and energies of Earth

**Platinum:** metal of highest frequency; attuned to higher realms; carries Goddess energy

**Rhodochrosite:** women's healing stone for past trauma, abuse, self-hatred; attuned to the heart center, the inner child, and the Goddess

**Rose Quartz:** women's stone for self-love/self-worth; heals the heart center, self-image, and trauma from abuse

**Ruby:** Goddess stone of passion, energy, and protection from negative forces; disconnects negative entities from one's energy field

**Selenite:** attuned to the Goddess and the moon; carrier of healing energy for all energy centers

**Serpentine:** helps to activate the kundalini safely; restores energy in the physical body

**Shell:** connects to the Mother of the Seas and carries healing ocean energies of Gaia

**Silver:** sacred to the moon and the Goddess; a Priestess metal

**Turquoise:** stone of protection and healing; increases life force; repels the Evil Eye and all forms of negativity; invites luck

### Fragrance and the Soul

The word *perfume* comes from ancient uses of ceremonial incense and means "through smoke." Burning fragrant plants or hanging them over doorways was believed to keep people or dwellings free of negative influences. Fragrance has long been associated with inviting benevolent influences and favors of the gods, and the sweeter or more pungent, the greater the propensity to attract the highest energies. Only the sweetest and finest scents were worthy of offering to the deities, and wearing fragrance was considered a high offering when one approached the altar or stepped into sacred space.

Aromatics were part of religious life around the globe and offered in temples during ritual. In the ancient world of the Egyptians, perfume oils and ointments made from scented plants and spices were distributed only by high priests, a practice and art that went hand in hand with spiritual office. Fragrances of antiquity were synonymous with medicine and used as such. Hebrews used fragrant oils to bless dwelling spaces and people, especially the sick. Afflictions of the nervous system responded positively with these applications that we now call aromatherapy. In ancient translations, the words *perfumer* and *apothecary* were sometimes interchangeable.

In Greek tales and culture, female magicians were portrayed as experts in the art of making potions and perfumes. During Rome's height of power, fragrances were used in every corner of life, and perfume was applied to all areas of the body including the soles of the feet. Greek athletes used specific scents on different parts of the body for peak performance.

Like mystics throughout the ages who have spoken of sound and color as nothing less than a spectrum of frequencies, author and chemist G.W. Septimus Piesse described fragrances as having corresponding musical notes; plants ranging from verbena to patchouli pulsate on the musical scale and contribute to life's complex and subtle symphony.

Many Christian, Sufi, Hindu, and Jain saints have been said to exude heavenly fragrances while living as well as after death. St. Francis of Assisi was reported to radiate the scent of lemons and St. Catherine sweet violets. According to mystics of both ancient and modern times, each of us carries a signature fragrance within the soul. If this is true indeed, is it any wonder why our sense of smell connects us to our deepest memories and accompanies our most powerful human experiences?

# *A Renaissance of Sacred Beauty*

Adornment is usually associated with women, and because of this, modern women who choose not to paint their faces or clothe their bodies with the latest fashion trends are often seen as less desirable. Each woman, according to Goddess philosophy, is unique and not beholden to cultural whim. However, if one chooses to use cosmetics, sacred intention can bring purpose to our most mundane activities and heal wounded feminine identity. Adorning the body for self-empowerment and honoring Deity rather than exclusively for self-enhancement can invoke the

Goddess within. Invoking the Goddess within enables us to see beauty where we once saw imperfection, and when we are able to see our true beauty we can spread that beauty wherever we go. We cannot rely on social preference and greed to change; we must take responsibility for our own self-image. We decide whether or not society's dysfunction should be our own. Each time we dislike ourselves, we degrade the Goddess within. Each comparison to manmade, profit-inducing preference defaces the body's temple.

Won't you join me in a renaissance of beauty based on spiritual love for self and the Goddess within? An approach to beauty that revives the mysticism of cosmetics so we are living offerings to a Higher Power? Won't you join the pampered Sisterhood? After all is said and done, Goddess Earth is a lady. She wears the billowing cloth of the heavens, the jewels of the storm, and the incense of blooms and summer nights. Let's celebrate being Her mirrors in physical form!

*sacred space for everyday cosmetics*

## Vanities as Altars

What we put on our bodies delights our senses and praises the Goddess within, but it can also raise our frequency. This means that our beauty routine can be sacred, and that haphazard drawer or bag of cosmetics can play an integral part of daily self-blessing. Here are a few ideas for turning a tiny corner of your bathroom or bedroom into consecrated space where self-empowerment and beauty go hand in hand.

1.  Mount a shelf on the wall or designate a corner where your cosmetics and everyday jewelry can be dedicated to a new mindset of self-care that includes Spirit and the Goddess. Inexpensive but lovely jewelry or stationary cases make wonderful storage places for make-up, etc. and don't take up too much room on a counter (see image on page 191.)

2.  Add an inspiring framed print or statue, a decanter of rosewater, or a candle to your sacred cosmetic space so you are reminded daily of a higher intention.

3.  If you already have the luxury of a true vanity, consider making it an altar to your wellbeing and the Goddess within.

4.  You may wish to use a special mirror for your daily beauty routine, one that is a reminder of the beauty within and that reflects the ancient belief that mirrors are psychic tools for divination and portals to other realms.

5.  Consider using only pure products on your skin, including those not tested on animals. Up to 500 chemicals may be used in *one* fragrance alone (i.e. shampoo, soap, etc.) and everything we put on the skin is absorbed into the body. Most of all, reputable mineral make-up, essential oil perfumes, and natural soaps are made from ingredients from the earth itself—what nature intended.

6.  Consider using the simple recipes later in this chapter to make your own fragrances and bath crystals.

## Step into the Day as a Priestess

1.  Even if you are pressed for time, invoke protection when applying your eye make-up. Call on the angels or the guarding mothers and grandmothers going back into time as you line or color your eyes. Be reminded of the power of your own glance.

2.  As you apply your lip color, honor the power of your voice and the words that come from your mouth. Remember the breath and the breath of life.

3. When you paint your nails, consider honoring the index finger, the finger of power. You can paint that nail a different color or only paint that particular one on each hand or just one hand.

4. Place a special ring on your power finger before leaving the house or before spiritual work. It is your symbol of Priestess status.

5. When you apply perfume, imagine a shield of angelic or Goddess light within the fragrance enveloping you in protection, beauty, and grace. Anoint your brow, heart, navel, and palms of your hands.

6. As you brush or comb your hair, set an intention for the day and set it into action with your movement. Unleash some magic!

**honoring the power finger**

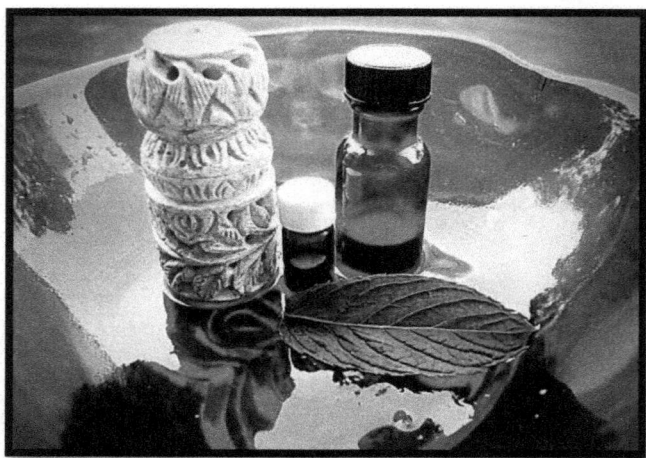

# *Anointing Oils and Sacred Perfume*

## Modern Aromatherapy & Sacred Uses of Essential Oils

Essential oils are steam-distilled essences of plants, roots, barks, leaves, grasses, berries, and fruit rinds and are infused with the very essence of Gaia. A plant's essential oil is its life force and innate immune system that prevents it from disease, and from a spiritual perspective, the blood of the Earth Mother. In the ancient world, aromatic plants were infused in oils and distilled to extract a concentrated essence. They were used for ceremony, anointing the sick, clearing sins or past trauma, and blessing physical dwelling places.

Modern in-depth studies have shown that all living beings possess frequency—in short, cellular vibratory levels. Each essential oil is considered to also possess frequency that is measured by megahertz (MHz). Oils with higher frequency are most valuable when applied to our spiritual lives and can stimulate the pituitary and pineal glands which some believe to play a role in spiritual, mystical, and/or psychic experience. Essential oils can be combined with energy work, Reiki, hands-on-healing, prayer, chakra clearing, sound healing, and gemstone healing. Vibrational or spiritual aromatherapy affects the vibrational frequency of a person and includes the subtle realms of emotional and spiritual wellbeing. On a practical note, vibrational aromatic therapy can also be highly beneficial for healing deep emotional traumas and can be applied to get to the energetic or root cause of physical and/or emotional health complaints.

**Fast Fact***:* Essential oils range in frequency from 53 MHz (basil) to 320 MHz (rose).

Aromatherapy which includes practical, clinical, cosmetic, and vibrational applications is an extensive study and its intricacies are another book entirely, but here is a brief reference guide to essential oils potentially valuable to your Goddess path and spiritual life. For sake of relevancy and space, I have included only their energetic properties with occasional physical properties when they pertain to women's health. See Resources for reputable suppliers and study courses and Recommended Reading for further inquiry.

**\*Note**: *If you are pregnant or nursing, many essential oils* *are contraindicated, so please take precaution and use after pregnancy and breastfeeding, or only under the strict supervision of a professional aromatherapist. If you have moderate-severe allergies and/or asthma, you are best to avoid chamomile (Roman or German), and oils containing menthol (all mints and eucalyptus). As a rule, do not apply near the face. Anyone can be allergic to anything, therefore, discontinue use if you should develop a rash, etc.*

### Energetic Properties of Sacred Essential Oils
...

**Angelica Root (Angelica archangelica):** woody and sweet; invites angelic protection; reinforces the energy field; *Note: angelica in diluted form is available for a fraction of the cost and contains the same properties

**Atlas Cedarwood (Cedrus atlantica):** balsamic, woody with a hint of spiciness when aged; protects the energy field from outside influences; raises one's frequency; wonderful oil to add to meditation blends

**Balsam Fir, Silver Fir (Abies alba):** evergreen scent like a Christmas tree; cleanses the energy field of negative thought-forms; protects the energy field from unwanted outside influences; grounding to the entire individual on all levels; good oil to use before or after spending time with a group of people (excellent for therapists, massage therapists, energy workers, teachers, caregivers, etc.); unblocks emotions stored in the energy centers of the body

**Basil (Ocimum basilicum):** pungent and brightly herbaceous; encourages receptivity to self-worth, courage, and good outcomes to endeavors—also instills hope on a cellular, physical level; supports (adrenal) life force; repels evil influences

**Benzoin (Styrax benzoin):** warm, vanilla-like, balsamic; inspires spirituality; protects the energy field; a good oil for anointing during prayer or ritual; stimulates the finer spiritual senses; energetically, provides balm to individuals, especially women attempting to heal past abuse or trauma

**Bergamot (Citrus bergamia):** citrus, sweet and fruity with a green undertone; increases frequency of the physical body; dissolves fear locked in the energy field; instills happiness and hope

**Birch, Sweet (Betula lenta):** similar to wintergreen and root beer, sweet with minty undertones; cleanses the energy field; helps one move into the present time and leave emotional baggage behind; helps restore life force in cases of physical and emotional depletion after periods of prolonged stress; protective against negative energies and repels entities clinging to the aura and psyche; *Caution: Birch essential oil contains high levels of methyl salicylate, the chemical precursor to aspirin; those allergic to aspirin should not use this essential oil on the skin and advised to seek alternatives (i.e. eucalyptus, peppermint, spearmint, or ginger)for this purpose. Birch essential oil should only be used on occasion in small amounts. Avoid regular or long-term use.*

**Cacao (Chocolate) (Theobroma cacao):** chocolate, nutty, and sweet; helps transform fear into trust in a Higher Power and personal strength reserves; promotes self-love and forgiveness; resonates with the heart center; helps to stimulate feel-good endorphins, namely serotonin production in the brain

**Cedar (Juniperus virginiana):** earthy evergreen scent of red cedar; grounds emotions and clears negative thoughts; refreshes the energy field and increases life force; protective; invokes the Earth element

**Chamomile, Roman (Chamaemelum nobile):** fruity and brightly herbaceous; assists in the healing of childhood emotional wounds, helps align the energy field with the healing aspects of nature and the Devic kingdom; inspires hope, helps one process pain from the past, beneficial during times of deep disappointment; *Note: Roman Chamomile in diluted form is available for a fraction of the cost and contains the same properties

**Cinnamon Bark (*Cinnamomum zeylanicum*):** sweet, spicy, and pungent; attracts opportunity, success, and abundance; instills hope and renewed passion; Cassia, an inexpensive close relative to true cinnamon, can be substituted. *Caution: Cinnamon bark and cassia essential oil can cause burns and skin irritation when used improperly. Avoid contact with mucus membranes including eyes, nose, and mouth as well as the genital area. Do not use on skin unless highly diluted in a blend. Vapors should not some too close to the eyes or nose as* *they can cause irritation. Applied to hair is okay. If applied to potpourri or candles, just simply dispense from bottle.*

**Clary Sage (*Salvia sclarea*)** grassy and herbaceous; brightens the spirits, dispels melancholy; dissolves thought forms; for times of emotional, physical, or spiritual transition; for multilevel balance, including hormones

**Cypress (Cupressus sempervirens):** earthy evergreen, cedar-like; unsurpassed for life transitions including losses and death of loved ones; protective and strengthening; invokes the Earth element and sacred to Hekate and Artemis

**Frankincense (Boswellia carteri):** resinous, slightly musty with citrus undertones; for spiritual pursuits, meditation, and strengthening the auric field; defuses obsession; helps one to cope with grief and despair

**Geranium (Pelargonium graveolens):** like the flower with citrus and rose undertones; supports women's self-love/self-worth/positive self-image and aids in self-acceptance; soothes the grief-stricken heart, and provides connection to the Goddess; attuned to mother energy; for doing inner child work; valuable oil for female hormonal imbalances or hormonal transitions

**Jasmine Absolute (Jasminum officinale):** sweet, deep floral; powerfully feminine even in inexpensive diluted forms; attuned to the energies of the Goddess, the moon, and the psychic realms; supportive to female sexuality/sexual response; invites higher energies including angels *Note: jasmine in diluted form is available for a fraction of the cost and contains the same properties

**Juniper Berry (Juniperus communis):** pungent, sweet evergreen; helps to dispel negative energies, entities, and thoughtforms; also helps to clear fixations/fears; provides protection during sleep and night terrors; for exorcism; supports the kidneys, adrenals, and lungs; purifies body, mind, and aura

**Lavender (Lavendula angustifolium):** green, refreshing floral without overpowering sweetness; clears the energy field after providing Reiki or other energy work; good oil to use after a day spent with a large group of people; helps to open the psychic eye and invites spiritual insights during the dream state; helps to stimulate serotonin in the brain, thus reducing anxiety, sugar and carbohydrate cravings

**Myrrh (Commiphora myrrha):** deep, resinous with smoky undertones, earthy; eases fear and helps to induce a meditative state; useful for grief or facing death and all issues surrounding transition; calms the central nervous system; *Note: myrrh in diluted form is available for a fraction of the cost and contains the same properties

**Neroli/Orange Blossom (Citrus aurantium bigaradia):** herbaceous floral with citrus undertones; helps us connect to the spirit world and invites angelic influences; calms fears; *Note: neroli in diluted form is available for a fraction of the cost and contains the same properties

**Oakmoss (Evernia prunastri):** earthy, soil-like with green undertones; attuned to the element Earth and the Goddess as Gaia; resonates with faerie; very grounding

**Palo Santo (Bursera graveolens):** sweet and woody; clears negativity and promotes healing; attuned to shamanic and ancestral energies; used for protection during psychic work

**Patchouli (Pogostemon patchouli):** soil-like, woody with herbaceous undertones; attuned to the element of Earth and the Goddess as Gaia; very grounding; attracts abundance; uplifts; helps to sharpen concentration and focus yet calming to the nervous system

**Rose Absolute (Rosa damascena) or (Rosa centifolia):** like the flower, some varieties sweeter than others; the highest frequency known and capable of elevating any oil mixed with it; clearing and elevating to the energy field; used for women's grief, self-love/self-worth/self-image issues; the quintessential oil of Goddess energy and sacred to Aphrodite, Venus, the Blessed Mother/ Lady Guadalupe and Mary Magdalen; helps to balance hormones during PMS, perimenopause, and menopause; *Note: rose in diluted form is available for a fraction of the cost and contains the same properties

**Sage (Salvia officinalis):** green and herbaceous, pungent; clears negativity from spaces and the energy field; invokes physical energy when inhaled

**Sandalwood (Santalum album):** warm and earthy with subtle sweetness; attuned to the moon and excellent for meditative states; traditionally used in Hindu temples;

invites higher energies of sages, saints, and spirit guides; helpful for cystitis and urinary tract infections; calms the nervous system and soothes the effects of deep grief; *Note: Sandalwood in diluted form is available for a fraction of the cost and contains the same properties

**Spikenard (Nardostychys jatamansi):** valerian-like, musty, slightly woody; used for anointing and inviting higher energies; considered an oil of Christ Consciousness; invokes deep peace; sacred to Mary Magdalen; regulates the autonomic nervous system and helps to turn off the fight or flight stress response

**Vetiver (Vetiveria zizanoides):** deep and earthy, root and soil-like; offers deep connection to the element of Earth and the Goddess as Gaia; for times when the spirit needs deep peace and retreat from the mundane world; grounding and restoring; helps to balance estrogen and progesterone in the body

**Ylang Ylang (Cananga odorata):** sweet and heady, similar to jasmine without jasmine's vanilla-like undertones; attuned to the Goddess and the moon; connects to the angelic realm and invites higher energies; supportive of women's sexuality; balancing and calms stormy temperaments; regulates adrenaline; helps the body and psyche to receive and accept pleasure

## *Aromatic Alchemy: Using Sacred Essential Oils*

Essential oils can be sprinkled on dried leaves and natural materials to create a homemade potpourri or rubbed onto candles and allowed to dry before lighting for a lovely fragrance. You can also dab corners of your sacred space with essential oils or add them to distilled water to make a fragrant room spritzer. Most of all, you can make your own sacred blends to use on your body as well as your own Goddess spas.

In clinical and vibrational applications, quality essential oils should be used, not only for safety but to ensure integrity of frequency. Please note that chemical fragrances have very little frequency which means zero spiritual properties. Even adding one chemical single note with a blend of natural essential oils will lower its frequency. Essential oils, like the human aura, can fluctuate depending upon environmental changes, thought patterns, emotions, and surrounding energies. Before you use essential oils or blend them, you may wish to say a prayer, play beautiful music, or meditate, for essential oils have been shown to increase their frequency by 10 MHz when positive thoughts or prayer accompany use.

On a very practical note, in the world of essential oil marketing, only 5% plant material is required for a company to legally state that an essential oil is "100% pure." Please be aware of misleading labels. See Resources in the back of this book for reputable recommended essential oil companies.

*Note: Essential oils should never be taken internally or directly applied to the skin without dilution. If you are pregnant or nursing, many essential oils are contraindicated, so please take precaution and use after pregnancy and breastfeeding OR only under the strict supervision of a professional aromatherapist. If you have moderate-severe allergies and/or asthma, you are best to avoid chamomile (Roman or German), and oils containing menthol (all mints and eucalyptus). As a rule, do not apply near the face. Anyone can be allergic to anything, therefore, discontinue use if you should develop a rash, etc. Avoid contact with varnished surfaces and fine furniture.*

## Quick Use Reference for Blessing and Meditation Oils

1. Simply dilute essential oils of your choice with a ratio of 1-4 drops essential oil to 1 teaspoon of any light vegetable oil* for on-the-spot one time use. To make a larger lasting batch, add 30-50 drops of essential oil to half an ounce of light vegetable oil and store in an amber or cobalt bottle in a cool place out of direct sunlight. *Grapeseed, light olive, and almond are good choices.

2. Use on the body as perfume, apply to energy centers (chakras), or dab into the hair (*avoid clothing- the vegetable oil base will stain fabrics.*)

# Blessing and Meditation Oils

### Priestess Blessing Oil
**(sweet and resinous with vanilla-like undertones)**

1 drop ylang ylang essential oil
2 drops benzoin essential oil
1 drop Peru balsam essential oil
blended into ½ teaspoon of light vegetable oil.
Use immediately.
or
10 drops ylang ylang
20 drops benzoin
10 drops Peru balsam
blended into ½ ounce of light vegetable oil. Store in an
amber or cobalt bottle and keep out of direct sunlight and
away from heat.

### Gift of the Goddess Blessing Oil
**(a grassy floral)**

1 drop clary sage essential oil
1 drop geranium essential oil
1 drop ylang ylang essential oil
1 drop diluted neroli essential oil
blended into ½ teaspoon of light vegetable oil.
Use immediately.
or
10 drops clary sage essential oil
6 drops geranium essential oil

10 drops ylang ylang essential oil
10 drops diluted neroli essential oil
blended into ½ ounce of light vegetable oil. Store in an amber or cobalt bottle and keep out of direct sunlight and away from heat

### Desert Bride Blessing Oil
**(sacred resins balanced with sweetness)**

1 drop frankincense essential oil
1 drop myrrh essential oil
1 drop ylang ylang essential oil
blended into ½ teaspoon of light vegetable oil.
Use immediately.
or
10 drops frankincense
10 drops myrrh
8 drops ylang ylang
blended into ½ ounce of light vegetable oil. Store in an amber or cobalt bottle and keep out of direct sunlight and away from heat.

### Sagewind Blessing Oil
**(a grassy, "green" floral)**

1 drop of sage or
1 drop clary sage essential oil
1 drop ylang ylang essential oil
blended into ½ teaspoon of light vegetable oil
Use immediately.

or
3 drops sage
2 drops clary sage
8 drops ylang ylang
blended into ½ ounce of light vegetable oil. Store in an
amber or cobalt bottle and keep out of direct sunlight and
away from heat.

### Angels Blessing Oil
**(deeply sweet and woody)**

1 drop angelica root essential oil
1 drop ylang ylang essential oil
blended into 1 teaspoon of light vegetable oil
Use immediately.
or
10 drops angelica root
10 drops ylang ylang
blended into ½ ounce of light vegetable oil. Store in an
amber or cobalt bottle and keep out of direct sunlight and
away from heat.

### Lavender Fields Blessing Oil
**(herbaceous with a hint of fruitiness)**

1 drop lavender essential oil
1 drop Roman Chamomile essential
blended into 1 teaspoon of light vegetable oil
Use immediately.
or

10 drops lavender
8 drops Roman Chamomile
blended into ½ ounce of light vegetable oil. Store in an amber or cobalt bottle and keep out of direct sunlight and away from heat.

### Winter Spice Blessing Oil
**(a seamless blend of fir, spice, and bright citrus)**

1 drop balsam fir essential oil
1 drop clove essential oil
1 drop tangerine essential oil
blended into 1 teaspoon of light vegetable oil
Use immediately.
or
8 drops balsam fir
4 drops clove
10 drops tangerine
blended into ½ ounce of light vegetable oil. Store in an amber or cobalt bottle and keep out of direct sunlight and away from heat.

### Summer Garden Blessing Oil
**(bright, pungent herbs with sweet floral overtones)**

1 drop basil essential oil
1 drop lavender essential oil
1 drop geranium essential oil
1 drop ylang ylang essential oil
blended into 1 teaspoon of light vegetable oil

Use immediately.

or

2 drops basil

4 drops lavender

2 drops geranium

blended into ½ ounce of light vegetable oil. Store in an amber or cobalt bottle and keep out of direct sunlight and away from heat.

### Autumn Fires Blessing Oil
**(earthy spiciness)**

1 drop nutmeg essential oil

1 drop clove essential oil

1 drop patchouli essential oil

blended into 1 teaspoon of light vegetable oil

Use immediately.

or

2 drops nutmeg

3 drops clove

3 drops patchouli

blended into ½ ounce of light vegetable oil. Store in an amber or cobalt bottle and keep out of direct sunlight and away from heat.

### Winds of Change Blessing Oil
**(grassy, minty, and sweet- clean and bright)**

1 drop spearmint essential oil

1 drop clary sage essential oil
1 drop ylang ylang essential oil
blended into 1 teaspoon of light vegetable oil
Use immediately.
or
5 drops spearmint
5 drops clary sage
8 drops ylang ylang
blended into ½ ounce of light vegetable oil. Store in an
amber or cobalt bottle and keep out of direct sunlight and
away from heat.

### *Sacred Sleep Blessing Oil*
**(lavender and fir duet)**

1 drop lavender essential oil
1 drop balsam fir essential oil
blended into 1 teaspoon of light vegetable oil
Use immediately.
or
8 drops lavender
5 drops balsam fir
blended into ½ ounce of light vegetable oil. Store in an
amber or cobalt bottle and keep out of direct sunlight and
away from heat.

*If your soul was a fragrance, what would it be?*

*Mary Magdalen, the patron of perfumers*

# Aged Perfumes

Though the art of perfume-making is complex and can involve many layers and steps, you don't need to be a professional aromatherapist or perfumer to enjoy the art of fragrance blending. Making perfume oil requires some knowledge and a little time for it to age. If you are new to this, you may find the how-to formulas here a wonderful way to begin your own journey into the world of organic perfumes. If you are experienced in blending your own fragrances, the following recipes might be lovely to try. *Note: These recipes are for concentrated formulas and despite the small amount, they are powerful and will last a long while.

### Quick Use Reference for Aged Perfume Oils

1. Fill an empty amber or cobalt aromatherapy bottle with ½ ounce oil such as grapeseed, light olive, or almond.

2. Depending upon desired strength, add up to 120 drops of essential oil to the vegetable carrier oil, adding one essential oil at a time and swirling or rubbing the closed bottle between your hands to blend well (don't shake upside down). You can also add essential oils to a base of rosewater for a spray perfume.

3.  When the blend delights your nose, allow to "set" for a month in a cool, dark place before using. Perfume oils must mature for best results. Blends can smell quite differently with time due to the rich complexity that transpires. Some fragrances deepen and improve with age, some lasting for years. (I have sacred blends 6-10 years old that have become deeper and more concentrated, and two drops will last almost 24 hours.) *Note: perfumes with citrus oils will not have a very long shelf life, though some fixative oils such as resins will act as a preservative.*

4.  Consider using a "fixative" essential oil in your perfume blends to give them depth and tenacity (lasting power.) Frankincense, angelica root, myrrh, oakmoss, vetiver, and benzoin are all good choices that mix well with many essential oils.

### *Moon Garden Perfume*
**(a "green" floral with a nice balance of brightness and depth)**

30 drops pre-diluted Roman Chamomile essential oil
20 drops ylang ylang essential oil
8 drops clary sage essential oil
10 drops lavender essential oil
1 drop geranium essential oi
1 drop angelica root essential oil
to ½ ounce light vegetable oil for a perfume oil
or rosewater for a spray

### *Spiced Cocoa Perfume Oil*
**(a delicious-smelling blend of chocolate and spices with a hint of licorice*)**

30 drops cacao essential oil

2 drops nutmeg essential oil

10 drops clove essential oil

5 drops ylang ylang

3 drops cardamom essential oil

1 drop anise seed essential oil*

to ½ ounce light vegetable oil

*if you do not like the scent of licorice or anise, omit this oil*

### *Night Embers Perfume Oil*
**(intensely spicy, sweet, and woody)**

1 drop cassia essential oil

10 drops clove essential oil

10 drops pre-diluted angelica root essential oil

20 drops ylang ylang essential oil

20 drops amrys essential oil

to ½ ounce light vegetable oil

### *Earth Goddess Perfume Oil*
**(earthy like freshly-turned soil tempered with some sweetness)**

25 drops patchouli essential oil

20 drops amrys essential oil
2 drops vetiver essential oil
10 drops ylang ylang essential oil
2 drops cedar essential oil
8 drops myrrh essential oil

### Anointing and Daily Self-Care

Using sacred blends can become part of your everyday routine. Before you dress in the morning or when you step from the shower, anoint your heart, wrists, navel, and pubic bone with your chosen fragrance. This is also a wonderful way to end the day before going to sleep. As you anoint your body, see every part of yourself as sacred ground. You may wish to say a prayer or a simple affirmation such as, "I am protected this day (or night) by the Great Mother. I walk in Beauty."

# *Bath Crystals and Dusting Powders*

Sacred bathing mirrors spiritual traditions and gives us opportunity to infuse an everyday activity with spiritual intention. From the Hindu ritual of immersion in the Ganges to Christian baptism, bathing purifies not only the body but the energy field. If you prefer showers over baths, consider using bath crystals in a foot bath after a long day. Birthdays, sacred days, milestones, times of mourning, or recovery from an illness are ideal times for a sacred bath. Sinking into a scented bath pulsating with essences from our Mother Earth is a return to the womb on the deepest spiritual level possible.

Dusting powders for the body are lovely to layer the energies of fragrance, especially after a bath, foot bath, or shower. Once you try these beautiful bath salts and powders, you may never use chemical-laden or talc-based products again.

### Quick Use Reference for Bath Crystals

1. Add up to 50 drops of essential oil to one cup of Epsom salts and ¼ cup of evaporated sea salt, fine Celtic gray or Himalayan pink salt.

2. Stir ingredients in a bowl and mix well. Funnel into an air-tight glass container such as a mason or canning jar (can be purchased at craft stores.) For freshness and fragrance, use within 6-8 months. If you'd like to make a large batch, just double or triple the recipe requirements.

3. Use ¼ cup per bath or footbath. Sprinkle into water and swish with your fingers to distribute.

# *Goddess Consciousness*

## *Forest Pool Bath or Foot Bath Crystals*
**(refreshing scents of evergreen and a hint of sweetness)**

10 drops balsam fire essential oil
10 drops juniper essential oil
5 drops ylang ylang essential oil
2 drops cypress essential oil
per cup of Epsom salts blended with ¼ cup evaporated sea
salt or Himalayan pink salt

## *French Fields Bath or Foot Bath Crystals*
**(lavender mingled with grassy sage)**

20 drops lavender essential oil
6 drops clary sage essential oil
per cup of Epsom salts blended with ¼ cup evaporated sea
salt or Himalayan pink salt

## *Chocolate and Flowers Bath or Foot Bath Crystals*
**(sweet chocolate aroma with floral femininity)**

25 drops cacao essential oil
5 drops ylang ylang essential oil
15 drops diluted rose absolute essential oil
per cup of Epsom salts blended with ¼ cup evaporated sea
salt or Himalayan pink salt

## *Pink Moon Bath or Foot Bath Crystals*
**(jasmine with rosy overtones)**

## *Goddess Consciousness*

20 drops rose geranium, diluted rose absolute, or
rosewood essential oil
10 drops diluted jasmine absolute essential oil
per cup of Epsom salts blended with ¼ Himalayan pink salt

## *Winter Twilight Bath or Foot Bath Crystals*
**(clean and crisp, minty pine)**

30 drops pine needle essential oil
10 drops peppermint
per cup of Epsom salts blended with ¼ cup evaporated sea
salt or Himalayan pink salt

## *Purification Bath or Foot Bath Crystals*
**(menthol vapors with herbs and citrus)**

10 drops eucalyptus essential oil
5 drops peppermint essential oil
5 drops lemon essential oil
1 rosemary essential oil
per cup of Epsom salts blended with ¼ cup evaporated sea
salt or Himalayan pink salt

## *Flaming Rose Bath or Foot Bath Crystals*
**(a sexy floral spiced with ginger)**

10 drops rose geranium essential oil

# *Goddess Consciousness* ⭐

12 drops ylang ylang essential oil
1 drop ginger essential oil
per cup of Epsom salts blended with ¼ cup evaporated sea
salt or Himalayan pink salt

## *Sahara Rain Bath or Foot Bath Crystals*
**(desert resins with a hint of sweetness)**

10 drops myrrh essential oil
2 drops ylang ylang essential oil
3 drops frankincense essential oil
per cup of Epsom salts blended with ¼ cup evaporated sea
salt or Himalayan pink salt

## *English Garden Herbal Bath or Foot Bath Crystals*
**(scent of pungent herbs touched with fruit and florals)**

10 drops lavender essential oil
8 drops geranium essential oil
8 drops Roman chamomile essential oil
1 drop white thyme essential oil
1 drop rosemary essential oil
1 drop basil essential oil
per cup of Epsom salts blended with ¼ cup evaporated sea
salt or Himalayan pink salt

## Quick Use Reference for Body Powders

1. Add up to 15 drops of essential oil to 1 cup of pure

corn starch in a bowl. Stir very well with a fork, flattening each bead of essential oil until it dissolves into the corn starch.

2. Funnel into a grated cheese shaker and cover tightly. (Cheese shakers can be found in any kitchen section of department stores or craft stores.)

3.  Place a small strip of clear packaging tape over the holes and seal after each use. *Note: body powders with essential oils are not recommended for use on the face.*

## Chocolate Lavender Body Powder
**(cocoa and lavender bliss)**

15 drops cacao essential oil
5 drops lavender essential oil
mixed well into pure corn starch

## Sahara Rain Body Powder
**(sweet desert resins)**

5 drops frankincense essential oil
8 drops myrrh essential oil
2 drops ylang ylang essential oil
mixed well into pure corn starch

### *April Snow Body Powder*
**(clean, sweet evergreen and mint)**

4 drops peppermint essential oil
4 drops ylang ylang essential oil
2 drops pine needle essential oil
mixed well into pure corn starch

### *Flaming Rose Body Powder*
**(sexy floral with a touch of ginger)**

4 drops rosewood essential oil
3 drops ylang ylang essential oil
2 drops geranium essential oil
1 drop ginger essential oil
mixed well into pure corn starch

### *French Fields Body Powder*
**(grassy floral)**

6 drops lavender essential oil
5 drops clary sage essential oil
2 drops geranium essential oil
mixed well into pure corn starch

# *The Goddess Home Spa:*

## Suggested Combinations, Perfumed Candle Rubs, and Aromatic Room Sprays

# Suggested Trios
## Combining Perfumes, Baths, and Powders

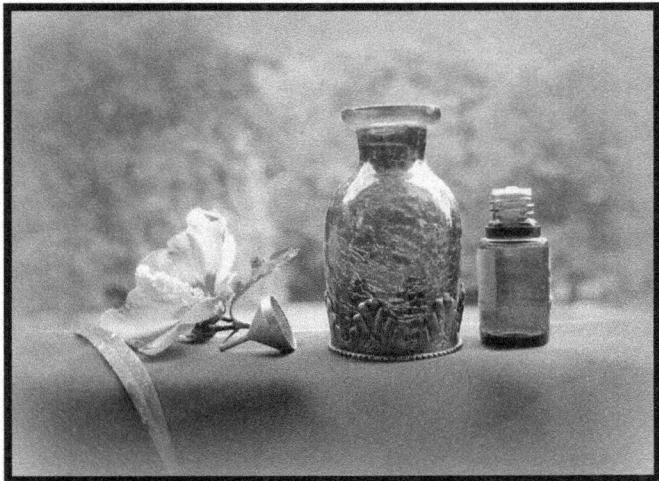

-Chocolate and Flowers Bath Crystals/Chocolate Lavender
Dusting Powder/Spiced Cocoa Perfume

-Pink Moon Bath Crystals/Flaming Rose Dusting
Powder/Flaming Rose Perfume

-French Fields Bath Crystals/French Fields Dusting
Powder/Moon Garden Perfume

-Winter Twilight Bath Crystals/April Snow Dusting
Powder/Earth Goddess Perfume

-Purification Bath Crystals/April Snow Dusting
Powder/Moon Garden Perfume

**-English Herbal Garden Bath Crystals/French Fields Dusting Powder/Moon Garden Perfume**

**-Sahara Rain Bath Crystals/Sahara Rain Dusting Powder/Night Embers Perfume**

# *Aromatic Sprays for Sacred Space*

Because using essential oils can be a little intimidating before learning the basics, I chose to include this section here. Using incense and fragrance in consecrated space is as ancient as humankind's communion with Deity. Scenting a room or sacred space keeps good energy flowing in and out, places you in an invisible bubble of protection, and inspires peace. Spraying aromatics into the air is also beautiful way to consecrate your sacred space and everyday environment from the home office to the bedroom. Using essential oils makes it easy and personalized. Here are a few wonderful ways to bring sacred scents into your life:

### Quick Use Reference for Purifying Room Spritzers

1. Fill a small-medium size misting/spray bottle halfway to three-quarter full with distilled water (found in any supermarket where spring water is sold.)

2. Add approximately 50-60 drops of essential oil. Shake well before each use.

3. Spray into the air to clear a room of accumulated energies. The effects are similar to smudging. You can also spray a cloud of fragrance around yourself, eyes closed, of course.

## Room Spritzer Blends

### *Energy Mist*
(citrus scents with ginger and hints of grass- bright and pungent)

25 drops lemongrass essential oil
25 drops sweet orange or tangerine essential oil
5 drops ginger essential oil
to distilled water

### *Passion Mist*
(sweet chocolate spice)

20 drops of clove essential oil
15 drops ylang ylang essential oil
15 drops cacao (chocolate) essential oil
2 drops of nutmeg essential oil
to distilled water or rosewater

### *Full Moon Mist*
(intoxicating sweet lemon with a hint of lavender)

30 drops ylang ylang essential oil
30 drops lemon essential oil
1 drops lavender essential oil
to distilled water or rosewater

### *Prophesy Mist*
(bright and a little euphoric)

20 drops lemon essential oil
30 drops anise seed essential oil
to distilled water

### *Purification Mist 1*
(woody sweetness with forest pine)

20 drops palo santo essential oil
10 drops frankincense essential oil
20 drops pine needle essential oil
to distilled water

### *Purification Mist 2*
(pungent herbs)

20 drops eucalyptus essential oil
20 drops spearmint essential oil

10 drops basil essential oil
to distilled water

## *Wood Spirit Mist*
(fragrant cedar and pine)

30 drops cedar essential oil
10 juniper essential oil
10 drops pine needle essential oil
to distilled water

## *Renewal Mist*
(refreshing and bright citrus and grassy undertones)

40 drops pink grapefruit essential oil
5 drops tangerine essential oil
10 drops lemongrass essential oil
to distilled water

# Scented Candle Rubs

### Quick Use Reference for Scenting Candles

1. Simply rub essential oils along the candles of your choice and allow them to dry for at least three hours

before you burn them. Store in an air-tight box and use within a week for best results.

### Full Moon Candle Rub
(sweet and haunting with delicious lemon)

4 drops ylang ylang essential oil
5 drops lemon essential oil
per candle

### Sacred Earth Candle Rub
(freshly-turned soil and pine needles)

5 drops patchouli essential oil
2 drops balsam fir essential oil
per candle

### Fire and Spice Candle Rub
(baking spices like Grandma's kitchen)

4 drops clove essential oil
1 drop nutmeg essential oil
per candle

## Goddess Consciousness

### Sweet Lavender Candle Rub
(sweet lavender)
4 drops lavender essential oil
3 drops ylang ylang essential oil
per candle


### Midsummer Candle Rub
(fragrant herbs with an undertone of citrus)

1 drop basil essential oil
1 drop spearmint essential oil
1 drop lemongrass essential oil
per candle


### Chocolate Lavender Candle Rub
(cocoa floral)

4 drops cacao essential oil
2 drops lavender essential oil
per candle
*Note: *due to cacao's dark-colored essential oil, choosing dark-colored candles is recommended to avoid unsightly staining.*

## How to Make Time for Soulful Beauty

A beautiful way to honor your inner Goddess is reserving time to nourish your senses and your spirit. Here are a few suggestions for incorporating the information and ideas in this chapter into your life.

1. Mark a date on your calendar every month for a home Goddess spa appointment. Arrange your schedule accordingly as if you have an appointment at a salon, gym, etc. Reserve time to honor your body and the Goddess.

2. Design your spa time from choice of music to what you will wear afterward. You may wish to include a prayer at the beginning and end of your Goddess spa time.

3.  You may wish to choose a theme for your spa time and choose your blessing oils or perfumes, spritzers, bath crystals, and body powders accordingly.

4.  Aside from the monthly spa date, choose a bath or a footbath with the same intention during any work week or on a weekend. Use a fragrance or blessing oil daily. Bits of self-care add up to a more balanced and blessed you!

5.  Consider creating a spa with friends and include a ceremony of your choice.

## 10

## Soul Sustenance: Sacred Herbs, Food, and Goddess Kitchens

The kitchen is not often considered to be a spiritual place, but it should be. It is where we nourish ourselves on a daily basis and where we gather with loved ones. Even if we do not indulge in the art of cooking, we all eat and fill our cups with steaming-hot coffee or fragrant tea. In essence, our kitchens are where Earth energies are concentrated and where nourishment from our planet fills our bellies.

Seeing the kitchen as a place of sustenance and magical

potential can bring new meaning to our relationship with food and give us an inspiring platform to honor the Goddess. Once we make a connection between food and spirit, we are fully nourished. In our age of obesity, illness, toxic soil and chemicals, eating disorders, fast food, and reality shows glorifying competition or gluttony in the kitchen, this connection is needed now more than ever. Too many human beings have forgotten how to define nourishment and rarely make time for it.

As with essential oils, frequency also plays an important role in what we put into our mouths. Studies using Kirlian photography to show energy emanating from organic versus non-organic produce demonstrate the difference in integrity between the two. Skeptics claim that the moisture in the photographed subject is what creates the "illusion" of the aura; however, many argue that if this was the case, then why do inanimate objects also demonstrate energy on film? Despite the controversy, it is surely something to think about. On a purely practical level, putting better food into our bodies—whole, satisfying food with higher frequency—could only help the body run better in much the same way higher-octane fuel helps the performance of our vehicles. We are willing to do it for our cars, then why not our precious, physical bodies?

This chapter offers inspirations, insights, and practical knowledge—mystical lore of food, a Medicine Woman Herbal, and easy recipes for soul-nourishing teas, warm flavored milks, and energized waters. You will also find ways to turn any kitchen into inspiring and nurturing sacred space.

# The Enchanted Kitchen

Deep in the memory of childhood, somewhere along the line we heard about fairy godmothers, witches, and Wise Women who lived in enchanted cottages. In most instances, the common vision of such a place included a cozy hearth, drying herbs, and magical brews. This fairy tale image comes down to us from the simple fact that in times gone by, women served as healers in the community. They used herbs to help the sick or injured, and there was nothing hocus pocus about it. Their understanding also encompassed spiritual uses of plants, which in reality is an art that is more practical than it is mystical when we see it for what it truly is—working with energy. In essence, the biological is mystical, and in my opinion, there is nothing more magical than that!

In our modern era, some of us incorporate the knowledge of our ancient mothers and value the wisdom of the green world by not only using herbs for medicinal and energetic purposes but by fostering a corner of enchantment in our kitchens. You need not be a seasoned clinical herbalist or a green witch to integrate herbs or sacred intention into your busy life. Here a few suggestions to bring some spirit, magic, and higher frequencies into your kitchen:

# *Goddess Consciousness* ⭐

1. Designate a little time at least one day a week to preparing something...a soup or meal, a sweet treat, or a magical tea. Consider playing beautiful music while you cook. Classical, Gregorian chant, relaxation spa CDs, Native American flute, meditation or Tibetan singing bowls, medieval polyphony, sacred music, or nature sounds are all wonderful choices to choose from. The lovely harmonies and peace will find their way right into your food and nourish the soul.

2. Consider creating an herb pantry and putting all of your grains, legumes, and medicinal herbs into Mason or jelly jars and storing them on shelves to display. Empty bookcases make wonderful corner pieces where everything you need is at your fingertips along with connections to the earth and its bounty.

3. Pick herbs, wildflowers, garden blooms, etc. and hang them upside down to dry in the kitchen. A bouquet of roses left over from Valentine's Day or a small branch of oak leaves blown down after a storm make lovely dried bouquets. Dried plants bring a breath of fresh air into your kitchen and can be placed in vases, jars, pitchers, tea pots, bowls, and cups or hung beneath a shelf, on the wall, or over a door. Bringing in fresh items to dry each year is a lovely symbolic way to discard what is no longer needed to usher in the new. If you live in an urban or suburban area and do not have access to wild plants, perhaps you can purchase

your flowers, greenery, and already-dried items at your local florist. If you live in a more countrified locale but for whatever reason cannot comb the waysides, meadows, or woods, perhaps you can ask a friend who gardens to put aside some plants for you to dry. If you gather wild plants yourself, remember to bring heavy clipping shears and gloves, for some stems are thorned or too woody to handle with bare hands.

4. Bring the energy of the Earth Goddess into your kitchen by finding corners to display found wonders such as birds' nests, river stones, winter branches, and feathers. Consider gathering long twigs or thin, windblown branches from your lawn and placing them in an old pickling jar or earthenware crock; string them with clear or single-color holiday lights all through the winter (or year) for an inviting, magical touch.

5. If you are drawn to images of the Wise Woman/Crone, Earth goddesses, or fairies, consider framing a piece of artwork or a photograph that speaks to you and hang it near your herb and/or grain stock.

*Note: Be mindful if you have four-legged family members; certain plants are harmful to cats and dogs, so place them out of reach to be safe. Also, keep children away from plants that are not in the edible herb family, especially wild berries, for many are poisonous and not for human consumption.)*

## Fragrant Drying Herbs/Plants

Anise Hyssop
Bee Balm
Cedar
Eucalyptus
Hydrangea
Juniper
Lavender
Marjoram
Poplar Branches w/ Buds
Red Staghorn Sumac Berry (from the staghorn sumac
tree, *not* poison sumac!)
Red Clover
Rosemary
Roses
Sage
Sagebrush
Sassafras Leaves
Thyme/Lemon Thyme
Verbena
Yarrow

## Colorful and Decorative Drying Herbs/Plants

Bittersweet Vine
Chili Peppers
Concord or Fox Grapes
Corn Stalks

Fireberries or Firethorn
Goldenrod
Lotus Seed Pods
Milkweed Pods
Mountain Ash/Rowan berries
Moss
Mullein Stalks
Privet Berries
Pussy Willow
Roses
Rose Hips
Spanish Moss
Sunflowers
Thistles/Sow Thistles
Wild Plum/Sloe
Willow/Curly Willow
Winter Cherry/Japanese Lantern

# Magic, Superstition, and Our Romance with Food

**Sacred Nourishment**

Even when we're on the run, taking a second or two to silently acknowledge the earth's bounty and the Goddess of sustenance can nourish our spirits as well as our bodies. A few words of Goddess "grace" before eating can be as simple as silently giving thanks to the plants, vegetables, grains, and fruit for growing and providing nourishment, and if you eat meat, the animals who gave their lives for our sustenance.

Below is a list of common foods and brief references to their mystical history, and when appropriate, their connections to the Goddess.

## Magical Folklore and Foods of the Goddess

**Amaranth:** *History*: sacred to the Aztecs and Artemis; used in rites to summon the spirits and the dead

**Apples**: *Lore/History*: symbol of immortality and the soul; sacred to Artemis/Diana, Athena, Hera, Aphrodite, Dionysos, Apollo, Venus, and Zeus; consumed at Samhain, the Celtic New Year which was also called Feast of Apples; Nordic peoples buried their dead with apples as a symbol of resurrection; was halved and eaten by the bride and groom at Gypsy weddings; cut in half a star or pentagram is revealed which represents the five elements; used for divination and love spells; unicorns were believed to dwell beneath apple trees

**Apricots:** *Lore/History:* a symbol of female genitalia, especially in medieval France; eaten to invoke lust and passion

**Bananas:** *Lore/History:* once a food stuff forbidden to be consumed by women (Hawaii); eaten to increase fertility and sexual potency; offered to the gods; attracts prosperity

**Beans:** *Lore/History:* ancient Romans associated the souls of ancestors with the bean, therefore were eaten at funerals; carried on the person as a protective amulet; used in ceremonial rattles

**Beets:** *Lore/History:* offered to Apollo at Delphi

**Blackberries:** *Lore/History:* sacred to Brigit/Brigid, goddess of Poetry, Fire, and Healing

**Blueberries:** *Lore/History:* eaten for protection or placed on the property for the same reason; guards against psychic attack

**Bread:** *Lore/History:* sacred to the Grain Mother; the word *lady* is derived from *hlaf-dig* or "giver of the grain"

**Buckwheat:** *Lore/History:* stored in the kitchen to prevent poverty or scarcity

**Cabbage:** *Lore/History:* planted by a bride and groom to ensure good luck in the marriage

**Cacao/Chocolate:** *Lore/History:* food of the Aztec and Mayan gods; drunk by nobility and priests; ceremonial beverage; the species of chocolate we consume today is not the same species the ancients used

**Celery:** *Lore/History:* eaten to increase psychic powers or stimulate prophetic dreams

**Cherries:** *Lore/History:* sacred to Maya, virgin mother

of Buddha; used in love spells and divination

*Coffee:* *Lore/History:* used in rites of exorcism and healing in pre-Islamic Ethiopia; coffee beans were symbols of the life-giving yoni

*Coconuts:* *Lore/History:* for protection; a symbol of chastity; offered to Hindu gods, the three "eyes" of the coconut shell representing those of Shiva; invokes courage

*Corn/Maize:* *Lore/History:* personified as Corn Mother, the patron of plenty; attracts good luck and keeps evil influences from newborns and women in labor

*Dates:* *Lore/History:* sacred to Hekate, Isis, Apollo, Artemis, and Ra; eaten to increase fertility and sexual potency

*Eggs:* *Lore/History:* symbol of the Germanic goddess Eostre, deity of springtime and the fertility of the season, hence the custom of Easter eggs; also sacred to Mary Magdalen symbolized in a myth regarding Christ's resurrection

*Figs:* *Lore/History:* used in ancient divination practices; eaten to ensure fertility; ancient symbol of female sexuality and genitalia (the seeded womb)

*Garlic:* *Lore/History:* used in exorcisms of evil or vampiric spirits (stealers of psychic energy); sacred to Hekate and offered at crossroads; repels envy and the negative energy of the Evil Eye

*Grains:* *Lore/History:* sacred to the Earth Mother and Her divine son who took the form of wheat, rye, barley, and oats; keeps evil at bay

*Grapes:* *Lore/History:* sacred to Hathor and Dionysos; symbol of ecstatic inspiration and fertility; considered by Gnostics to be the forbidden fruit in the Garden of Eden

*Honey:* *Lore/History:* sacred to the Great Goddess and her ancient priestesses called *melissae* or bees

*Leeks:* *Lore/History:* eaten to repel evil influences

*Lemons:* *Lore/History:* hung in the home to attract good fortune; juice added to purification baths and full moon rites

*Lettuce:* *Lore/History:* protective when grown in gardens

*Limes:* *Lore/History:* twigs were carried to guard against the Evil Eye

**Milk:** *Lore/History:* the cow was sacred to the Mother Goddess in the Mediterranean as well as India which continues to this day; primordial creation substance

**Mulberries:** *Lore/History:* guards a garden against lightning; magician's magical wands were often made from wood from the mulberry tree

**Nuts:** *Lore/History:* eaten to increase prosperity and fertility; Scottish divination tools; certain nuts such as almonds symbolized the yoni, woman's sacred gateway of life

**Oats:** *Lore/History:* eaten to attract money

**Olive:** *Lore/History:* sacred to Athena/Minerva and a symbol of wisdom and peace; oil was burned in temples and used in sacred anointing; brides in ancient Athens wore olive leaf crowns for fertility

**Onions:** *Lore/History:* used in ancient Egyptian rituals of oath-taking; protective like garlic but not as potent energetically

**Oranges:** *Lore/History:* attracts love and inspires physical beauty; carrying flowers from the orange in bridal bouquets is linked to old fertility rituals during which the orange blossom was a symbol of virginity and fertility

**Papaya:** *Lore/History:* eaten and shared between lovers

**Peach:** *Lore/History:* originated in China and believed to be from the Tree of Life sacred to the Goddess; linked to female fertility; in Chinese lore, a peach pit worn around a child's neck will keep demons away

**Pears:** *Lore/History:* used in love spells; legends say that witches reveled beneath pear trees

**Peas:** *Lore/History:* attracts money and increased profits from business

**Persimmon:** *Lore/History:* burying the green unripe fruit and offering it to the earth was believed to bring good luck

**Pineapple:** *Lore/History:* attracts love, luck, and money

**Plum:** *Lore/History:* inspires love and protects the household when its branches are hung over the door

**Pomegranate:** *Lore/History:* ancient symbol of the womb due to its many seeds; sacred to Persephone where the fruit is food for souls in the afterlife

**Potato:** *Lore/History:* associated with the goddess of

## the Pomegranate

*The pomegranate, also called the Chinese apple, has long been associated with the Goddess, especially in her Underworld aspect. The fruit was especially sacred to the Greek goddess Persephone—Mistress of the Dead, but also associated with the Roman Goddess Juno— Mother of Heaven, and the Babylonian goddess Ishtar—divinity of love, sexual power, and war. The blood-colored fruit was representative of the womb, and its ruby-like seeds were eaten to increase fertility, abundance, and luck. It was believed that souls after death were nourished by pomegranate seeds which prepared them for rebirth. The pomegranate is often eaten at the time of Samhain, the Celtic new year when the door between worlds is left ajar and the dead come back; consuming three glistening pomegranate seeds at this time is said to ensure good fortune in the coming year. From a more scientific perspective, the juice from the fruit has been shown to be especially beneficial to women's health including vitamin fortification during pregnancy, easing chronic cystitis, lowering the risk of breast cancer, and preventing post-menopausal osteoporosis.*

fertility in South America

**Quince:** *Lore/History:* symbol of female fertility in ancient Greece and eaten by brides; sacred to the goddess Venus; attracts love and happiness

**Radish:** *Lore/History:* protects against the Evil Eye when carried; invokes lust when consumed

**Raspberries:** *Lore/History:* bramble branches were believed to keep out ghosts and were hung over the door after a death in the family to keep the spirit of the deceased from re-entering

**Rice:** *Lore/History:* tossed over newly-married couples to bless them with fertility; rice is used as an offering in Hindu and Jain puja rituals

**Salt:** *Lore/History:* sacred symbol of rebirth and purification; thrown over the shoulder to dispel bad luck and halt death; eaten before leaving to go on a journey

**Sesame Seeds:** *Lore/History:* believed to hold secrets and lead to hidden treasure, hence the password command, "open sesame"

**Strawberries:** *Lore/History:* brings luck; food of lovers

**Sugar Cane:** *Lore/History:* purifies sacred space before ceremonial use; used in love spells

**Tamarind:** *Lore/History:* attracts love

**Tomatoes:** *Lore/History:* protects any area where planted or placed; once called "love apples"

**Turnips:** *Lore/History:* were the original Jack-o-lanterns with the insides hollowed and lit with a candle on Samhain, the Celtic New Year (known to us as Halloween); used to scare away evil influences

**Wheat:** *Lore/History:* represents abundance and attracts money; symbolic of the fruitful earth

**Wine:** *Lore/History:* once symbolic of the Goddess' menstrual blood, therefore, the blood of life; sacred to Dionysos/Bacchus

# The Wise Woman Herb Pantry

Herbs—those fragrant little beings we use to tame winter colds and flavor our food can also be our most sacred offerings. When we pluck minty sprigs or sprinkle golden flowers into water to make a tea, we invite the very energies of Goddess Earth into our bodies and our souls. The rain-scented soil, the summer sun, and the dew that sustained the living plant becomes part of our own flesh. All of the cosmic caretaking of the plant devas and the Green Mother that breathed life into the herb is also poured into us.

Herbs are also nature's apothecary. What shamans, Wise Women, and lay people have known for centuries about plants and their curative powers is now being proven in reputable clinical studies. Combining ancient knowledge

251

with cutting-edge sophistication, clinical herbalism is the way of the future. As women, we have innate capacity to understand the ways of plants, and working with them is a beautiful way to keep our bodies and psyches in better balance.

Plants, like all living beings, possess frequency and spirits that interact with our own. They are also deeply interconnected to the unseen energies of the earth, the invisible caretakers of the green world only visible to the developed psychic eye. Plants and trees are our greatest allies, and once we get to know them, we develop relationships with them that can change our lives on the deepest cellular level. Plants can help us find equilibrium, guide us to wellness, and provide our bodies with what we need to heal ourselves. They can be strong teachers who can accompany us through physical or emotional crisis yet be gentle friends who delight us with their presence in the form of taste, fragrance, and beauty. Herbalism—medicinal or spiritual—is a complex science and art, one that takes a lifetime of study to fully master, but all of us can work with plants. The following herbal is a brief reference guide to significant plants that can enhance your life. Information herein refers to internal use (tea, tincture, or capsules) unless otherwise noted. *Most importantly, be sure to use herbs of finest integrity; most spices and some herbs on the commercial market are irradiated, which renders them inferior for medicinal use. Spices are most vulnerable to this process that deactivates their powerful benefits.* See Resources for reputable suppliers and Recommended Reading for deeper study.

# *A Wise Woman Herbal:*
# *Medicinal and Energetic Uses*

**\*Note**: *If you are pregnant or breastfeeding, taking certain medications including blood thinners, or are planning to undergo surgery, consult with your doctor about ingesting herbs, for many are contraindicated.* **Disclaimer**: ***This list of***

*herbs and the information herein is not intended to diagnose or treat illness, or to replace conventional medical treatment.*

## Alfalfa

**Properties:** useful for arthritis, weak appetite, and mineral deficiency; rich in minerals such as calcium and potassium; richest source of life-nourishing chlorophyll; soothing and nourishing for disorders of the colon; supports the blood and recommended for anemia; increases the body's alkalinity and balances overly-acidic conditions *Note: contraindicated for estrogen dominance, estrogen-dependent cancers, and transplant survivors on anti-rejection drugs*

**Energetic uses:** encourages groundedness and inner stability

## Anise Seeds

**Properties:** increases breastmilk; excellent remedy for indigestion, stomach pain or upset, and intestinal discomfort; helps reduce cough and congestion; licorice-like flavor

**Energetic uses:** lifts the mood; instills hope and inner calm; cleanses the energy field of pessimism and feelings of defeat; provides a sense of grounding and stability

## Betony, Wood

**Properties:** for neuralgia associated with shingles; improves liver function; reduces anxiety and nervous extremes; supportive during stress

**Energetic uses:** places a shield around a person and strengthens psychic defenses; will keep nightmares and night terrors away

## Birch

**Properties:** pain reduction; diuretic for non-cardiac and non-renal fluid retention; anti-inflammatory properties in arthritic conditions, cystitis, and gout; may be helpful in lowering cholesterol; improves digestion

**Energetic uses:** protection, detachment of entities from the energy field

## Blackberry Leaves

**Properties:** cleanses the blood and liver; lessens inflammation of gums, mouth, and throat; used as a mouthwash; relieves diarrhea; may be helpful for cardiovascular diseases; prevents and reduces free radical damage to cells; *Note: excessive consumption is not recommended

*Energetic uses:* encourages resilience and charging forward with goals after disappointments and failure; protects the energy field from outside influences; sacred to Brigid, ancient goddess of art and poetry, fire, and healing

## Black Tea

*Properties:* rich in anti-oxidants; improves circulation; lowers cholesterol; may reduce tooth decay; soothing to the stomach; calms diarrhea; according to reputable clinical studies, black tea reverses abnormalities of the blood vessels and may prevent stroke and cardiovascular disease; lowers bad cholesterol; *Note: *tea inhibits the absorption of iron and drinking it between meals is advised*

*Energetic uses:* encourages courage and strength of spirit `

## Bladderwrack

*Properties:* good source of iodine and may improve thyroid function; mineral-rich and nutritious for the skin, hair, and nails

*Energetic uses:* holds the energies of the sea; cleansing

to the energy field and encourages second sight

## Burdock Root

**Properties:** blood purifier due its cleansing action on the liver, kidneys, colon, and skin; for gout, skin troubles, cancer, and infections; also a blood builder and useful for anemia

**Energetic uses:** protective and combats negativity, lower energies, and malevolent outside influences

## California Poppy

**Properties:** non-opiate/non-addictive with sedative properties for tension, insomnia, pain, and anxiety; excellent for children's colic; relaxes muscles throughout the body; a good remedy for migraine, tension headaches, back pain, sciatica, and shingles pain; can be taken internally and applied externally for pain in general; balancing properties for stressful times or when one is in addiction withdrawal, including cigarette cessation

**Energetic uses:** helps one to ground and have his/her own mind regarding spiritual matters; encourages self-reliance in all situations; available as a flower essence

(See Resources)

## Cardamom Seeds

**Properties:** relieves indigestion, flatulence, and improves digestion of proteins, starches, and milk products; allays nausea; found to be cancer-fighting and prevents new cancer cells; helps constipation; promotes better circulation; strengthens libido

**Energetic uses:** inspires passion for life and ambition, and dissolves apathy; supports the heart chakra

## Chamomile, Roman

**Properties:** calms the nervous system and digestive tract; promotes peaceful sleep; reduces menstrual pain; relaxes muscles throughout the body; useful in fevers, infections, cold/flu, and gastroenteritis; lessens nausea during pregnancy; natural antihistamine properties; effective in cases of cystitis and bladder inflammation; a primary women's herb for menstrual and hormonal imbalances, PMS, menopause and perimenopause; ideal herb for children's digestive woes; its Latin name translates to "matrix, mother, womb"

**Energetic uses:** encourages happiness and lifts melancholy; dissipates anger; instills hope; balances moods; helpful in physical digestive distress from emotions; promotes self-acceptance, especially for women or girls prone to eating disorders or self-harm; available as a flower essence (See Resources)

## *Cinnamon*

***Properties:*** used in Chinese and Ayurvedic medicine for thousands of years; lowers bad cholesterol; improves memory; promotes healthy circulation; balances blood sugar levels in both reactive hypoglycemia and diabetes; fights E. coli; cancer fighting properties especially for cases of lymphoma and leukemia; encourages weight loss; kills systemic candida and helps to restore beneficial flora in the intestines; strengthens the immune system on every level; *Note: be sure to use true cinnamon (*Cinnamomum zeylanicum) *rather than cassia, which is very similar to cinnamon and sold as such. See Resources for suppliers.*

***Energetic uses:*** attracts opportunity, success, and abundance; inspires confidence, stability, and comfort

## *Cloves*

***Properties:*** digestive remedy par excellence and increases digestive enzymes; reduces food putrification in the bowel; anti-fungal, anti-bacterial, and anti-viral properties; immune strengthener; for acute viral and bacterial infections; inhibits *listeria* bacteria and combats food poisoning in general; lowers the risk of cancer, including the lung; eliminates and prevents systemic candida and unhealthy flora in the intestines; **\*Note:** *a pinch in a morning shake, hot or warm water, or coffee/tea is a nice way to get a dose of cloves*

**Energetic uses:** inspires trust in others and self; encourages renewal of body and spirit; invokes inspiration and aspiration

## Comfrey Leaf

**Properties:** soothing to the organ systems including digestive, respiratory, and urinary; rich in minerals and very fortifying to the body's nutrition and metabolism; strengthens bones and knits broken ones; soothes on contact whether it be skin or digestive tract; useful for ulcers, inflammation, and excessive heat in the body; helps arthritis, bronchitis, bladder inflammation, and diarrhea; as a douche, heals vaginal yeast infections and applied externally as a foot bath or tincture for fungal conditions of the feet; **\*Note:** *not to be confused with* **comfrey root** *which is controversial and not recommended for internal use. Also, comfrey leaf may bring skin conditions to a head* *which can lead to a boil or cyst; this is the plant's way of clearing the problem on the deepest level.*

**Energetic uses:** comforts during times of emotional distress and helps to inspire self-nurturing; promotes healing at the energetic level; holds the earth and the Earth Mother's healing green energy; supports the heart and root chakras

## Damiana

**Properties:** supports the reproductive system in both women and men and strengthens orgasmic response; nourishing to the adrenals; useful for discomfort during perimenopause and menopause; calming to the nervous system, improves bowel function and useful for constipation; lifts the mood

**Energetic uses:** bestows a feeling of being nurtured and warmed from the inside out; instills hope; opens the psychic eye

## Dandelion

**Properties:** promotes detoxification of liver, kidneys, and blood; increases bile and other digestive juices; helpful for gout and arthritis; good to sip when starting a cleaner diet or after indulging in too much holiday food, alcohol, and sugar

*Energetic uses:* cleanses negative emotions from the energy field and also those held in the bodily tissues; helps overly ambitious, busy, or scheduled individuals to slow down and relax; available as a flower essence (See Resources)

## *Elder (berries and flowers)*

*Properties:* Berries: improve immune function; very useful for fevers, cold/flu, and infections; Flowers: beneficial for bronchial spasms related to asthma, allergies, and colds/flu; useful for melancholy depression and anxiety; for sore throats, inflamed gums, or as an eye wash for conjunctivitis

*Energetic uses:* inspires strength and courage when fears are dominant in the psyche; encourages self-esteem; connects us to the realms of faerie; brings protection to the energy field/aura when needed

## *Eucalyptus*

*Properties:* Aboriginal plant medicine for infectious fevers; helpful for cold/flu, chickenpox, measles, typhoid fever, malaria, scarlet fever, bronchitis, pneumonia, ear infection, bleeding gums, thrush, sore throats, and sinus problems; Chinese medicine uses eucalyptus for tuberculosis of the lungs, inflamed and aching joints, neuralgia, and migraines; will clean the air of infectious agents

*Energetic uses:* helps us to accept life's circumstances and go with the flow more easily

## *Fennel*

*Properties:* excellent for digestion and improving the absorption of nutrients; increases breastmilk; muscle relaxant and useful for menstrual cramping; breaks up mucus in the lungs; helps gout, arthritis, and painful joints

*Energetic uses:* promotes healing and psychic protection

## *Fenugreek Seeds*

*Properties:* for diabetic conditions; lowers blood sugar; lowers bad cholesterol while raising beneficial cholesterol; increases breastmilk; for chronic bronchitis and wet coughs; breaks up systemic congestion; induces childbirth; improves digestion; strengthens appetite;

*Energetic uses:* attracts abundance, especially financial; cleanses emotions no longer useful for our highest good

## Ginger Root

*Properties:* kills bacteria and useful in cases of food poisoning; excellent for nausea, travel sickness, and morning sickness; stimulating to the circulation and warms the body; kills candida and balances yeasts in the body; prevents certain cancers, especially colon cancer; speeds digestion and helps food absorption; reduces sinus inflammation; useful for colds/flu and stomach cramps; excellent for muscle and joint pain; recommended for pain associated with arthritis, sprains, and fibromyalgia; increases libido, increases feel-good endorphins, especially dopamine *Note: *will neutralize antidepressant medications and herbals intended to utilize serotonin*

*Energetic uses:* inspires a positive, fighting spirit when faced with obstacles and challenges; provides fiery energy of protection around the energy field/aura; supports the first, second, and third energy centers/chakras and increases *prana* or life force

## Goldenseal

**Properties:** lowers blood sugar and highly useful for diabetes; cleanses the bowel and blood; stimulates liver function; excellent mouthwash for gingivitis and inflamed gums; kills candida and balances healthy flora in the large intestine

**Energetic uses:** inspires one to leave the past behind after emotional cleansing; encourages tears and letting go

## Green Tea

**Properties:** reduces risk of many cancers; rich in antioxidants; lowers bad cholesterol and raises beneficial cholesterol; reduces risk of heart disease and improves artery function; lowers blood pressure *Note: tea inhibits the absorption of iron and drinking it between meals is advised*

**Energetic uses:** bestows grace of spirit and inspires wealth; opens the heart chakra and encourages compassion and gentleness; invokes emotional courage when one feels vulnerable and helps us to allow love into our lives

## Hawthorn Berries

**Properties:** strengthens the heart and improves circulation; balances fluids in the body (diuretic); reduces hardening of the arteries and useful in all heart conditions including arrhythmias; may be helpful for rosacea when both the berries and the flowers of the hawthorn are used; calms the nervous system and quells agitation

*Energetic uses:* used in times of grief, loss, and transition to heal the emotional heart; helps one cope with disappointment; helps balance intense emotions; opens the heart chakra

## Hyssop

*Properties:* improves immunity and helps the body fight infections; helpful for congested lungs; lowers fevers; helpful in cases of nervous debility, asthma, and spasms of the stomach and digestive system; speeds healing of cold sores (herpes simplex)

*Energetic uses:* cleanses the mind and heart of guilt; encourages forgiveness, especially for oneself; purifies the energy field of emotional baggage

## Irish Moss

*Properties:* improves metabolism and thyroid function; rich in minerals; extremely soothing to the digestive system and inflamed skin conditions when applied externally; useful for bronchitis and respiratory ailments; nourishing to the kidneys; soothes bladder and urinary tract infections; makes a wonderful hydrating skin "cream" when applied to the skin and will "set" make-up when applied beforehand

*Energetic uses:* invokes happiness and a more carefree attitude; connects one to the energy of the ocean and healing force of the seas; helps one to retrieve deep soul memories

## Jasmine Flowers

*Properties:* gentle and healing herb for the female reproductive system; useful for PMS, headaches, heavy menstrual bleeding, and cramping; strengthens women's orgasmic response and libido; may also decrease uterine fibroids; good for sinusitis and respiratory infections

*Energetic uses:* encourages mental clarity and stamina; inspires deeper thoughts about life and purpose; connects an individual to her innate feminine wisdom; resonates with the energies of the night and the moon; inspires beauty, happiness, and hope; attracts angelic influences

## Juniper Berries

*Properties:* promotes flow of urine and helps to heal urinary tract infections; nourishing to the bladder and non-diseased kidneys*; excellent for improving immunity and fighting infection; useful for bronchial congestion, cold/flu, and allergies; stimulates weak appetite, improves digestion, and helps flatulence; increases peristalsis of the digestive tract, especially the large intestine; may help arthritis; lowers blood pressure; supports the adrenals and the liver; **\*Note:** *not recommended and contraindicated for kidney disease*

*Energetic uses:* powerful eliminator of lower energies and entities; protects the energy field/aura; removes astral and psychic attachments and emotional "threads" from other people; protective herb when placed on the person or placed by one's bedside

## Kava Kava

*Properties:* ceremonial herb used for centuries as a powerful, non-addictive sedative; relaxes the smooth muscles of the body; helps production and utilization of many neurotransmitters including serotonin and GABA; excellent for insomnia, anxiety/panic attacks, and hormonal-related nervousness; promotes a sense of well-being, positive outlook, and calms the fight or flight response; calms excessive adrenalin and cortisol production during or after stress; reliable pain reducer and effective for Chronic Fatigue Syndrome, fibromyalgia, headaches, migraine, ADHD, and convulsions **\*Note:** *kava kava should never be combined with alcohol or medications including antidepressant drugs or drugs used to treat Parkinson's Disease; not recommended for anyone with compromised liver or kidney function. Also, although it is a root, kava kava is never prepared as a decoction but as an infusion in hot (but not boiling) water.*

**Energetic uses:** opens the psychic eye and stimulates visions, creativity, and prophetic dreams; dispels evil influences and encourages good fortune

## *Lady Slipper*

**Properties:** Native American remedy for afflictions of the nervous system including nervous debility, severe anxiety, and insomnia; lessens spasms and pain; useful for women's hormonal transitions including perimenopause, menopause, and PMS \*Note: lady slipper is an endangered plant; please use cultivated sources (See Resources)

**Energetic uses:** connects us to a higher source of inner strength and wisdom; resonates with femininity and spiritual innocence

## *Lavender Flowers*

**Properties:** unsurpassed tonic for the nervous system and useful for nervous exhaustion, digestive spasms and upset; fragrant put powerful anti-infectious properties valuable in cases of strep throat, typhoid, cold/flu, tonsillitis, chest infection, and infections of the bowel; useful for headaches including migraine; muscle relaxant; reduces anxiety, dread, panic attacks, trembling, nervousness, and stress; lowers fevers when consumed hot

**Energetic uses:** dissolves thought forms, especially those created by jealousy; opens the higher chakras including the third eye and crown; attracts angels; calms stormy emotions; available as a flower essence (See Resources)

## *Lemon Balm*

**Properties:** affects the limbic system of the brain, therefore highly useful in cases of emotional extremes; strengthens memory and improves concentration; helpful for insomnia if drunk throughout the day; calms the digestive system and improves liver and gallbladder function; recommended for PMS, menstrual cramps, and emotional mood swings; may decrease tinnitus (noise in the ears), migraine, and dizziness; useful for coughs and respiratory complaints, sinus problems, and allergic reactions; ideal children's herb due to its gentle but effective action in cases of stomach and intestinal cramping; also highly useful for nervous exhaustion and *hyper*thyroidism; *Note: those with *hypo*thyroidism should not take large amounts of lemon balm or long-term

**Energetic uses:** helps to restore youthful enthusiasm and emotional vitality; especially helpful for burnout and recommended for caregivers, worriers, and depleted individuals; inspires courage and self-reliance; protects energy field/aura during sleep and prevents night terrors, nightmares, and visitations

## *Lemongrass*

**Properties:** has antifungal and antibacterial properties; Ayurvedic applications of lemongrass include Parkinson's Disease, Alzheimer's Disease, and disorders of the nervous system; nerve tonic; excellent herb for insomnia or fitful sleep; may fight cancer cells; helps to balance intestinal flora and combat systemic candida

**Energetic uses:** stimulates second sight/psychic ability; clears deep regrets, promotes forgiveness and honesty with others and oneself; helps us to integrate life experiences; inspires peace and contentment; brightens the spirits

## *Licorice Root*

***Properties:*** useful in soothing digestive distress and promotes healing of ulcers; gently improves bowel function and lessens constipation; for bronchitis, congested lungs, sore throat, and cold/flu; supports the adrenals and endocrine system in general; helps balance non-diabetic blood sugar swings and raises blood sugar; raises blood pressure, therefore good for hypotension*; *Note: *contraindicated for high blood pressure*

***Energetic uses:*** encourages grounding and stability; clears bitterness and feelings of resentment; invokes the wisdom inherent within the soul or Higher Self/Goddess Self; nourishing and supportive of the solar plexus chakra

## *Linden*

***Properties:*** muscle relaxant and nervous system ally for times of stress, tension, and pressure; may prevent heart disease and relax coronary arteries; excellent for excitable children, colic and fevers; may be helpful in cases of mild-moderate depression; reduces high blood pressure; helps ease menstrual discomfort

***Energetic uses:*** dissolves emotional blocks and helps

reserved individuals to express or receive love; opens the heart chakra and inspires universal, humanitarian connectedness; encourages peace within; attracts angels

## Marshmallow Root

**Properties:** unsurpassed for reducing inflammation in the gentlest way possible and useful for inflammatory bowel conditions, digestive upsets including heartburn; highly useful for cystitis, bladder inflammation, and kidney stones; increases the flow of breastmilk; good remedy for sore throat, lung irritation, coughs, and chronic bronchitis

**Energetic uses:** calms heated emotions, fears, and agitation; opens communication and helps one to cope with loneliness or isolation

## Motherwort

**Properties:** calming women's herb that is nourishing to the female reproductive system; useful for repressed or sluggish menstrual flow; normalizes menstrual cycle; helps to balance the body during perimenopause and menopause; quiets nervous heart palpitations; relaxes the heart muscle and prevents blood clots; may be helpful for depressive states accompanied by anxiety; *Note: contraindicated for anyone on blood thinners or women who are trying to conceive*

**Energetic uses:** gently bestows feelings of equilibrium; envelopes the energy field with loving, maternal energy and protection; helps to heal the cellular effects of any form of sexual abuse or violence; encourages the acceptance of one's sexuality; helps women to make peace with their own bodies

## Mugwort

**Properties:** for stomach and intestinal problems including spasms, diarrhea, constipation, and nausea; for irregular menstruation; may help relieve programmed emotional patterns *Note: not recommended for long-term use*

**Energetic uses**: induces psychic dreams and opens the psychic eye; invites spiritual dreams and information from the spirit worlds; offers protection of the energy field/aura and banishes evil influences; may be useful for astral projection or soul travel; sacred to the goddess Artemis and connects us to the pristine places in nature where feminine energy is dominant; available as a flower essence (See Resources)

## *Mullein (leaf and flowers)*

**Properties:** Leaf: powerful antibacterial and antitumeral properties; useful to combat pneumonia and staph infection; antispasmodic properties; excellent herb for the lungs including for congestion and asthma; improves, opens, and deepens the breath; Flowers: mullein oil made with the flowers of the mullein plant is a reliable remedy for earache and wax accumulation

**Energetic uses:** helps us to connect to the inner voice that guides us in the right direction; channels light into the energy field and helps to bring clarity where there is confusion; clears guilt and the weight of the past; inspires us to remain true to what is right in our hearts; available as a flower essence (See Resources)

## *Nettles*

**Properties:** unsurpassed to supply the body with needed minerals; excellent blood builder and plant source for iron; helps to restore vital energy after illness, stress, transition, or shock; energizes the body and oxygenates the cells; removes uric acid and helpful for kidney stones, gout and arthritis; cleans the blood of toxins; balances blood sugar; may be helpful for some forms of eczema; excellent herb to fortify hair, skin, and nails; **\*Note:** *It is recommended to infuse nettles for four-12 hours to bring* *out the most of their beneficial minerals and nutrition.*

**Energetic uses**: showers the aura and spirit with vitality; blesses exhausted souls with the restorative emerald-green energy of the earth and the Earth Goddess; resonates with the heart chakra; inspires renewal and rejuvenation

## Oatstraw

**Properties:** nutritious nerve tonic; for nervous debility, anxiety, adrenal exhaustion, and overtired/overworked states

**Energetic uses**: supports the spirit with energy to endure; restores vital energy to the soul and chakras after illness, loss, or psychic depletion (and the extreme—psychic attack)

## Olive Leaf

**Properties:**  helps to lower blood pressure in cases of hypotension; relaxes the blood vessels in the body; improves circulation; useful in cases of angina; may be useful for diabetes; strongest plant-based antibiotic and unsurpassed for infection, malaria, and typhoid fever; also has antiviral properties; strengthens immunity in general

*Energetic uses:* restorative to the body and mind; instills harmony and inner peace; helps to replenish life force and vitality; available as a flower essence (See Resources)

## Pau d' Arco

*Properties:* sacred herb with powerful anti-cancerous properties; for chronic and acute viral conditions; cleans the blood; kills systemic candida and restores healthy intestinal flora; useful for diabetes, parasites, and skin conditions

*Energetic uses:* detaches parasitic energies/entities from the energy field; encourages getting to the root cause of physical illness and breaks up old emotional wounds and patterns deep in cellular memory

## Peppermint

*Properties:* helps the body find balance and encourages homeostasis; cools or warms the body when needed; tonic for the whole body when cases of depletion after physical or emotional stress or illness; acts as a sedative or a stimulant, depending upon the body's needs at the moment; allays nausea; calms spastic bowel conditions; lessens pain in muscles and digestive system; excellent for headaches, cold/flu, and heart palpitations; general heart tonic; recommended for travel sickness, herpes simplex, and sore throat; may be useful for tuberculosis; **\*Note:** *peppermint is contraindicated for stomach or duodenal ulcers, and some people with hiatal hernia see an increase in symptoms after ingesting peppermint*

***Energetic uses****:* clears and strengthens the mind, lifts the blues, and ideal for overtired students; inspires happiness and hope; enforces resilience; available as a flower essence (See Resources)

## *Raspberry Leaves*

***Properties:*** female hormone regulator; for water retention, especially related to hormonal shifts; allays morning sickness; tones the female reproductive system and prepares the body for pregnancy; increases fertility and chances of conception; helps to prevent miscarriage; reduces leg swelling and cramping during pregnancy; helps to prevent post-partum depression by balancing hormones and neurotransmitters after pregnancy; excellent tonic tea for women, men, and children; useful for stomach aches and diarrhea; helps to balance hormonal shifts during the menstrual cycle, perimenopause, and menopause

*Energetic uses:* offers protective and healing energy

## Red Clover Blossom

*Properties:* blood cleanser and useful for tumors due to sterol-beta-sitosterol; excellent for the female reproductive system and recommended for pelvic inflammatory disease; also for heavy periods, vaginal infections; estrogenic action makes it a wonderful herb for later stages of perimenopause and into menopause; lessens hot flashes, improves bowel function, and calms stomach and intestinal pain; valuable in cases of atherosclerosis; for tension headaches and stress-related allergies or asthma; for some skin conditions, especially children's eczema; helpful for osteoporosis; **Note:** *contraindicated for estrogen dominance and estrogen-dependent cancers*

*Energetic uses:* clears the energy field and especially helpful for empaths who take on the emotional or physical problems of others; helps one to weather the storms of life with inner calm; available as a flower essence (See Resources)

## Rooibos/African Red Bush

***Properties:*** contains extremely high amount of anti-oxidants; useful for asthma, allergies, and boosting immunity; similar to black and green tea in effect (minus the caffeine content) and slows the aging process, inhibits cancer, and slows the progression of serious conditions including Alzheimer's Disease and perhaps AIDS; reduces systemic inflammation; good for insomnia and digestive discomfort

***Energetic uses:*** strengthens the energy field/aura in the same way it strengthens the body's immune and cellular function; provides a spiritual fortress for one's spirit

## *Rose*

***Properties:*** *whole flowers and petals*: gentle but effective hormonal regulator for women; antibacterial, antifungal, and antiviral properties; fortifies the lungs to fight infections; excellent for colds/flus and for restoring healthy intestinal flora after the use of antibiotics; for PMS, menopause, and perimenopause discomforts; decongests the female reproductive system; calms frayed nerves, heart palpitations, and lightens emotional stress; balances acidity within the digestive tract; *Rose Hips:* wonderful source of vitamin C; *Note: Be sure to obtain unsprayed/organic roses for internal consumption. See Resources.*

***Energetic uses:*** brings balm to broken hearts and helps one to cope with death, loss, break-ups, transitions, loneliness, and the effects of past abuse be it physical, emotional, verbal, or sexual; blesses a woman with the ability to be comfortable with her own body, sexuality, and self-image; promotes self-forgiveness and forgiveness; lifts the spirits; invokes Goddess energy

## _Rosemary_

**Properties:** increases circulation to the brain, therefore strengthens the mind, memory, concentration, and thought processes; supports the adrenals*; useful for everyday fatigue or after illness; affects the nervous system and revitalizes spent reserves; excellent for bronchitis, spasmodic coughs, and asthma; useful for varicose veins; prevents chilblains by improving circulation to extremities; promotes the digestion, especially the digestion of fats; stimulates the liver and clears the body of toxins; recommended for mouthwashes and douches as it counteracts inflammation and yeast overgrowth; reliable treatment for head lice when applied externally; stimulates appetite *Note: _individuals with adrenal exhaustion should be cautious with rosemary and only use small amounts, for it can be too stimulating to already-depleted glands_

**Energetic uses:** inspires creativity; instills hope and a happier outlook on life; revives the spirit after dejection, rejection, and failure

## St. John's Wort

**Properties:** highly effective for Obsessive Compulsive disorders, some forms of depression, anxiety, and phobias; antiviral properties; *Note: *despite promising studies regarding St. John's Wort and HIV, it is not recommended for HIV patients due to possible drug interactions. Also, St. John's Wort can make the skin photosensitive and one can sunburn easily. Take precaution with sun and tanning bed exposure while using St. John's Wort*

**Energetic uses**: stimulates the psychic centers; inspires laughter and joy; vibrationally resonates with the healing and uplifting energies of the sun; promotes courage; instills the desire and ability to live in the present moment

## Slippery Elm

**Properties:** more a foodstuff than a herb, slippery elm soothes and repairs the digestive system from mouth to rectum; highly useful for acute and chronic bowel conditions and diseases including IBS, Crohn's Disease, colitis, ulcertative colitis, constipation, and diarrhea;

helps top heal ulcers and balances excessive acidity;

*Energetic uses:* comforts the emotionally-worn heart and spirit and gives strength during times of emotional vulnerability

## Spearmint

*Properties:* similar to peppermint but spearmint has a more warming quality, gentler action, and a sweeter scent especially good for children and sensitive systems; relieves many digestive troubles including sluggish digestion, stomach pain, nausea, belching and flatulence; may help female hormonal balance, especially for PMS

*Energetic uses:* ushers in a sense of lightness and hope yet helps one to remain grounded

## Stevia

*Properties:* sugar substitute; helps to balance blood sugar; fights yeasts/candida; makes a beneficial mouthwash to prevent plaque and improve gum health; can be used in tiny a mounts to sweeten herbal teas and beverages; **\*Note:** *stevia is often found in liquid form, but the clear variety (processed) has no medicinal value; same for the powdered stevia found in* the sugar aisle. For medicinal integrity, use only the dried herb.

*Energetic uses:* fills the heart chakra with gentleness and happiness; strengthens the energy field/aura

## Turmeric

*Properties:* like its cousin ginger, turmeric possesses powerful antiflammatory properties; strengthens and soothes digestive function and helps inflammatory bowel conditions; decreases arthritis pain and that associated with syndromes such as fibromyalgia; supports the liver and gallbladder; reduces inflammation that can lead to heart disease *Note: a pinch in a morning shake is a nice way to get a dose of turmeric*

*Energetic uses:* used in Hawaiian magic; invokes protection; resonates with the solar plexus chakra and increases *prana* or life force

## White Oak Bark

*Properties:* excellent for eliminating parasites in humans; helps to also flush the urinary tract, therefore useful for bladder infections and kidney stones; will decrease or stop bleeding in cases of hemorrhoids, nosebleed and heavy menstrual periods but will treat only the symptoms for temporary relief; reliable first aid disinfectant, wound wash and protectant when applied topically; will also draw out splinters and bee stings when made into a paste with flour and water

***Energetic uses****:* helps us to connect to our inner strength, resolve, and stability; resonates with ancestral energies and the wisdom keepers of all traditions; protective and strengthening; instills patience and healing knowledge

## *Wild Cherry Bark*

**Properties:** excellent remedy for coughs, sore throats, and bronchitis; for colds/flu, diarrhea, intestinal pain or upset, and nausea; calming and warming, cleansing and fortifying; strengthens immunity

***Energetic uses:*** supports the solar plexus and heart chakras/energy centers; deepens love for others and self, encouraging compassion and patience; inspires creativity

## *Yarrow Flowers*

**Properties:** useful hormonal regulator for women and useful in preventing or lessening PMS; regulates the menstrual period; stimulates appetite by supporting the liver; relieves indigestion by increasing digestive enzymes; promotes sweating when taken hot and good for colds/flu, especially when accompanied by body aches; promotes a restful night's sleep; balances blood pressure; reduces fluid retention and inflammation; nerve tonic; helps to relieve nosebleed, heavy menstrual periods, and hemorrhoids

**Energetic uses:** one of the most valuable herbs to open the psychic eye, promote visions, and fill the energy field with protective light; helps strengthen invisible boundaries of those who are easily drained by others; helps empathic people to not "bleed" their energy; available as a flower essence (See Resources)

# The Rose: Metaphor & Medicine

The lovely rose has deep roots in the Sacred Feminine and many ancient Goddess connotations from Venus to the Blessed Mother. In the ancient world, the flower was associated with the sacred *yoni* or vagina. As Sufi poets before them, troubadours in France used this sexual-sacred symbolism which lingers in French culture to this day as *la rose*, a reference to the hymen or state of virginity. Roses are also significant and symbolic in alchemical philosophies; the red representing masculine elements and the white representing the feminine, both applied as metaphor for sacred unity. Medicinally, the rose is a powerful plant ally for women and can be used as herbal medicine for hormonal imbalance, PMS, perimenopause, uterine problems, mood swings, and weak immunity. Mirroring and giving credence to the age-old connection between roses, love, and sex, clinical aromatherapy studies have shown that the scent of rose essential oil (Rosa damascene) stimulates dopamine, the neurotransmitter most abundant in the brain when a person is joyfully in love or infatuated. This neurotransmitter is also responsible for giving us ambition and courage, and in women, strong orgasmic response. Genuine rose essential oil possesses the highest known frequency of 320 MHz. Rosewater, the most economical way to enjoy the scent of rose, can help soothe the energy center of the heart during grief, loss, and separation.

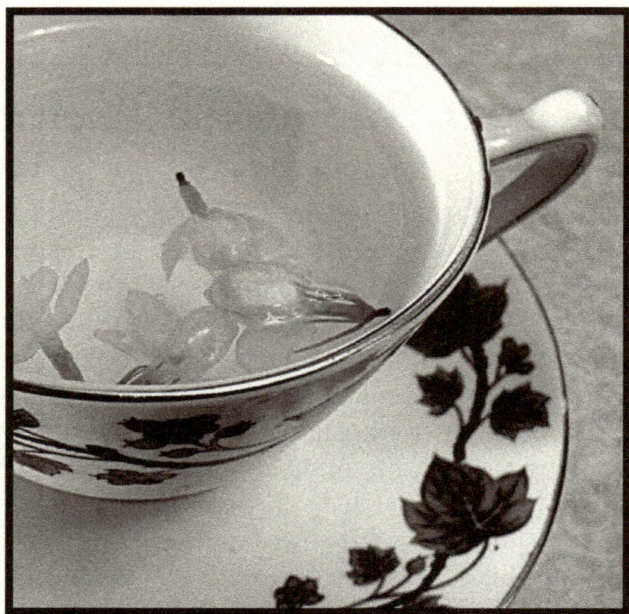

★
★
★

## Blessings in a Cup:
### Inspiring Teas and Nourishing Beverages

What better way to bring a touch of magic into our daily lives than to make libations from our herbal friends? Herbal libations offer invaluable benefits for our health and magic for all of our senses. When blended and prepared, teas can be delightfully nourishing and display an array of jewel-toned colors. Their fragrances haunt us with memories of summer fields, autumnal orchards, or forgotten childhood days. They can even awaken the sixth sense and bless us with psychic dreams.

On a practical note, always use fresh spring water or well water that is free of chlorine, etc. For best results, make your tea right before use. Any leftover tea makes good iced tea and can be stored in the fridge for up to four days. You can also pour leftover brew into your bath for its energetic value.

Aside from tea, fragrant herbs and spices can make lovely soul-nourishing drinks when warmed and can be made with milk, almond milk, coconut milk, or rice milk. Below you will find some inspiring and easy recipes. Infusing your blends with higher intention can be a spiritual practice unto itself.

## The Wise Woman Way

1. Before placing herbs into a cup, pot, or teapot, aloud or silently acknowledge the plants and thank them for their spirit medicine and healing energy. Give special thanks if you are using the root of a plant, for its very life was sacrificed when it was pulled from the ground. Hold the herbs in your hands for a few moments while you say a prayer, offer a blessing, request healing, or infuse them with universal love or just plain good thoughts.

2. Once the herbs are in the water, you may simply say, "in the name of the Goddess," or "in the name of _____(insert any higher power you are drawn to.)"

## Quick Use Reference for Preparing Herbal Teas

**Infusions:** The infusion method of preparing herbal teas steeps the dried or fresh aerial parts (leaves, flowers, soft stems) of a plant to bring out its beneficial properties without boiling them. As a rule, infusions are made from herbs that are *not roots or barks*. *Examples of infusion herbs:* lavender, jasmine flowers, hyssop, and peppermint. *Note: *one exception is kava kava root, which is prepared as an infusion.* Infusion times vary and a few herbs do best with cold infusions rather than hot. Certain plants need longer or shorter periods of time to steep, but most of the time, 10-20 minutes is all that's needed. *An exception is nettles, which are recommended to steep for at least four hours to bring out the most of their nutrition.* Most infusions can be consumed hot, cold, or room temperature, though some herbs work best when taken hot.

**Decoctions:** The decoction method of preparing herbs involves simmering dried or fresh roots, rhizomes, barks, berries, and woody stems for a period of time in order to bring out their beneficial properties. As a rule, most need 15-25 minutes of simmering (after boiling point) for their best effects. Most decoctions can be consumed hot, cold, or room temperature, though some herbs work best taken hot. *Examples of decoction herbs:* marshmallow root, wild cherry bark, white willow bark, hawthorn berries.

**Ratio:** Most preparations require 1-2 teaspoons of dried herb per cup of water. You can decrease the amount for a weaker tea. If you are using teabags in a teapot, use 1 teabag per person.

**Straining:** Teas can be strained with a strainer or cheese cloth.

**Helpful additions:** a mortar and pestle, strainers of various sizes, lovely tea cups or delightful mugs, good local honey or raw honey

# *Teas for Women's Wellbeing*

...

## *Rose Petal Infusion*

### Overnight method:

Fill a 1-quart Mason jar with ½-3/4 cup of dried organic roses/rose petals. Pour boiling water over the herbs, filling the jar halfway. Stir the herb mixture and then fill the rest of the jar with water until full. Put lid on and cover with a towel overnight. Strain and drink 1-2 cups a day for a fragrant immune-booster and hormonal balancer. Ideal during hormonal swings, PMS, perimenopause, and the week before your period. Also wonderful during cold/flu season to give you an extra edge. If preferred, add honey to taste. Refrigerate for up to 4 days. Individual portions can be reheated.

### Quick method:

6 teaspoons of dried organic roses/petals infused in 3 cups of boiling water for 20 minutes. Strain before drinking. If preferred, add honey to taste.

...

## *Nourishing Nettle Infusion*

### Overnight method:

Fill a 1-quart Mason jar with ½-3/4 cup of dried nettles. Pour boiling water over the herbs, filling the jar halfway. Stir the herb mixture and then fill the rest of the jar with water until full. Put lid on and cover with a towel overnight. Strain and drink 1-2 cups a day for a powerhouse mineral drink that your body will thank you for. Refrigerate for up to 4 days. Individual portions can be reheated.

### Quick method:

6 teaspoons of dried nettles
infused in 3 cups of boiling water for 20 minutes. Strain before drinking.

...

## Bright Spirits Tea

### Overnight method:

Fill a 1-quart Mason jar with 1/4 cup of lemongrass and 1/3 cup lemon balm. Pour boiling water over the herbs, filling the jar halfway. Stir the herb mixture and then fill the rest of the jar with water until full. Put lid on and cover with a towel overnight. Strain and drink 1-2 cups a day for a lovely mood lifter and nerve soother. Add honey to taste. Refrigerate for up to 4 days. Individual portions can be reheated.

### Quick method:

2 teaspoons lemongrass and 4 teaspoons lemon balm infused in 3 cups of boiling water for 20 minutes. Strain before drinking. Add honey to taste.

...

## Winter Support

1/4 cup elderberries, 1 cinnamon stick, 5 cloves, 1 tablespoon crushed juniper berries (use mortar and pestle or the back of a spoon), 1 teaspoon cut or powdered licorice root simmered in 1 quart of water for 20 minutes. Licorice will sweeten the brew, but if you'd like, add some honey to taste. Strain and drink 1-2 cups a day for defense against colds/flu. Also good to drink if you are already under the weather. Refrigerate for up to 4 days. Individual portions can be reheated.

## Flower Power Inner Peace Tea

**Overnight method:**

Fill a 1-quart Mason jar with 1/4 -1/2 cup lavender and 1/2 cup of jasmine flowers and then pour boiling water over the herbs, filling the jar halfway. Stir the herb mixture and then fill the rest of the jar with water until full. Put lid on and cover with a towel overnight. Strain and drink 1-3 cups a day for a fragrant and calming tea. Add honey to taste. Refrigerate for up to 4 days. Individual portions can be reheated. *Note: only use high quality lavender flowers from a herbal supplier, *not* a craft supplier.

**Quick method:**

2 teaspoons lavender and 4 teaspoons jasmine

infused in 3 cups of boiling water for 20 minutes. Strain before drinking. Add honey to taste.

...

## Marshmallow-Elm Soother

2 tablespoons slippery elm course-cut or powder and ¼ marshmallow root simmered in 1 quart of water for 20 minutes. *Strain while still warm because the mixture thickens more as it cools.* If preferred, add honey.  This mucilaginous brew soothes the entire digestive system and can be a go-to formula for any tummy or bowel distress, including heartburn. Also valuable for sore throats, rattling coughs, or allergies. Both herbs are nutritious food stuffs that the body assimilates well. Drink 1-3 cups a day and refrigerate for up to 4 days. Individual portions can be reheated. *Note: if brew is too thick, simply add hot water to desired thickness and stir well. Keep in mind that the thickness of both herbs is what makes them work well, so don't thin them out too much.

# Psychic Infusions & Enchanted Brews

### Soothsayer's Tea

(*drink regularly to strengthen the psychic eye, before doing psychic work, or before bed for psychic dreams*)

1 teaspoon lavender, 1 teaspoon yarrow, 1 teaspoon mugwort, and 1 teaspoon spearmint
infused 3 cups of hot water for 20 minutes, strained, and sweetened to taste.

### Angel's Breath Tea

(*fragrant tea attracts higher energies; drink to raise your frequency or commune with angelic intelligences*)

1 tablespoon jasmine flowers, 1 teaspoon lavender, 1 tablespoon organic roses/petals
infused in 3 cups of hot water for 20 minutes. Add 1 capful of culinary orange flower water, stir, strain, and sweeten with honey to taste.

### Protection Tea

(*drink to strengthen your energy field/aura and keep negative influences from entering your space*)

1 tablespoon crushed juniper berries (use a mortar and pestle or the back of a spoon) and 1 tablespoon birch

bark infused in 2 cups of boiling water for 20 minutes, strained, and sweetened with honey to taste.

...

# *Seasonal Libations*

### *Breath of Spring Tea*
*(a fragrant, pick-me-upper)*

**Overnight Method:**

Fill a 1-quart Mason jar ¼ cup lemongrass, 2 tablespoons crushed juniper berries (use a mortar and pestle or the back of a spoon), 2 teaspoons damiana, and ¼ cup spearmint and then pour boiling water over the herbs, filling the jar halfway. Stir the herb mixture and then fill the rest of the jar with water until full. Put lid on and cover with a towel overnight. Strain and drink 1-2 cups a day for a fragrant tea. Good for waking up sluggish adrenals yet calming to the system. Refrigerate for up to 4 days. Individual portions can be reheated.

**Quick method:**

2 teaspoons lemongrass, 1 teaspoon crushed juniper berries, and 2 teaspoons damiana
infused in 3 cups of boiling water for 20 minutes. Strain before drinking. Add honey to taste.

### Hunter's Moon Tea
*(a lovely wine-colored blend using autumn berries and fruits)*

¼ cup elderberries, 2 tablespoons hawthorn berries, 3 thick apple segments with skins, 1 broken cinnamon stick or 2 teaspoons of cinnamon bark chips, 4 clove buds, ½ cup of apple cider simmered in 2 ½ cups of boiling water for 15-20 minutes. Strain and sweeten to taste. Refrigerate for up to 4 days. Individual portions can be reheated.

### Ruby Winter Spice Brew
*(a festive crimson tea perfect for celebrations or dismal, cold days to add warmth and color)*

1 star anise, ¼ cup hibiscus flowers, 1 cup fruit-sweetened apple-cranberry juice (*not* cocktail), 2 broken cinnamon sticks or 1 tablespoon cinnamon chips, 1 slice of fresh ginger root, a pinch of cardamom (seeds or powder), a few peppercorns, 1 capful of pure vanilla extract, a dash of nutmeg simmered in a quart of boiling water for 20 minutes, strained, and sweetened to taste. Double or triple amounts as needed for gatherings. Refrigerate for up to 4 days. Individual portions can be reheated.

### Sacred Trees Brew
*(a tea with pleasant bitterness and earthiness; lovely*

*brew to drink when honoring the earth or when you need to feel more grounded)*

1 tablespoon white willow bark, 1 tablespoon wild cherry bark, 1 teaspoon white oak bark, 1 tablespoon birch bark, and 1 tablespoon pau d'arco bark simmered in a quart of boiling water for 10-15 minutes, strained, and sweetened to taste. Drink 1-2 cups a day. Refrigerate for up to 4 days. Individual portions can be reheated.

### Summer Meadows Tea
*(a delightful infusion of herbs from summer fields)*

Fill a 1-quart Mason jar ¼ cup red clover blossoms, ¼ cup chamomile flowers, and 1 tablespoon yarrow. Pour *warm* water over the herbs, filling the jar halfway. Stir the herb mixture and then fill the rest of the jar with water until full. Put lid on and cover with a towel overnight. Strain and drink 1-2 cups a day for a fragrant tea that is also wonderful for the digestive system. Refrigerate for up to 4 days. Makes a lovely iced tea, but individual portions can be reheated.

**Quick method:**
1 tablespoon red clover blossoms, 1 tablespoon chamomile, and 1 teaspoon yarrow
infused in 3 cups of boiling water for 20 minutes. Strain before drinking. Add honey to taste.

# Nourishing Milks

(*Note: *these can be made with cow's milk or dairy-free alternatives such as coconut, almond, or rice milk; substitute according to taste or diet specifications.*)

### Creamed Chamomile

Place 2 teaspoons chamomile flowers in 2 cups of milk of choice and warm over low heat or a double boiler until hot. Allow to sit for five minutes before straining and if preferred, sweeten with honey. Drink warm.

### Peppermint-Honey Milk

Place 1 teaspoon peppermint and 1 teaspoon of honey in 2 cups of milk of choice and warm over low heat or a double boiler until hot. Allow to sit for five minutes before straining. Drink warm.

### Rose Milk

Place 2 teaspoons of organic roses/petals in 2 cups of milk of choice and warm over low heat or a double boiler until hot. Allow to sit for five minutes before straining and if preferred, sweeten with honey. Drink warm.

### Creamed Winter Chai

Place 1 teaspoon of chai spice* in 2 cups of milk of choice and warm over low heat or a double boiler until hot. Allow to sit for five minutes before straining and if preferred, sweeten with honey. Drink warm. *Note: *if* *you can't find chai spice blend, make your own with a dash of cinnamon, a pinch of black pepper, a dash of nutmeg, 1 star anise, a pinch of fennel seeds, and 2 cloves)*

### Golden Spice Milk

Place ¼ teaspoon ground turmeric, 1 thin slice of fresh ginger *or* a pinch of powdered ginger in 2 cups of milk of choice and warm over low heat or a double boiler until hot. Allow to sit for five minutes before drinking and if preferred, sweeten with honey. Drink warm.

### Jasmine Milk

Place 1 teaspoon of jasmine flowers in 2 cups of milk of choice and warm over low heat or a double boiler until hot. Allow to sit for five minutes before straining and if preferred, sweeten with honey. Drink warm.

### Lavender Milk

Place 1 teaspoon of lavender flowers in 2 cups of milk of choice and warm over low heat or a double boiler until hot. Allow to sit for five minutes before straining and if preferred, sweeten with honey. Drink warm.

### Lemongrass Milk

Place 1 teaspoon of lemongrass in 2 cups of milk of choice and warm over low heat or a double boiler until hot. Allow to sit for five minutes before straining and if preferred, sweeten with honey. Drink warm.

### Spiced Cocoa

Wisk or stir together 1 teaspoon of unsweetened cocoa powder, a dash of ground cloves, ¼ teaspoon cinnamon, a dash of nutmeg, and 2 ½ teaspoons of honey in 2 cups of milk of choice and warm over low heat or a double boiler until hot. Allow to sit for five minutes before drinking and if preferred, sweeten with more honey. Drink warm.

### Lavender Cocoa

Wisk or stir together 1 teaspoon unsweetened cocoa, ½ teaspoon lavender flowers, and 2 teaspoons of honey in 2 cups of milk of choice and warm over low heat or a double boiler until hot. Allow to sit for five minutes before straining. Drink warm or hot.

### Creamed Licorice-Spice

Place ½ teaspoon powdered licorice, a pinch of powdered ginger, and a dash of cinnamon in 2 cups of milk of choice and warm over low heat or a double boiler until hot. Allow to sit for five minutes before drinking. Drink warm.

# Consecrated Waters

Water is necessary to life and a conductor of energy. It is the blood of the earth, and its fluidity resonates with our ever-changing emotions. Although associated most often with Christianity, holy waters are found in most religious faiths. The consecration of water for anointing, sprinkling, baptizing, and sacred bathing is universal. Similar in intention, when we drink water charged with prayer, invocation, the moon or the sun's energy, gemstones, or fresh plants, we energize our bodies and infuse our spirits with liquid light.

In his groundbreaking book *The Hidden Messages of Water*, scientific researcher Masaru Emoto presents stunning images of water under the microscope that reveals the effects of thought, intention, emotion, and music on water's crystalline structure. These microscopic variations amaze the eye and bring attention to the fact that water, like everything else, has *consciousness* capable of responding to its environment.

When we see water as living energy with soul-intelligence, we realize that everything we put into it also leaves its energy imprint and consciousness. Gemstones, sunlight, moonlight, and plants can charge water and create an elixir for the soul as well as physical wellbeing. Consecrated waters are easy, fun, and magical, and most of all, you can feel the difference after using them. Some people feel more vitality in their bodies while others feel more alert mentally; some develop psychically while others reach a deeper state of meditation or communion with Earth energies. Sometimes the results vary—but the constant factor is that we always receive what we need from sacred water. Consecrated waters can be ingested, poured into the bath, spritzed into the air or onto the body for vibrational purification, and used to bless sacred space. They are also beautiful to behold, especially when created with crystals or floating flowers.

## Moon Water

The energy of the full moon is best, but the waxing moon a day or two before the full moon—or a day or two after—is also a good time to make moon water.

**Used for:** reducing inflammation in the body, opening the psychic eye, easing anxiety or tension, inducing sleep

**How to do it:** Fill a glass jar with spring or purified water, seal it, and then place it outside where it will be exposed to the moon's light. Leave it there overnight and collect it early in the morning. Repeat the same process with the same jar of water for another night or two. Store your moon water in the fridge between "moon charges" and then afterward as you use it.

**How to use it:** You can add some moon water to your teas or drink it straight. Drinking it before bedtime can bring you enchanted or psychic dreams. Pouring it into a sacred bath, especially coupled with essential oils, creates a powerful and healing spa. If you don't like baths, consider pouring some moon water into a foot bath or splashing it onto your skin after a shower.

**Variation:** Place a clean quartz crystal, amethyst, or rose quartz into your jar of water before placing it in the moonlight.

## Sun Water

**Used for:** revitalizing the body, especially during or after illness, stressful periods, or during the winter; sharpening focus or creativity; fortifying the solar plexus and heart chakras; for watering plants to make them healthier

**How to do it:** Fill a clear or colored* glass jar with spring or purified water, seal it, and place it outside in the morning sun. Noon's light is also good. Allow your jar of water to absorb the sun's light throughout the day, but be sure to collect it at sundown. *Note: choosing an appropriate color for your sun water can also add another healing component- color therapy.

*Red glass*: for increased energy, passion, zest for life, sense of grounding and security

*Orange glass*: for increased creativity, sexual life force, encourage conception, inspire hope

*Yellow glass*: increase mental sharpness and ideal for students, teachers, writers, researchers, etc. Also encourages self-confidence and strong emotional boundaries; brings hope and happiness to the energy field\

*Green glass*: for healing, opening, or balancing the heart chakra and revitalizing the physical body

*Blue glass*: for decreasing inflammation in the body, encouraging communication and speaking our truths, calming frazzled nervous systems

*Purple glass*: for opening the psychic eye, supporting spiritual studies, and balance between the physical and the spiritual, between the passions and the spirit

*Pink or rose-colored glass*: for bringing peace to the energy field, as well as renewed wonder and innocence; good for healing the past including the trauma of abuse

**How to use it:** You can add some sun water to your teas or drink it straight. Drinking it in the morning can bring you more energy and determination for the day. Pouring it into a sacred bath, especially coupled with essential oils, creates a powerful and healing spa. If you don't like baths, consider pouring some sun water into a foot bath or splashing it onto your skin after a shower.

**Variation:** Place a clean quartz crystal, amethyst, or rose quartz into your jar of water before placing it in the sunlight.

*Crystal Waters*

**\*Note:** *Many gemstones and crystals are suitable and safe to make charged waters, but many are not. Please be sure to learn more about a particular stone before making a crystal water. Rule of thumb: metallic, blue, green, blue-green, and unpolished stones are toxic and should never be used for consecrated waters or ingested. For safety, only use the recommended gemstones in this listing.*

**Used for:** wellbeing on the physical, emotional, and spiritual levels.

**How to do it:** Place a crystal in a glass jar or large bowl and fill with spring or purified water. You may wish to use moon or sun water. Cover and allow it to sit for 24 hours. After your water is charged, keep it in the fridge as you use it, but be careful the stones don't fall into your cup or glass as you pour.

**How to use it:** Drink 1-2 cups a day or use in a bath. Pouring it into a sacred bath, especially coupled with essential oils, creates a powerful and healing spa. If you don't like baths, consider pouring some crystal water into a foot bath or splashing it onto your skin after a shower.

**Variation:** If you would like to charge water with a stone that is not suitable (too toxic) for crystal water, simply place it by the jar of water for the period of time. Its energy will be transferred.

## Gemstones for Crystal Waters and their Properties

**Clear Quartz:** "universal" stone for balance of body, mind, and spirit; resonates with all energy centers/chakras; fills the energy field and bodily cells with living light; fortifies the nervous system and promotes hair and nail growth; strengthens connective tissue

**Rose Quartz:** gentle stone that is healing to the emotions; calms aggression, anger, frustration, resentment, grief, heartbreak, hate and self-hate, and all issues surrounding abuse; resonates with the female reproductive system and heart chakra; supports the physical heart

**Amethyst:** stimulates the psychic or third eye; inspires spiritual devotion; connects one to the higher realms of frequency; supports addiction recovery, balances brain waves and the nervous system; increases oxygen and oxygen utilization in the blood

**Ametrine:** counters self-sabotaging patterns; encourages one to have their own mind; improves brain function and problem solving; improves metabolism and supports the endocrine system; soothes digestive imbalances

**Herkimer (Quartz) Diamond:** stimulates consciousness expansion and useful for pursuits involving astral projection, soul journeys and working with vortex energy;

purifies spaces and environment; balances the effects of radiation therapy or exposure

**Fluorite:** helps to bring clarity during highly-charged emotional times; sharpens the mind, memory, and thought processes; lessens fear of the unknown or the future; balances brain waves and hemispheres; fortifies collagen, teeth, and bones

**Aquamarine:** encourages us to speak and live our truths, integrate past experiences and emotions attached to them; soothes angry and resentful states; soothes sore throat and throat conditions involving hoarseness of the voice; lessens anxiety and nourishes the nerves; helps herpes and allergies; supports the immune system and increases its ability to fight infections; soothes skin problems including eczema and psoriasis

**Aventurine:** brings joy and willingness to trust the future; improves circulation; promotes cellular repair; increases *prana* or physical life force and stimulates healing

**Sugilite:** counteracts pessimism and low confidence; dissipates worry; helps sleep disorders including sleep walking, night terrors and nightmares

## "Singing" Waters

Waters charged with music, meditative frequencies, or sounds from the natural world offer their own brand of wellbeing. Consecrating water with sound is easy and beneficial to the body and spirit. Here are a few suggestions:

~Recordings of calming classical music
~Live or recorded Tibetan singing bowls
~Live or recorded crystal singing bowls
~Live or recorded meditation bells
~Live or recorded shamanic drumbeats
~The human voice- chant, toning, or prayer
~Recordings of nature sounds such as songbirds

**Used for:** balancing the nervous system and getting out of fight or flight mode; deepens meditation and spiritual awareness; promotes healing; helps us tap into our inner all-knowing/wise Goddess or Higher Self

**How to do it:** Fill a jar with spring or purified water and place near a speaker for approximately an hour so the water can absorb the vibrational benefits of your chosen recording. If you are a musician, you can place the jar of water on top of the piano or near you as you play an instrument or sing. You can also play a meditation bell, hand drum, and singing bowls, OR chant, tone, or pray aloud near the water. For live sound, twenty minutes or more will give your water a lovely charge.

**How to use it:** Drink 1-2 cups a day or use in a bath. Pouring it into a sacred bath, especially coupled with essential oils, creates a powerful and healing spa. If you don't like baths, consider pouring some sound-charged water into a foot bath or splashing it onto your skin after a shower.

## 11

# Touching the Universe:
# Woman's Sexual Fire

In ancient times, the sensual and the sacred were looked upon as two halves of the same spiritual whole. Religion was deeply rooted in the celebration of the turning seasons, especially apparent in the cults of Dionysos, Aphrodite, Astarte, Baal, and Bast. Seasonally observed, this ecstatic worship focused on the growth rhythms of the land and deities believed responsible for the bounty. Celebrants left populated cities to revel in the wild. Dancing, drinking, and ecstatic music catalyzed sexual activity. Madness replaced reason more often than not, but for a chosen few, lack of inhibition cultivated by intoxicants and sacred sound begot powerful mystical experiences. Any child conceived during these nights of ecstasy was believed to be a child of the Goddess.

Prostitution, now considered to be a degrading drain on society, had two faces—one with a higher calling that was once seen as a holy and respectable contribution to ancient matriarchal civilizations. Unlike the modern world of greed, lust, drug traffic, and abuse, ancient temple prostitution was a life of spiritual service to Deity and was distinctly different and separated from common brothels. Servants of the Goddess entered a house of worship while they were young girls to learn the revered arts of ritual, dance, and adornment. Lifetime service and devotion to Deity began with a ritual sacrifice of virginity. Any sexual act performed after this holy sacrifice was consecrated and dedicated to the Goddess. Men who returned from war found pleasure as well as emotional healing in these Priestesses. To have intercourse with a temple prostitute was to directly commune with the all-creating, all-knowing Mother of the Universe.

Medieval Hindu temples of India still awe and even shock those who visit these testimonies of art, religion, and sacred sexuality. Such elaborate temples are the remains of a forgotten time when pleasure of the body opened the gates to enlightenment and bliss. This concept of spiritual salvation was and still is idealized in the marriage of Lord Shiva and the goddess Shakti; the sexual union of these two equal forces sustains the world.

Hindu women wear the red bindi upon their foreheads not only to signify marital or caste status but as a symbol of their sacred femininity or Shakti (Goddess) power. The crimson bindi signifies the moon and the third eye, and above all, the vagina in all its holiness. Some sources say the bindi was originally imprinted with menstrual blood signifying a woman's magical potency. Our biological functions and lunar correspondences with menstruation led to the first calendars, and our modern words such as menopause, menses, menstruation, and menarche stem from the prefix *men*, meaning 'moon' and 'month'. Sexual and menstrual fluids were considered spiritual elixirs, and words relating to menstruation translated to "sacred", "deity", or "spirit." The Greeks termed it cosmic "red wine" and the Hindus called it *soma,* the nectar of immortality.

The human body is the temple of the Goddess, and woman is its gateway. When we are attuned to Her, we bless our partners with Shakti, the universal life force. When sexual expression is experience as spiritual offering, we make love in Goddess Consciousness. When we are in this space, we realize that we—as women—do not need to seduce, entice, or tease, but enlighten. If your partner is male, you have the power to ignite the Goddess flame within him. If your partner is female, you have the power to magnify her Goddess energy. Either way, when both individuals reach an equal state of spiritual awareness, the energy raised and exchanged becomes part of the Creative Force of the universe. This means that a single, shared thought becomes a seed of psychic energy that can eventually manifest on the physical plane. Sexual power consciously applied can aid us in manifesting what we need in our lives, including abundance and healing on any level.

Sexual expression and spiritual enlightenment have gone hand in hand in Eastern religious teachings since ancient times. This philosophy, concentrated in Tantric Yoga, has been practiced for thousands of years to attain Nirvana. True Tantra is a spiritual joining of male and female energies to achieve enlightenment through the awakening of the Shakti—the Goddess Force known as kundalini. The kundalini energy is believed to sleep at the base of the spine until it is activated by various spiritual practices including meditation, yoga, and sacred sexual union. This serpentine two-fold energy holds both solar (masculine) and lunar (feminine) energies which entwine and pass through the chakras until it reaches the crown which is considered the gateway to God. Once this cosmic force illumines and opens this center, supreme knowledge can be at our fingertips. Women are seen as natural Shakti channels, and it is interesting to note—contrary to many beliefs that our monthly blood is impure—in Tantric "Left-Hand Way" sects, a woman is considered to be in full spiritual power during menstruation, therefore, capable of activating her partner's kundalini energy.

With practice, you will know when the kundalini begins to rise by the intense physical and psychic heat that is very different from mere sexual arousal. Some women have visionary experiences during conscious lovemaking, and that sacred time can yield much power and epiphany. For many, sexual expression can be a way to God/dess while others strive for celibacy in order to achieve a state of concentrated spirituality. In the instance of the latter, it is commonly believed that orgasm leads to loss of prana or life force; it is also seen as a distraction. But not everyone can or should lead celibate lives.

The sexual force *creates life*; therefore, it is the life force within. Non-emotional, recreational sex does indeed lead to loss of prana over time while sexual expression with someone we love replenishes energy and increases the body's cellular vitality. Love is the universal force; ultimately, not merely emotion but energy. This energy is manifested as human emotion, and because of this, love can be the most powerful of experiences. In essence, love is the healing God/dess Force. This Force flows through us, igniting every cell of our bodies with cosmic energy. When we unite with a beloved, the sexual force evolves from basic instinct to God/dess power. When we see sexuality as the ultimate creative force of Deity, we no longer need to use it as a weapon or rely on it for self-esteem. Instead, we protect and value it.

Many Tantric techniques require great physical and mental discipline; though these teachings are beautiful, mystical, and very useful, many couples find the techniques to be too complex, rigid, cryptic, or time-consuming. There are other ways to achieve spiritual awakening and unity during lovemaking. Sexual love with or without Tantric discipline can be an avenue to psychic awakening and deep mystical experience.

Despite the fact that many Eastern teachings exclude the same-sex couple, homosexual Tantra exists. Often, only the heterosexual union is valued due to the common belief that that female and male, yin and yang, are needed for spiritual balance. In reality, regardless of gender, each of us carries both male and female energies within our bodies and psyches. The true mystical goal is to unite both energies in order for a state of sacred androgyny to exist. The higher planes of consciousness and being have no divisions; the higher one advances within the spiritual realms, gender comes less and less significant. Gender is necessary on this physical plane for one purpose and that is for biological procreation. Blending both female and male energies within is a natural process as we advance.

On the following pages, you will find sensual meditations for two that will awaken the Goddess within you and your partner. If you have plants or indoor trees in your living space, you may consider using these techniques or making love near them. The life force in plants resonates with the life force between lovers. If you want to charge crystals and stones with your lovemaking, place them near you or in the soil of your plants. You can also keep these crystals, wrapped in cloth or placed in a pouch. After a month, the stones will be infused with your love energy and can be used for personal healing or sun/moon waters (see Chapter 10).

If your sexual self has been wounded by abuse, rape, shame, guilt, or fear, allow the Goddess to take this burden from you. Ask for assistance in taking back your power and realizing that no person, organized human-made religion, or opinion can touch the shining, inviolate self that manifests in your sexuality. If your sexual power has been degraded, healing is possible, and only love can heal; evil cannot exist where love lives. If you cannot love yourself, love the Goddess within until you fully know that you are one and the same. Ultimately, the Lover within is all we ever need.

## The Cradle

The Cradle is a beautiful way for two people to connect spiritually before lovemaking or any other time. When applied to female-male unions, this meditation helps to awaken the Goddess energy within the man and empowers the woman. In female-female unions, it brings both women back to the womb and intensifies connection with the Universal Mother.

To begin, with your back supported against a wall or headboard, sit with your legs parted in a V while your partner lies on his/her back between them. This "birthing position" is important metaphorically as it is physically. Take a deep breath; upon exhalation, have your partner inhale. Slowly, create a free-flowing breathing pattern that is uninterrupted when you inhale the other exhales. As you exhale, visualize light emanating from your yoni. Have your partner imagine breathing in this light. Do this long enough so you can feel the Goddess energy entering your partner. This exchange of psychic energy can be felt as warmth, tingling, or pulsing and enables both of you to share life force. If your partner is male, this yonic force can awaken his own inner Shakti. If your partner is female, be sure to switch positions and begin again. Male-female couples can also change roles, but the effects of The Cradle are best experiences when the man remains receptive. On the other hand, lesbian couples benefit more when both partners have a chance to receive.

# *Did you know . . .?*

## *Virgin*

*The word "virgin", due to mistranslations, has come down to us to define a person who has never had sex. However, the ancient meaning of the word simply connoted an unmarried woman.*

*Food for thought...*

## The Clitoris

### Biological fact...
The clitoris is the only human organ with the sole purpose of providing pleasure.

### Etymology:
from kleitoris (Greek) meaning "Goddess-like, divine"

### Energetic significance...
The clitoris holds concentrated Goddess or Shakti energy

# The Yoni

The yoni or vagina is considered the sacred gateway of life; the word *yoni* means source and womb. It is often portrayed in tear drop or almond-shaped forms but can be portrayed as an upside down triangle. In Hinduism, the goddess Kali has been called Cunti, an ancient title of honor that comes down in our present age as a degrading slang word without the "i". Yonic symbols in Hinduism represent the Mother of the Universe and are often part of ritual worship, especially the Yoni Puja which includes elaborate

**the yoni mudra**

libations, offerings of incense, spices, and flowers. Natural yonic rock formations in the southwestern United States were sacred to Native peoples, and women's rites often took place near them.

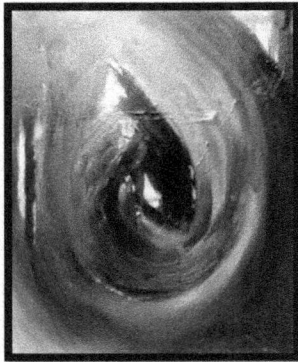

# *The Diamond*

The Diamond is a wonderful continuation to The Cradle. Any couple can use it, but the lesbian couple benefits by this particular meditation especially due to the fact that the Goddess energy is doubled. If your partner is male, it is best to use The Diamond after The Cradle while his inner Goddess energy is freshly awakened.

To begin, with backs supported, sit across from each other on the floor or bed with your legs parted in a V, feet touching so both of you form a diamond shape with your bodies. (Variation: sit in a chair across from each other with your knees touching.) Lift your head up as if you are looking at the stars and close your eyes. This physical formation directly invokes the Divine Feminine within and calls down the Goddess Force of the universe.

Now consciously imagine projecting light energy from your heart and yoni simultaneously to your partner as your partner does the same. Totally surrender to the giving and receiving of sacred lover's energy. When and if you feel this energy reach a peak, offer the power between you to the Goddess and allow Her energy to enter the diamond formed by your bodies. If you are both in a heightened state of awareness, you will sense this Force coming downward in a column of energy.

## *Goddess Fire*

The Goddess Fire kundalini technique can be especially intense, so be sure your partner is of like-mind before attempting this sexual meditation.

With both partners moving in harmony during lovemaking, begin very slowly, breathing together. Inhale and exhale at the same time, creating a wave of synchronized breath. A shared pattern of breath helps you move as one consciousness. As you breathe, feel the life force of your beloved's body. Feel your own breath originating deep inside your body from the sacred wellspring inside your yoni. Feel your breath beginning here and then rising upward. Be keenly aware of the friction between your and that of your partner's. As you increase rhythm, visualize a fire burning in gold where your physical forms are joined. When you inhale, imagine this shared fire rising upward toward the head in serpentine movement. After a few moments of this, you may feel an explosive increase in desire; at this point, do not increase your rhythm but continue to visualize the river of Goddess fire ascending toward your brow. If you feel a wave of anxiety or momentary fear, try to work through it. This is a sign that the kundalini is awakened and Shakti is activated. The intensity may reach a point where you fear combustion, but rest assure, you are safe. Do not suppress the energy, even if you are afraid. Surrendering to the force of Shakti is necessary for it to ascend fully. If you work through it, all anxiety should turn into euphoria. Once you get this far, it is natural to forget your breathing pattern. Let it all go and just be in the moment of power and pleasure.

With or without orgasm, you might see spirit lights, have a vision, come to a realization, or enter a state of spiritual ecstasy. If you and your partner are in sync on many levels, you might even share the same spiritual or psychic experience. Your Shakti energy can be very healing to your partner as well as yourself. Be sure to allow for stillness and silence afterward so your partner can absorb your energy. Do not worry about being drained; the Goddess Fire technique allows all energy to be replenished.

★

# Water and Flowers

The Water and Flowers meditation uses the sound of water and high-vibrational fragrance to stimulate the psychic centers of both partners. To begin, play a nature recording of ocean waves or heavy surf, rain without thunder, or a babbling brook. Fill a medium to large bowl with petals from highly scented flowers such as roses, carnations, hyacinth, lilacs, wisteria, or jasmine if you can obtain it. The sweeter and more dominant the fragrance, the higher the vibrational level of the plant, therefore capable of raising your own energetic frequency.

Press the palms of your hands against your partner's and close your eyes. Absorb each other's energy in loving silence. Everyone has small energy centers in the palms of their hands, but if you are a holistic healer, artist, or musician, these centers are probably more developed and project a considerable amount of life force. When you feel fully connected to your beloved, open your eyes. Study each other lovingly for long moments and listen to the sound of the water. When you feel ready, take a handful of fragrant petals and sprinkle them gently over your partner's hair and skin, pressing ever so slightly so the perfume is released with your touch. Continue and have your partner do the same until the bowl is emptied and a deep communion has been experienced.

## *Goddess Consciousness* ⭐

Press your foreheads together and visualize warm white light pouring into each other. When you feel united spiritually, share a slow kiss, allowing your souls to meld.

# *The Feminine Four*

*Disclaimer and Author's Note:*

*The following chapter takes a fun but meaningful look at how the elements Earth, Air, Fire, and Water manifest in our spirits, personalities, and passions. This material is not based on clinical psychology or professional personality typing, nor is it intended to profile or stereotype any individual. The following information—my own personal observation and study from 1989 to 1998— is inspired by ancient elemental principles of temperament, Humorism of the Greeks, and the work of twelfth century visionary, Hildegard von Bingen. This work is my personal take on the elemental philosophy as it pertains uniquely to women, and additions such as the concept of a Rising Element—along with names I have given each elemental personality—are purely for personal use and creative purposes.*

12

# *Elemental Identity: Finding Yourself in Earth, Air, Fire, and Water*

**Threads of the Soul and Our Elemental Essence**

The elements are the building blocks of nature, therefore, our very existence. Earth and its sustenance sustains our physical lives. Water is necessary for our survival and is a major component in our biological makeup. Fire enables us to cook and provide warmth, and also build, create, mold, and progress in industry. Air is our minute-to-minute link to life. When we look at these forces in simple, pragmatic terms, it is no wonder why we have an undeniable need and desire to be near them. This need manifests in the passion for gardening or cooking, vacationing near the water, nesting by a fire with a lover, or breathing deeply on crisp autumn days. We search for these elements outside of us because they are also inside of us—parallel psycho-spiritual forces interwoven in the complex tapestry of our preferences, goals, challenges, careers, and relationships. Each and every human being is a child and partner to Earth, Air, Fire, and Water.

The ancients saw this intricate connection and built their philosophies upon the four elements. The Greeks had an elaborate healing system based on the four humors of the physical body. This system called Humorism, had wide-reaching influence in Roman, Islamic, and European medicine up until the nineteenth century. In addition, elemental philosophy is the cohesive of Ayurvedic and Chinese medicine, esoteric teachings, and divination systems such as astrology and palmistry. The ancients in India, Greece, Persia, Samaria, Italy, and the Americas all constructed their own versions of the roles of the elements, but all came to the same conclusion that we are all related to these natural forces.

Certain Tribal nations designed their camps around Earth, Air, Fire, and Water. These home-based divisions also included animal totems as guardians of the four directions. Death rituals around the world also incorporated the elements, some which continue to this day: burial in the womb-like earth, cremation by purifying fire, dissolution in the sea or other body of water, and natural disposal in the wilds to be consumed by birds. It was believed that which-ever element physically or spiritually births an individual also embraces the person at death, thus, completing the circle.

A few cultures including the Greeks mentioned a fifth element in their beliefs which is commonly referred to as *ether* or Akasha. Akasha is revered by Hindus as one of the three universal principles and is believed to permeate everything in the manifested worlds. The fifth element is also linked to the Hebrew *ruach* which means breath, wind, or spirit in motion. Mystic Madame Blavatsky brought the Akashic concept to the West and drew connections between cultural interpretations of this basic life force. She viewed the fifth element and subtlest element as energy that manifests thought into the material world and forms the universal soul of humankind.

Drawing upon the ancient philosophy of the four elements, we can find ourselves in all of them. As human beings we are complex in nature, and our moods, interests, and challenges are constantly shifting. Earth, Air, Fire, and Water are moving within our personalities, but a dominant element can usually be defined. Though equally balancing all four energies should be our goal, until then, most of us can be identified by one of the four. Sometimes we spend years in tune with one particular element then move into another. During this transition, choose the element which you believe is strongest at the time. If you are the rare woman who is equally developed in two or more elemental energies, then finding your governing element is not possible—you can simply choose which energy you wish to work with at a particular time.

## How to Use This Chapter

This elemental system is not intended to be a basis for psychological profile, nor is it intended to confine you into categories, labels, or classifications, but rather a tool to access your inner Priestess. I did not include quizzes or questionnaires to help you determine which element you are most aligned with. None of us truly ever fit into any one "category", so I avoided these approaches to enable you to freely explore the many facets of yourself.

Some elements have two distinctly different profiles which often seem opposite of each other, so be sure to read each elemental personality before deciding which one is your primary element. Bear in mind that you will probably see bits of yourself in each, and no single profile will be your exact match.

## Source

We consume fruit and flesh

Of the fields;

Are we not earth?

Beneath bodily soil,

Our spirits are of the wind;

Are we not air?

Impassioned, we dance

To the heart;

We burn with love as our fuel;

Are we not fire?

Over waves of laughter

And rocks of turmoil,

We flow urgently toward the Destination;

Are we not water?

# Priestess of the Seasons: The Earth Sister

*Beloved Earth, whose breath I long for,*
*Breath of April wind and lilac...*
*Do you remember braiding my hair with daisies*
*When I was a child? Do you remember*
*The virgin's heart you pierced with beauty...*
*Beloved Earth, who put the seasons in my soul?*

Hello Earth Sister! Phew, I had a difficult time tracking you down, but now that I have your attention, welcome to your world. Take a break from your typically busy day, find a comfortable chair, and take a new, exciting look at yourself. This chapter begins with you because your element Earth is the foundation of our being. The earth is our home. All of life is cradled within this beautiful, ever-changing yet constant element that is yours. Like your element, Earth Sisters tirelessly keep this planet running. You dedicate your life to hard work and might be inclined to sacrifice anything that threatens to deter you from achieving your goals or protecting your loved ones. You get things done, go beyond the call of duty, and have a fierce competitive edge when you need it. In short, the world would probably explode in chaos without women like you who are the glue of society. You are the ones to call in a crisis, the ones who look death defiantly in the face, raise children, uphold homes with timeless wisdom, and the ones who break long-held records. Perhaps, you never really knew the importance of your car pools, activism, rallies, long-winded lectures, or even your homemade brownies!

Yes, you have a broad range of professional capabilities. The Earth Sister may be a full time mother and homemaker, dedicated wife, massage therapist, herbalist, holistic practitioner, politician, environmentalist, activist, florist, athlete, or real estate agent. You may also express your passion as a chef or cook, teacher, coach, horticulturist, business owner, songwriter, writer, or natural perfumer. If you have a gift for words, you may write books or lecture. If you are a poet, you are one with purpose. If you are a feminist or an athlete, you may be a modern Amazon. Many Earth Sisters choose medicine, go into the military, or choose a religious life.

Whether you are on the ambulance corps or in the office, you face things head on. You are a woman who might build her own house, relish a camping trip even in the rain, and grow her own organic vegetables with brilliance.

My maternal great grandmother was such a woman. She was an independent practical nurse at a time when few women ventured outside the home. She was a firm believer in the human spirit, and when anyone around her was dying or in despair, she would simply say, "Where there is life, there is hope." She knew the secrets of herbs, received her monthly horoscope when few people knew what astrology was, and believed in karmic law which prompted her to yell, "Reaction! Reaction!" when one of her grandchildren behaved badly. She was a woman who had seen much tragedy in her life but always managed to be a pillar of strength for those around her even when her own foundation was crumbling. Perhaps this is the most profound quality of the Earth Sister—tenacious strength that enables survival at all costs.

Another Earth Sister, a dear friend of mine, decided one day to pack up and move to Hawaii. She took only a few belongings and her dog. She rebuilt a small studio bungalow and enjoyed her earth-centered life without electricity. Even though she now has electricity, she still gathers wild fruit by hand, collects local crafts, and lives with a loyal family of adopted animals.

If you are a strong, reliable Earth Sister your price for all of this energy might be the fact that everyone around you forgets that you have your own needs; *you* may forget you have needs. You may become a victim of self-neglect, exhaustion, or bitter regret if you live your life for everyone else until you cannot do it anymore or illness makes the choice for you. Another price to pay may be injury. If you are an active or competitive Earth Sister, you may barter common sense for perfection and use your body even when it is injured. If you are an athlete or dancer, you might perform with an injury and later regret it. You may also be a mother or caregiver who tries to do it all in one day, balancing the needs of your household until you succumb. No matter what area you invest your energies in, overexertion can be a price.

Emotionally, you can be exceptionally grounded. You usually have a stable nature and may even act as mediator for those around you. However, the world better run for cover when you have finally taken enough. Your anger has a tendency to build, perhaps even for years. When this repressed emotion finally does surface, it can be sudden. intense, and inconvenient as an earthquake—ten on the Richter scale without apology. Those around you have no other choice than to hide or take what's coming to them with grace. No one with a sound mind would think of opposing you, but there is that occasional someone who dares to challenge you. However, the odds of you winning the battle are in your favor. Your outbursts can last for short periods and afterward, people around you may cautiously crawl out to see if it's safe to re-enter your space. Usually, no one mentions it, and life goes on where it left off despite the occasional aftershock. Overall, dear Earth Sister, you are known for your reliability, practicality, and tenacity. You can also be known for your loyalty in work, friendship, and love. Your fidelity and constancy are immovable as a mountain once your heart finds the right partner. Your sexuality can be ardent and free-spirited, natural and necessary to your wellbeing. If you are a deeply religious or spiritual Earth Sister, you accomplish celibacy with the same passion.

Many Earth Sisters become mothers early in life or due to being raised in dysfunctional households with addiction, violence, or illness, forced to take on adult responsibilities.

Pregnancy, labor, nursing, raising children and having grandchildren affect you deeply. Earth Sisters can be their most powerful spiritually, creatively, and sexually during pregnancy. Of all the elemental personalities, the Earth Sister is the most present in her body and aware of its rhythms; pregnancy magnifies these instincts. Many are so in tune with their bodies that they know the time of conception and rarely need confirmation of pregnancy to validate what they already know.

Many Earth Sisters dedicate their lives to children even if they do not bear them. They are often adoptive, foster, or co-parents as well as teachers, daycare providers, and social workers or advocates for children's rights. On the other hand, many creative Earth Sisters see their art as their offspring and use their talent to affect the lives of others. Others are social activists or missionaries, one famous example is Mother Teresa. Still, there are Earth Sisters who channel their energy only into their work and are often criticized for not having or desiring children. Congratulations if you are such an Earth Sister. Yes, you are to be praised because you know what you want, don't want, and simply have a different purpose, one that is not inferior or selfish.

You probably go through many seasons in your life; periods of spring-like hope and ambition, times of summer-like productivity, autumn-tempered days of reflection, and idle winters of the soul when body and mind seek recuperation. No matter how long your "winters", there is always the day when new plans start the blood going like sap in a dormant tree. And no matter how endless your energy and invincible your ambition, there is a time when these resources wane only to be replenished.

Earth Sisters are the most constant of the elemental types. Your mundane preferences probably change little throughout your life. You most likely prefer a trifling bit of make-up or none at all and would choose a natural summer blush or tan over a cosmetic. You may be an Earth Sister who keeps her hair long or who prefers an easy, short alternative. The Earth Sister chooses fine china to proudly enhance the beauty of her home or the earthen appeal of pottery and ethnic wares. People remember your entertaining by the feast you prepare, the bread you bake, or your hostess flare.

The Earth-ruled woman's creativity emerges in painting, sculpting, craft-making, interior decorating, dancing, gardening, refinishing furniture, cooking, or coordinating events. If you are an artist, you probably enjoy the feeling of clay, wet paint, and other materials you work with.

Lastly and most importantly, your spiritual potential is powerful, wild, and shamanic with capabilities for hands-on healing/energy healing and reaching ecstatic states through dancing, drumming, and communion with nature. You are the Medicine Woman capable of communicating with animals and working with totems, healing with the medicinal and vibrational properties of plants, and experiencing powerful vision quests. You may be drawn to ancient religions, and the Divine Feminine may play an important role in your life or, on the other hand, you may be deeply dedicated to structured religion or follow no single path and prefer spirituality over creed.

As a daughter of the seasons, you hold the wisdom of the wilderness deep within you. You are the Priestess of the earth, and your mystical heritage reaches into the depths of history to the ancient Priestesses who entered trance and prophesized. Such Priestesses were found in the ecstatic worship of Greek deities such as Dionysos or Orpheus, timeless devotion to the Hindu goddess Kali, and the powerful ancestral traditions of the African sangoma.

Whether you are an Earth Sister or simply a woman who would like to commune more deeply with the element Earth, you might wish to buy a new plant and name it. Walk barefoot in a garden or through the grass after the rain. Buy a handful of flowers for your bedroom or desk.

Spend time among the trees. Catch fireflies and let them go. Take a walk with your dog or nap with your cat. Do anything to embrace the earth and allow her to embrace you.

## The Earth Sister at a Glance

### Vocational Possibilities

academics, activism, anthropology, archeology, aromatherapy, the arts, athletics, bodywork/therapeutic massage, caregiving, carpentry/construction, childcare, cooking, corporate positions, counseling, crafting, dance, education, finance, fitness, holistic health/healing, homemaking, horticulture, human rights, landscaping, law, medicine, military, music, office work, preservation, real estate, religious service, science, self-employment, social justice therapy/rehabilitation, travel, veterinary fields, writing, yoga instructor, zoology

### Potential Strengths

hardworking, pragmatic, stable, patient, ambitious, compassionate, committed, determined

### Potential Weaknesses

stubborn, competitive, self-sacrificing, materialistic, controlling

### Keywords

strong, reliable, nurturing, active, hands-on

# *Goddess Consciousness*

## Spiritual potential

shamanism, healing, trance, high magic, animal communication, yogic disciplines, mediumship

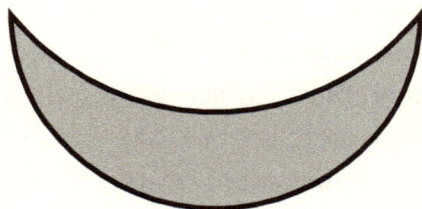

# *Daughter of the Phoenix: The Fire Gypsy*

*I am a child of the phoenix,*
*Daughter of the soul's changing fire.*
*With each descent, I will ascend*
*From my bed of ashes*
*Toward a triumphant heaven*
*With wings...*

Hello Fire Gypsy! Welcome to your world. I know you have projects to tend to and a friend needs one of your jokes today, but you'll be glad that you took this time to take another look at yourself.

While the Earth Sisters keep the world turning, Fire Gypsies color it and prevent us from dying of boredom. We may call Earth Sister during a crisis, but we call you,

343

too. While Earth Sister is bandaging someone's arm, you are telling your latest joke to the unfortunate soul who had the accident. You are the Pollyanna of the elemental women, the flower growing in the cement, a red rose in a black and white world. There is no passion quite like the Fire Gypsy's.

You are direct, confident in your abilities, and able to accomplish more than an eight-armed Hindu goddess when you focus your energy. Your intensity, humor, ambitious enthusiasm, and sense of self leave the rest of us uplifted, inspired, and sometimes a little envious. You blaze in the arts and entertainment, design, advertising, journalism, fashion, and teaching. Whether you are an interior designer or critic, your work stands out and speaks for itself. Your personality and charisma are important ingredients to your success, and you have more than one career. If you are such a Renaissance Woman, your resume' could give a potential employer a long night's reading. After all is said and done, Fire Gypsy, this world is better because of your humor, art, and sensuality. Your flame leaves a mark on everyone you meet, and your special gift is the ability to illumine the darkness.

Like your element Fire, you can be changeable and spontaneous. You may find it difficult to adhere to one thing until you profit by it. The boredom that drove you into fits as a child can make you restless at work, and sometimes your long-term security suffers. On the other hand, you may be so committed to one goal or project that you don't reserve energy to nourish other areas of your life. Many Fire Gypsies end up exhausted after intense periods of focused work. The tendency to burn the candle at both ends can compromise your physical and mental wellbeing.

Because you are eager to do everything with flare, some people around you are led to believe that you are not dependable or capable of emotional or spiritual depth. As a Fire Gypsy, it is likely that your emotions and spiritual hunger go very deep, so when you are faced with this assumption, you may get frustrated. You have an inborn philosophy that heaven is for the living, not the dead, and believe that enlightenment of any kind comes on the wings of joy and laughter.

You may also enjoy being a freelance psychiatrist (a good one, at that) but your own self-realization may not come until midlife or later. If you are a Fire Gypsy who keeps faces in her back pocket for every situation, you have many friends and can communicate with people from all walks of life. However, this versatility and social grace may also cultivate the inability to value solitude which is necessary for growth and spiritual progress. Nevertheless, when you look inward and find the still, unwavering flame of your soul, you find the rare beauty of silence that teaches you your greatest lessons. Your element Fire can be contained and soundless like a single candle in a holy place. Once you know how to direct, use, and control your special power, you are capable of becoming an incredibly enlightened, powerful being. Some Fire women are born into Goddess Consciousness; many female mystics and spiritual teachers begin life with their spiritual fire already developed.

Fire Gypsies make wonderful mothers, especially if they cultivate stability and patience in their children. If you are a mother, you are the woman who becomes your child's best friend. You are a grown-up kid yourself, so you find it instinctive to know what makes a child tick. You are an open-minded parent who loves roller coasters, bright colors, and fun. Your quality of youth not only makes you the coolest mother on the block but blesses you with the drive to oppose growing old mentally. You would think nothing of hopping on a merry-go-round at age ninety.

Yes, Fire Gypsy, you are the lover—playful, erotic, emotional, and experimental. You are also a fool for sentiment, flowers, and tender offerings. You either have many love affairs or an intense few that you shell-shocked. If you are a quick-tempered, dramatic, or hasty Fire Gypsy, you're likely to fill your empty periods of expected burnout with risky love affairs. Even if you are a stable Fire Gypsy, love relationships define your life and catalyze your deepest self-awareness. Your sexuality and emotions burn in harmony and can be very concentrated. You hunger, pine, and suffer deeply even during your heart's episodes of superficial infatuation. In the process of finding The One, you may leave behind broken hearts, but when you finally do find the right partner, your days of restlessness come to an end. The strength, power, and warmth of your heart can lead to monogamy and deep fulfillment if you allow real love to take its time.

Your sexual or emotional energy can be both the joy and the agony of your life, but once you harness its wildfire effect on your reasoning, it can bring you to ecstatic spiritual awakening. As a Fire Gypsy, your sexual energy is vitally and intricately woven within the intense fabric of your being. Ruled by Fire, you can reach Goddess Consciousness through lovemaking, and your Tantric potential will be discussed a little later.

Up until now, this portrait suggests that you are an enthusiastic, high-spirited, and unique woman. But where there is fire, there is ash; where there is light, there is darkness. Just as you are capable of experiencing great joy and pleasure, you are also capable of knowing periods of great upheaval, change, and metaphorical death. Like the beautiful and mythical bird, the phoenix, you can burn in your own fire only to ascend with vision and renewed strength. As a Fire Gypsy, you experience many "deaths" and many rebirths in your life. By the time you reach age twenty, you most probably experience your first bottom. Whether it is due to emotional pain, sexual crisis, or illness, it is during this time you turn inward for the first time. Anger, addiction, or the effects of childhood abuse may play a key role in your descents. During these times of inner devastation, you may believe that your life is in ashes and incapable of ever being rebuilt. Yet a deep inner will rarely accepts defeat. This central self makes you a daughter of the phoenix and makes your hell auriferous. If you bear the night's anguish, your temporary "death" on any level becomes the womb from which you are reborn. No matter how many times you experience destruction or destruction of self, you rise stronger and wiser. Like deadly lava, your anger, grief, or bitterness eventually prove to catalyze lush, new growth. What molten rock does for soil, tragedy does for the Fire Gypsy's soul.

Power is the very essence of the Fire Gypsy; this power can be very overwhelming not only to those around you but also to yourself. As a Fire Gypsy, sometimes you have to learn how not to burn yourself. Self-destructive Fire women often invite catastrophe or end up setting their lives on fire through rash decisions or power struggles. Like the destructive aspect of your element, this energy can be transformed into a positive force. Those who literally go to hell and back return with much to offer the world. You, dear lady of light, have the power to brand humanity with your vision and hard-earned truth.

Of all the elemental types, you manage to have fun through it all. On a mundane level, you throw a party even when you're in the trenches. Emotionally, you are often jovial, showing the world your best face even when you feel defeated. However, when you get angry, it can either be medicine or poison. When it's medicine, your heat burns the field so future harvests will be more abundant; when your anger is poison, you burn bridges that can never be repaired. You can verbally burn others and damage positive relationships. On the other hand, if you channel your anger in a positive way, you can accomplish great things in areas of injustice.

Being ruled by Fire, you naturally gravitate toward your element which means you enjoy candlelight in the dining room, bedroom, or work place. Some Fire Gypsies in the music business even record my candlelight. With this love and need to be by fire, you may love desert climates, hot summer days, making love by the fire, or witnessing the sunset.

As a Fire Gypsy, you most likely prefer the extraordinary, unique, or maybe even bizarre. Conservative living in any manner never attracted you and probably never will. Of all the elemental women, you are most likely to have a distinct personal style, a wardrobe of exotic clothing, or an eccentric collection of anything you have a passion for.

Your spiritual potential is no less unique. As a woman of Fire, you are especially capable of awakening the kundalini. This energetic force is believed to sleep at the base of the spine until it is activated. Once awakened, the kundalini ascends toward the head, igniting the chakras. Its destination is the crown chakra, the mystic's gateway, resulting in enlightenment. There are many ways to rouse this flaming spiritual energy inherent in each of us, including sexual union. Of all the elemental women, you are born with the ability to reach higher consciousness through sex. By nature, you are a potent Shakti, beautiful and strong counterpart to your male partners like the Hindu goddess who sustains Shiva's power. Like Shakti, Shiva—Lord of Dissolution, only destroys in order to create. It is believed that the sacred intercourse between Shakti and Shiva keeps the world in existence, and without Shakti, Shiva is powerless and inactive. If you are lesbian, this Tantric union is also possible. Though Tantric techniques most often focus on heterosexual union, lesbian Tantra exists and is very powerful.

Your mysticism is not for the weak. Fire Gypsies have the potential to experience spiritual ecstasy, intense visions, and concentrated kundalini arousal. If you are shamanic, your experiences might be profound. In certain shamanic cultures, there is a particular mystic who becomes initiated into her/his power when lightning accidently strikes them. If they live through the experience, they return to the world of the living with powers greater than any other shaman's. Lightning shamans are the most revered and feared of all Medicine Men/Women. This destructive/constructive dynamic is the very heart of your spirituality.

With or without lightning, your awakening can be quick, even frightening, but once you understand the nature of your element and energy, you can come in to your full power with balance and without fear. Fire Gypsies have the innate potential to see and/or read auras, heal with their hands, and manifest energies into the physical world.

Any woman whose Primary element is other than Fire and finds herself moving into Fire Gypsy energy (her Rising Element), long-buried anger can surface and make her feel out of sorts, even out of control. If you are one of these women moving into the energy of Fire, you may find this period very unsettling, even chaotic. Working with Water can help bring you back to a state of equilibrium; the Water principle can be very helpful. Spending time near a body of water, dipping your hands in a river or stream, swimming in a pool, creating a Water altar, or simply drinking more water can help quell Fire's effect on the emotions and the physical body. If you are a Fire Gypsy, this connection with water can also be helpful during periods of intensity.

To connect with Fire more deeply, try watching the moods of a candle flame and try to commune with the being within the light. Say a prayer at sunset or study the nature of lightning. Do anything that safely brings you closer to Fire and Fire to you.

## The Fire Gypsy at a Glance

### Vocational Possibilities

advertising, the arts, decorating, design, education, entertainment, fashion, graphic arts, journalism, management, metalsmithing, music, production, public speaking, self-employment, spiritual or religious leadership, storytelling, vibrational healing, writing

### Potential Strengths

passionate, positive, confident, humorous, energetic, creative

### Potential Weaknesses

impatient, sharp-tongued, opinionated, addictive, vindictive

### Keywords

confident, spontaneous, charismatic, unusual

### Spiritual Potential

Tantra, trance, magical arts, aura reading, Nirvana

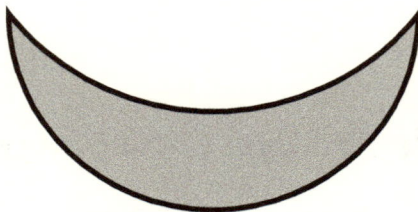

# Sister of the Siren: The Water Maid

*How long the journey of this soul*
*That wears the memory of waves*
*And forgotten faces of the deep...*
*Driftwood-soul, heart made wise*
*In the womb of the waters;*
*Driftwood-soul, now a voice*
*For the inaudible.*
*What I am, the wave has made.*

Psst...hey, you over there with that far-away look in your eyes. I'm sorry to interrupt your reverie, but now that I have your attention, welcome to your special corner of the world! Hello Water Maid.

I'm most certainly not the first to intrude upon your solitude; if you are true to your Water Maid nature, you most likely remember retreating into a sanctuary of drawing pencils, books, or daydreams while growing up. It is quite possible that no one around you had a clue about the wild world of your imaginings except a teacher who tried to focus your attention away from the sunny day outside the classroom window.

Even today you might have a bottomless imagination very similar to the Fire Gypsy's, but you might rather be tortured than allow anyone into the private chamber of your thoughts. Your dreams, secrets, and unspoken epics still create a shell for you to disappear into when the need and desire arises. Solitude can be your greatest necessity and your greatest source of pain. Overall, solitude is the Water Maid's greatest teacher.

It is safe to say that beauty entranced you from a very young age—music and its spell of harmonies, art's prism of colors, and poetry's waltz of words. Art and nature may have moved you more deeply than your peers. Of all the elemental women, you were most likely to have gotten goose bumps even at school concerts.

During your youth, those around you might have observed your depth of nature and sensed something about you that was "old", wise, or timeless. You lured people to you without intention and without saying a word like a siren in a Victorian painting. Even now as an adult, there is something sad, beautiful, or mystical about you that makes others want to be in your presence or to protect you.

At times this quality brings unwanted attention into your life. Like the elusive mermaid, some people want to catch you in their net for their gain. Throughout your life, your gentleness, shyness, or passivity may have made you especially vulnerable to physical, emotional, or sexual abuse.

As a daughter of the waters, you have the ability to reflect the moods of others. This unconscious mirroring probably makes you extremely perceptive and deeply sensitive. You absorb the emotions of others like a sponge. Needless to say, even as young girl, you knew that you were a psychic vessel that held whatever was poured into you.

Water Maid, I don't have to tell you that you often feel like a fish out of water in the presence of people. Even if you are outgoing on the surface, you might feel lonely in a crowd, isolated, and at times, rejected. If you have or had physical, mental, or emotional challenges, these feelings may be intense. It is not uncommon for Water Maids to have wounded or even crippled self-esteem. Unlike the Earth Sister, Fire Gypsy, and Sylph who are born with or are able to cultivate confidence, the Water Maid struggles sometimes her entire life. Acquiring self-love is a major challenge.

Many Water Maids are prone to melancholy or periods of deep loneliness, but many also gain strength during these times. If you are a creative woman, you probably feel that these experiences are often vital to your creative growth.

Illness, family addiction, depression, or debilitating insecurity might have caused you to lose your emotional footing during your youth. You might have felt as if you were swept into raging rapids with little control. It is possible that you turned inward in search of a safe harbor or developed false or self-destructive comfort patterns that later evolved into an eating disorder or addiction. If you were in a positive environment that fostered your special sensitivity, you might have channeled the depth of your emotions into playing an instrument, dancing, painting, writing, or pursuing spiritual interests.

If you are a Water Maid with a deep wellspring of emotion and creativity, you most likely have found your calling in the arts or are loyal to artistic activities. If you are a Water Maid with exceptional compassion, you might have found your calling in social service or caregiving. You may have a profound need to help others through service or art which nourishes you in return. There are many vocational possibilities for the Water Maid, but whatever you do, your work purifies our hearts and washes the wounds of the human condition. Where would we be without your cup of beauty always extended to quench our thirst? You, dear lady, are at home in music, art, teaching, counseling, writing, or anywhere your love of beauty and gift of compassion is needed.

You possess quiet intelligence and non-competitive ambition which often makes people unaware of your great capabilities. Unlike the Earth Sister, Fire Gypsy, and Sylph, your talents are overlooked until you build your confidence drop by drop. Sometimes people do not take notice of a serene river until it overflows its banks. You are no exception. Others recognize your power and ability only when you gain the self-esteem to challenge your boundaries.

There comes a day in every Water Maid's life when she realizes that her idealism conflicts with the ways of the world. If this realization comes during young adulthood, the Water woman often spends her twenties and thirties battling mistrust, bitterness, or disappointment. If this awareness comes at midlife, her very foundation could be washed away. Depression may result from disillusionment, and you may find yourself in a life-long pattern of submerging and re-surfacing. Each time you break the surface and face the sunlight you vow that the abyss will not call you down another time. However, each time you swim the depths you always return with invaluable self-knowledge. When you are in your true power, you rise each time a little wiser, stronger, or creative. Unfortunately, there are Water Maids who do not surface but succumb to the dark seas of their own souls. Suicide or the long suicide of addiction, or self-denial often claims the lives of many extraordinary Water women. The tragedy of this is that they use their immense power to destroy themselves.

The power of Water is immeasurable but worthless to the

Water Maid until she learns how to turn her power outward rather than inward. Once she does, she becomes a force to be reckoned with, often a force for positive change. There is nothing more beautiful or mighty than a Water Maid who controls the power of her own self.

As a Water Maid, you quench our parched daily existence, and your creativity and generosity can appear to be boundless. In reality, your inspiration can easily dry up for extended periods of time. Many creative Water Maids experience writer's block or lack motivation for months, sometimes years. It is the strange but expected paradox of the Water Maid; you may find it easy to quench, aid survival, but are often unable to quench yourself.

Your work and your emotions need a steady stream of new ideas, people, and activity to avoid stagnation. Without refreshing interludes and stimulating experiences to balance your required solitude, you can submerge into depression or apathy. However, like rains that eventually prevail, inspiration does return, and you surge once again with vitality.

You are the lady who uses the power of metaphor, symbolism, poetics, and mysticism in your daily life. While others speak of dreams, you sing, paint, write, and live them. You have the gift of memorizing ordinary moments and making them immortal through your creative work. You are the woman who can easily and vividly remember a childhood daydream, a lover's brief gesture, or the song of a bird on a lost summer day. We look to you to translate the emotions in our lives and give significance to mundane survival.

Emotionally, you are capable of experiencing great bliss as well as pain. When you feel, you *feel.* Your joy is rapturous, your laughter abundant, and your sorrow all-consuming. During periods of inner peace, you can be meditative, philosophical, and capable of great humor. Many Water Maids who are serious in their youth become more playful as they grow older and vice versa. Confidence is another blessing of growing older.

The Water woman usually feels quite uncomfortable with her own anger and avoids releasing it or even acknowledging it. Shyness or lack of self-worth can prevent you from confronting the source of your anger. If you funnel all of this energy inside yourself over time, you can be one of the many Water Maids who become resentful or even ill from unreleased emotion. This suppression can take a toll on your physical wellbeing. You may also find that you go through periods of insensitivity when you freeze your feelings for survival. Once you reach this state, spiritual work or counseling can have a positive thawing effect upon your emotions. As a woman of the waters, tears play an important role in your life and should never be repressed. If you have a fear of crying, remember that tears are your body's rain that thaws, washes, and restores the soul. Crying can be vital to your good health and serenity.

Some Water Maids drown others around them with their

problems and never truly learn to stand on their own two feet. Another tendency is to take things too personally, easily wounded by careless words and the behavior of others. This can be a real source of pain for you if you invest your self-worth in the actions or opinions of other people. Often the Water Maid utilizes her inborn powers only after she conquers her need for approval. Once she does, she can accomplish anything she sets her mind to.

Many Water Maids need the safe shore of a love relationship. You are most likely attracted to those with abundant energy and confidence. You may also have a history of attracting insensitive, violent, or abusive partners. If and when you find a person who energizes you without draining your life force and who understands your requirement for solitude and space, you discover eddies of potential within the relationship and yourself. Love and falling in love affect you deeply. Love can be a healing spring or a dark whirlpool for the Water Maid. If can be life-giving if the experience is positive; life-draining if it is negative. Like your element Water, you most likely need to be contained within the sure banks of a lover's presence in order to feel whole. You are a deeply passionate, even mystical lover. Some Water Maids suffer from sexual inhibition but once overcome, reach high summits of sexual experience. You can be erotic and spiritual, intense and gentle. As a lover and Water Maid, you possess a spell-binding gift which is the *willingness* to love unconditionally. Even if you suffer from insecurity, jealousy, dependency, or the need to control, your innate capacity to love can transcend these negative tendencies.

People may comment that you live a romantic life in general; romantic in the sense that you recognize and make room for beauty in all that you do. You may have a passion for sensuous fabrics, antiques, old books, or flowers. Aesthetic surroundings play an important role in your life as well as music, art, and cinema. If you are a bold Water Maid, your taste is probably avant-garde. If you are conservative, you are still lured to uniqueness. You may often feel that you were born in the wrong century and deeply long for a time and place you've never known.

Creative expression is probably a spiritual practice for you, and in many ways, your meditation. You most likely are able to transcend the mundane with pen, brush, camera, or musical instrument in hand.

It is also probable that your spirituality is your most intimate partner during your life's journey. You feel like a ship blown off course without it. You are a natural channel for higher forces and have potential to master Samadhi, the deepest level of meditation. You may also have potential in areas of mediumship, clairvoyance, astral projection, remote viewing, automatic writing or drawing, deep dream work, and hands-on healing. If you offer your spiritual services to others, you have to be careful not to deplete your energies or leave your energy field open to negative influences. Extra precaution to protect yourself is needed due to your openness and tendency to absorb other people's energy. You are the woman who can easily dip into the well of the Sacred Feminine and find serenity and authentic power. Once you learn to navigate the intensity of your seas, you can attain any spiritual quest on the horizon.

To commune with Water, take some time to skip stones on a lake, build a sand castle, take a bath by moonlight, or simply watch water in a glass catch sunbeams. Study paintings and myths of mermaids or undines or listen to a nature recording of rain or heavy surf. Do anything that brings you closer to Water and Water to you.

## *The Water Maid at a Glance*

### Vocational Possibilities

the arts, caregiving, education, entertainment (likely behind the scenes), holistic healing, homemaking, literary fields, medicine/nursing, psychic arts, social service, therapy/rehabilitation

### Potential Strength

perceptive, creative, reflective, intuitive, caring

### Potential Weaknesses

hypersensitive, insecure, suppressive, addictive, easily influenced

### Keywords

# *Goddess Consciousness* ⭐

creative, visionary, internal, solitary

## Spiritual Potential

mediumship, healing, astral travel, automatic writing, deep trance, Samadhi

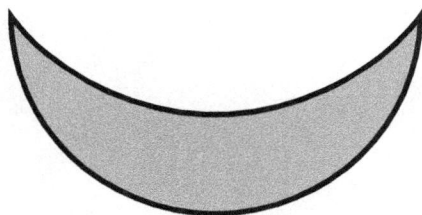

# Woman of the Winds: The Sylph

*On furious winds of thought I have flown...*
*On the winds of change my seeds have traveled;*
*Forever elusive, forever free,*
*My soul in flight.*

Hello daughter of divine thought! Welcome to your world. As a woman of air—the element that rules the mind—your intellect or refinement of spirit can be found realms above the average person. You are a lady of quicksilver, seeing miles ahead in a conversation and a bird's eye view of any given situation. You probably came out of the womb with a pocketful of plans or mystical visions.

There are two very distinct species of Sylph; one lives in the world of constant intellectual motion while the other inhabits the outer atmosphere of everyday consciousness.

Both are named after the *sylph* in occult literature, meaning a spirit of air. If you are the thinker, you are a disciple of higher education or a moving force in fields of science, medicine, law, invention, research, writing, astronomy, or aviation. If you are a mystic, you live in two worlds simultaneously and your work is most likely in the areas of psychic service or investigation, parapsychology, spiritual psychology, vibrational healing, or metaphysical ministry.

You are a catalyst for change. Your intellectual or visionary approach is like wind over water; your ideas create a ripple effect that is far-reaching. You are also equipped with limitless ambition. Your mind has no knowledge of doors, walls, or chains; you see beyond horizons and limitations. While the Earth Sister keeps the world turning, the Fire Gypsy makes it interesting, and the Water Maid nurtures its beauty, the Sylph keeps it progressing. Human advancement would be minimal without the boundless vision and mental stamina of the Sylph. You hunger for knowledge, and learning is your life's purpose. Whether you part the curtain of invisible worlds by changing consciousness or carry libraries inside your brain, you never cease to learn, inquire, and question. The Sylph pursues the unknown like a bird of prey.

You probably appear to be in another dimension most of the time and have difficulty remembering that you actually have a physical body to maintain. When the winds of inspiration call you, you might forget to eat or take care of yourself. Unless you have plenty of Earth in your personality, you probably have a tendency to neglect other mundane areas of life as well. Many Sylphs have messy houses or cars, and a growing list of chores that need to be done. Lack of time may also be a major factor. Sometimes you have so much on your plate that it is impossible to take care of things even if you *do* notice you haven't eaten or your fridge hasn't been cleaned out since Goddess knows when. Your mind and the realms of thought or spirit most likely come first before anything in your life, and your emotional life is no exception. Relationships play a minor role, or they may be compromised. Many Sylphs lead unattached lives, and of all the elemental women, find it easiest to live a celibate life. This may be by choice, or constant work makes the choice for them. If you are a spiritually-minded Sylph, you may feel that you do not need sexual expression or a significant relationship in order to feel whole. On the other hand, if you are a highly intellectual Sylph, you may feel detached from your emotions and not fully present in relationships.

Sylphs who are mothers are not abundant, but those who do have children often find it a difficult to balance their work with their role as parent. Again, if you have a weak connection to your opposite and balancing element Earth, your experience as mother can be challenging both to you and your child. Many Sylph mothers who dedicate most of their time to their work often compensate for their absence by providing their kids with an abundance of material things.

Your work or your hunger to always *know* may also make it seemingly impossible to relax. If you muster up enough Fire and actually go on vacation, you'll be the only one on the cruise ship distracted by loose ends at the office. If you don't physically take work with you, your mind is always working. Only when you get back home do you realize that you didn't even notice the sunset.

Due to emotional reservation, anger or irritation may the only emotion you allow yourself to give in to. You are professional and stable most of the time, but when your patience wears thin, your discontent can blow in like an unexpected storm. Many times a Sylph will not allow herself to surrender to anger in her personal life but will do so in her professional arena, or vice versa. Like a tempest, you may unleash your power, inspect the damage, and then get on with your life. You might also be hard on people who cannot keep up with the exquisite pace of your thoughts, plans, and ideas, or be short-tempered with those who do not share your unique vision or perspective. On the other end of the spectrum, if you are a medium of any sort, you might find everyday interaction with your partner tiresome and draining when you are dragged into petty arguments. You have the eagle's mind and vision, seeing the entirety of a situation with one glance; to you, picking at trivialities is not only a waste of time and precious energy but meaningless in the big scheme of things.

When it does surface, your anger may serve a purpose in breaking down walls between people or bringing the fresh air of new ideas where it is needed. Dear Sylph, sometimes your harsh winds are exactly what is needed to change minds and outdated systems. If you are political, your fierce side wedded with vision and sense of justice can make radical change where it is needed most. Many Sylphs were the backbone of the Women's Rights movement and Gay/Lesbian Liberation movement during the 1960s and 1970s. Alongside your Earth Sisters, you changed this world in many ways. If you are involved in environmental change, you may be a sweeping force in this area. Like the Earth Sister, you are the woman who will risk body and soul for a cause and will say what needs to be said and do what needs to be done. You are most effective when you apply your intellectual prowess; your greatest and most powerful weapon is your brain and/or spiritual vision.

As a woman of Air, freedom is your middle name. You avoid physical, emotional, and financial dependence. You often prefer your own company and need a great deal of breathing space if you live with someone. In turn, you are also able to give others their needed space. This need for psychic freedom also plays an intricate role in your emotions, or sometimes, disconnection from them. There may come a time in every Sylph's life when her heart goes to war with her mind. After she finds a cure, flies solo around the world, wins that court case or election, or proves life after death, she faces the biggest challenge in her life: feeling without being petrified. You may feel helpless in the face of love, all kinds. As an Air woman, your greatest lessons come through balancing the pragmatic with the unknown, the intellectual with the emotional, and the scientific with the spiritual. And nothing shortens the distance between these poles like love.

Love shakes you up and gives you claustrophobia until you are able to risk being vulnerable. Your fear of vulnerability can make you emotionally elusive, a bit out of reach, and in many ways, untouchable. If this fear leaks into your sexual life, you may find it challenging to unite body, heart, and mind. Of all the elemental women, your sexuality can be compromised by the fear of intimacy, making it difficult to enjoy being sexual, and you might find yourself going through the motions. This may cause you great pain you rarely admit to, or it may lead you to believe that you are not a sexual being, even asexual. However, you blossom sexually when you finally do allow yourself to learn emotional agility and to fully feel. As a Sylph, you are capable of ecstatic heights during lovemaking. If you are spiritual by nature, you are capable of total immersion in the Divine, even profound trance or out-of-body experience during intimacy.

When your heart and mind come to an agreement, creativity can blossom. I've heard many Sylphs complain that they are not creative, but as a woman of vision, you most certainly can be. The creative force is the Mother Energy of the sexual force; they are one and the same, despite manifesting separately. You will never be a lover of sentiment or be swayed by the emotional winds of others, but you are capable of uniting the opposing forces within when you realize the vast heaven of possibility at your fingertips. Your creativity most often manifests in words, especially the spoken word. Being a Sylph, your innermost power is connect to the breath, the life force. This means you can change and create with your voice. If you are true to your Air nature, you probably are or can be a great orator.

On the mundane level you probably do not have strong preferences. Unless you have a lot of Water and Fire in your elemental nature, the only thing you have a desperate need and passion for is knowledge. In the physical world, this manifests as books and you probably have a vast library.

Spiritually, you are capable of melding the mental realm with the spiritual. Your great mind power or connection to Spirit can give you the ability to bridge life's dualities. Being that your opposite element is Earth, at your most powerful, you can ground your spiritual energy and accomplish amazing things. You are capable of advanced abilities such as remote viewing, astral and consciousness projection, telepathy, telekinesis, angelic communication, and manifestation through concentrated thought. Those who accomplish teleportation or movement of physical objects using mind power are said to use breath as a tool. Being a woman of the winds, your breath is the key to your deepest meditation and spiritual progress.

If you are a Sylph who naturally lives in two worlds simultaneously, mediumship and interacting with the unseen forces are natural to you as breathing. Some of the greatest psychics and metaphysicians of the world are Sylphs. If you find it difficult to remain grounded, working with Earth will give roots to your wings when needed. As a Sylph, you have the inborn potential to accomplish psychokinesis which includes moving objects, bending metal, and cloud dissolution through will. The latter can also be extended to weather control, a global phenomenon common to powerful shamans.

To connect with Air, breathe deeply and become aware of the element when it enters your nostrils. Perch on a summit and watch the world below. Listen to a nature recording of winds or storms. Do anything that helps you connect to Air and Air to you.

## *The Sylph at a Glance*

### Vocational Possibilities

academics, astrology, astronomy, aviation, business, corporate positions, finance, historical studies, invention, law, mathematics, medicine, metaphysics, oration, parapsychology, physics, politics, psychic arts/service, psychology/spiritual psychology, research, science, theology, vibrational healing, writing

**Potential Strengths**

mentally alert, seeking, ambitious, leading, confident, visionary

**Potential Weaknesses**

non-emotional, not grounded, restless

**Keywords**

visionary, quick-thinking

**Spiritual Potential**

mind travel or remote viewing, mediumship, astral or consciousness projection, telekinesis, psychokinesis, telepathy, clairvoyance, manifestation, ceremonial magic, spiritual healing, angelic communication

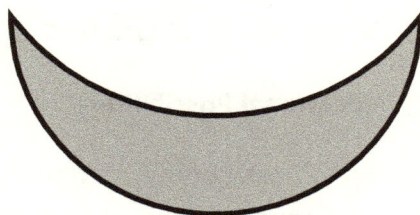

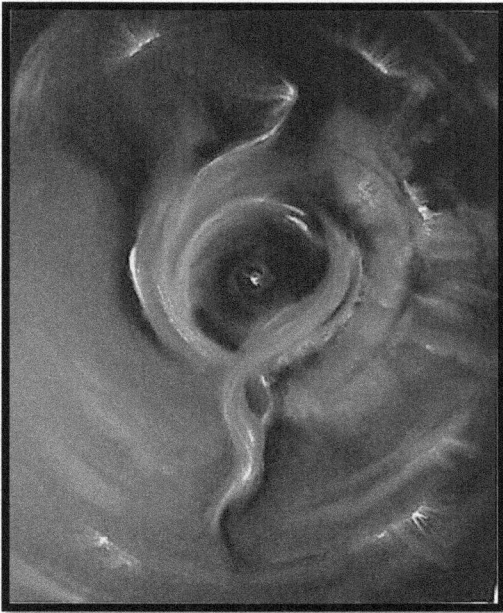

# Conclusion

Twenty-five years ago, the Goddess came into my life and turned it upside down with Her beautiful truths—truths about history, women's spiritual legacy, and most of all, myself and the reflection in the mirror. I was lifted from the mud of pain into the light where my soul opened beautiful and brilliant petals of possibility. Today, as I advance further into midlife and look at the landscape left behind, I see the constancy of these truths that have seen me through many spiritual paths, trial-and-error life choices, jobs and careers, romantic partners, changes and devastation, failures and unforeseen successes. Through it all, the Divine Feminine prevailed, providing a fiery core of sustenance that has nourished me well. Whenever I falter and forget, I look at the stars—infinite, eternal, and suspended by a power greater than themselves. And I am reminded that I, too, am in good hands.

Today is the clay, and we are the sculptors. So dear Sister-reader who holds this book in hand, let's create a masterpiece. Let's walk in Her name.

*Be*

*Free*

# Goddess Consciousness

With the silken threads of the seasons,

Gaia weaves the tapestry of our days.

At the loom of time, She braids the ages;

Each leaf, tree, and stone...a thread.

Each heartbeat, breath, and vision...a thread.

One thread severed from the Whole—

the death of Nature, the death of us.

# Resources

. . . .

## Herbal Suppliers

**Starwest Botanicals**
www.starwest-botanicals.com
bulk herbs by pound and ounce

**Frontier Co-op**
www.frontiercoop.com
bulk herbs by pound and ounce

**Maui Medicinal Herbs**
www.mauimedicinal.com
high-quality kava kava and other products

**Herbalist & Alchemist**
www.herbalist-alchemist.com
complete line of herbal tinctures

## Essential Oil Suppliers

**Young Living Essential Oils**
www.youngliving.com
highest quality therapeutic grade essential oils

**doTerra**
www.doterra.com

highest quality therapeutic grade essential oils

### Starwest Botanicals
www.starwest-botanicals.com
good selection of essential oils

### NOW Foods
www.nowfoods.com
high quality, affordable, and gas chromatography-tested
essential oils. Excellent prices for NOW essential oils can
be found at Swanson Vitamins
www.swansonvitamins.com

### Ananda Apothecary
www.anandaapothecary.com
excellent source for cacao (chocolate) essential oil

### Birch Hill Happenings
www.birchhillhappenings.com
private company with a wonderful variety of essential oils

### Eden Botanicals
www.edenbotanicals.com
lovely high-quality and exotic essential oils

### The Essential Oil Company
www.essentialoil.com
nice selection of rare absolutes

### Shaman's Dawn

## Goddess Consciousness

www.shamansdawn.com
Good source for palo santo spray and smudge sticks

# Clinical Aromatherapy and Aromatic Medicine Education

### Institute of Spiritual Healing and Aromatherapy (ISHA)
www.ishaaromatherapy.com

Highly recommended 240 hour course in aromatic medicine, vibrational aromatherapy, basic essential oil composition and chemistry, and ancient spiritual healing techniques. Recognized by NAHA (The National Association of Holistic Aromatherapy) and AIA (Alliance of International Aromatherapists)

### The East West School for Herbal and Aromatic Studies
www.theida.com

### Jeanne Rose Aromatherapy and All Things Herbal
www.jeannerose.net/courses.html

# Natural Perfumes & Cosmetics

### Amrita Aromatics and Apothecary
www.etsy.com/shop/AmritaAromatics
high frequency Earth-based and Goddess-inspired
artisanal perfumes and skin products

# Goddess Consciousness

### Ecco Bella
www.eccobella.com
luxurious gluten-free natural make-up and body care

### Herbs of Grace
www.herbsofgrace.com
rainbow assortment of loose mineral make-up

### Gabriel Cosmetics
www.gabrielcosmeticsinc.com
celebrity line of natural and organic make-up and skin care

### Henna King
www.hennaking.com
high quality henna products for hair and skin
Also henna-based nail and lip color

### Heritage Store
www.heritagestore.com
natural skin care, essential oils, and holistic products
based on the Edgar Cayce readings
Excellent source of rose water

# Goddess Inspirations

### Willowroot Wands
www.willowrootwands.com
Goddess wands, statues, jewelry and metaphysical
delights

### Spiral Goddess Grove
www.spiralgoddess.com
virtual Goddess temple

# *Recommended Reading*

. . . .

## *Goddess and Women's Studies*

**Ariadne's Thread: A Workbook of Goddess Magic** by Shekhinah Mountainwater

**When God Was a Woman** by Merlin Stone

**Pure Lust: Elemental Feminist Philosophy** by Mary Daly

**Blood, Bread, and Roses: How Menstruation Created the World** by Judy Grahn

**All Women Are Healers: A Comprehensive Guide to Natural Healing** by Diane Stein

**Casting the Circle: A Woman's Book of Ritual** by Diane Stein

**The Holy Book of Women's Mysteries** by Zuzsanna Budapest

**Shakti Woman: Feeling Our Fire, Healing Our World - The New Female Shamanism** by Vicki Noble

**The Woman's Encyclopedia of Myths and Secrets** by Barbara G. Walker

**Bond Between Women: A Journey to Fierce Compassion** by China Galland

# *Goddess Consciousness*

**The Legacy of Luna: The Story of a Tree, a Woman and the Struggle to Save the Redwoods** by Julia Butterfly Hill

**Woman and Nature: The Roaring Inside Her** by Susan Griffin

**The Woman with the Alabaster Jar: Mary Magdalen and the Holy Grail** by Margaret Starbird

**When the Drummers Were Women: A Spiritual History of Rhythm** by Layne Redmond

**The Spiral Dance: A Rebirth of the Ancient Religion of the Goddess** by Starhawk

**Portrait of a Priestess: Women and Ritual in Ancient Greece** by Joan Breton Connelly

**The White Goddess** by Robert Graves

**Naked Soul: Astral Travel and Cosmic Relationships** by Marlene Marie Druhan

**Birthing Fire: Meditations on the Sacred Feminine** by Marlaina Donato

# *Chant, Sound, & Toning*

**Chanting: Discovering Spirit in Sound** by Robert Gass and Kathleen A. Brehony

**Toning: The Creative Power of the Voice** by Laurel Elizabeth Keyes

# Goddess Consciousness

## Aromatherapy & Essential Oils

**Healing Oils, Healing Hands** by Linda L. Smith

**Essential Oils Desk Reference** (Essential Science Publishing) Gary Young

**The Aromatherapy Companion** by Victoria H. Edwards

**Aromatherapy for the Soul** by Valerie Ann Worwood

## Herbalism

**Flower Power** by Anne McIntyre

**Encyclopedia of Herbal Medicine** by Andrew Chevallier

**Back to Eden** by Jethro Kloss

**Healing Herbs A-Z** by Diane Stein

## Gemstones

**The Book of Stones: Who They Are and What They Teach** by Robert Simmons & Naisha Ahsian

**Gemstones A-Z** by Diane Stein

## Magazines & eZines

Sagewoman Magazine

# *Recommended Music*

*Origin of Fire- music of Hildegard von Bingen* -Anonymous Four

*108 Names of the Mother Divine, Sacred Chants of Devi, & Sacred Chants of Shakti-* Craig Pruess and Ananda-

*A Circle is Cast-* Libana

*Sacred Chants for Women & Return of the Goddess* –Lindie Lila

*Journey to the Goddess & Circle of the Seasons* –Lisa Thiel

*Soothsayer* –Marlaina Donato

*Ancient Mother* –Robert Gass

*Voice of the Blood- (music of Hildegard von Bingen) & Canticles of Ecstasy (music of Hildegard von Bingen)* -Sequentia

# *Bibliography*

Al-Rawi, Rosina-Fawzia. Grandmother's Secrets. NY,NY: Interlink Books, 1999

Ashley-Ferrand, Thomas. Shakti Mantras: Tapping into the Great Goddess Energy Within. NY,NY: Ballantine Books, 2003

Andrews, Ted. Sacred Sounds: Transformation Through Music and Word. St. Paul, MN: Llewellyn Publications, 1993

Austen, Hallie Iglehart. The Heart of the Goddess. Berkely, CA: Wingbow Press, 1990

Buonaventura, Wendy. Belly Dancing. London, Great Britain: Virago Press, 1983

Cahill, Susan (Editor). Wise Women. NY, NY: Norton and Company, Inc., 1996

Andrew Chevallier. Encyclopedia of Herbal Medicine. London, England: DK Publishing, 2000

Connelly, Joan Breton. Portrait of a Priestess. Princeton, NJ: Princeton University Press, 2007

Croutier, Alev Lytle. Harem: The World Behind the Veil. NY, NY: Abbeville Press, 1989

Cunningham, Scott. Cunningham's Encyclopedia of Magical Herbs. Woodbury, MN: Llewlellyn Publications, 2009

Druhan, Marlene Marie. Naked Soul: Astral Travel and Cosmic Relationships. St. Paul, MN: Llewellyn Publications, 1998

Editors. Ancient Wisdom and Secret Sects. Alexandria, VA: Time-Life Books

_____Mysteries of the Unknown. Alexandria, VA: Time-Life Books

Edwards, Victoria H. The Aromatherapy Companion. North Adams, MA: Storey Publishing, 1999

Eliade, Mircea. Shamanism: Archaic Techniques of Ecstasy. Boston, MA: Princeton University Press, 1964

Frankfort, Henri. Ancient Egyptian Religion: An Interpretation. Mineola, NY: Dover Publications, Inc., 1948

Gass, Robert. Chanting: Discovering Spirit in Sound. NY, NY: Broadway Books, 1999

Garrison, Omar V. Tantra: The Yoga of Sex. NY, NY: Julian Press, 1964

Gies, Frances and Joseph. Women in the Middle Ages. San Fransisco, CA: Harper Perennial, 1978

Grahn, Judy. Blood, Bread, and Roses. Boston, MA: Beacon Press, 1993

Guiley, Rosemary Ellen. Harper's Encyclopedia of Mystical and Paranormal Experience. NY, NY: Harper Collins Publishers, 1991

Hirschi, Gertud. Mudras. Newburyport, MA: Red Wheel/Weiser, 2000

Kalweit, Holger. Shamans, Healers, and Medicine Men. Boston, MA: Shambhala Publications, Inc., 1992

Kaufman, William Irving. Perfume. E.P. Dutton and Company, 1974

Keyes, Laurel Elizabeth. Toning: The Creative Power of the Voice. Marina del Rey, CA: DeVorss Publications, 1973

Khan, Hazrat Inayat. The Sufi Message of Hazrat Inayat Khan. London, Great Britain: Barnie Books, Ltd., 1962

Kidwai, Azra. Islam. Leicester, Great Britain: Silverdale Books, 2000

Kloss, Jethro. Back to Eden. Coalmont, TN: Longview Publishing House, 1960

Kumar, Acharya Sushil. Song of the Soul. Blairstown, NJ: Siddachalam Publishing, 1987

McIntyre, Anne. Flower Power. NY,NY: Henry Holt and Co., 1996

Monaghan, Patricia. The Goddess Path. St. Paul, MN: Llewellyn Publications, 1999

Mountainwater, Shekhinah. Ariadne's Thread. Freedom, CA: The Crossing Press, 1999

Picken, D.B. Shinto: Japan's Spiritual Roots. NY, NY: Harper and Row, 1980

Redmond, Layne. When the Drummers Were Women. NY, NY: Three Rivers Press, 1997

Rice, Edward. Eastern Definitions. Garden City, NY: Doubleday and Company, Inc., 1978

Ryman, Daniele. Aromatherapy. NY,NY: Bantam Books, 1991

Simmons, Robert. The Book of Stones. Berkely, CA: North Atlantic Books, 2007

Smith, Linda L. Healing Oils, Healing Hands. HTSM Press, 2003

Starbird, Margaret. The Woman with the Alabaster Jar. Santa Fe, NM: Bear and Company Publishing, 1993

Starhawk. The Spiral Dance. San Fransisco, CA: Harper San Francisco, 1979

Vishnu-Devananda, Swami. Meditation and Mantras. Motilal Banarsidass, 1999

Walker, Barbara G. The Woman's Encyclopedia of Myths and Secrets. San Francisco, CA: Harper and Row, 1983

Walker, Barbara G. The Woman's Encyclopedia of Symbols and Sacred Objects. San Francisco, CA: San Francisco, CA: Harper and Row, 1988

Worwood, Valerie Ann. Aromatherapy for the Soul.

Novato, CA: New World Library, 1999

Young, Gary. Essential Oil Desk Reference. Essential Science Publishing, 2004

# *Index*

Abortion, 100

Abuse, 186, 199, 274, 281, 306, 308, 318, 347, 355

Adornment, 173, 189

Affirmation, 121

Africa, 9, 105, 174, 175, 177

Age, 13-14

Agni, 64

Air (Element), 74, 364

Akasha, 331

Altars, 42-80, 192

Amaterasu, 36

Amulets, 52, 174, 179, 182

Androgyny, 317

Angels, 78, 202, 209, 270, 273

Anger, 46, 98, 126, 308, 337, 347-49, 351, 359, 367

Anointing, 70, 199, 217

Aphrodite, 52, 61, 64, 68, 71, 73, 184, 185, 242, 312

Apollo, 65, 67, 242, 243, 244

Archetypes, 167

Ariel, 65

Arizona, 44

Aromatherapy, 188, 196-233

Aromatics, 50, 187, 226-29

Artemis, 52, 55, 57, 60, 83, 101, 103, 104,183, 201, 242, 274

Artists, 325, 340

Ashes (loved ones), 48, 60, 67

Astarte, 52, 57, 312

Astral projection, 274, 308, 361

Astrology, 330, 336, 371

Athena, 77, 79, 175, 241, 246

Athletes, 188

Aura, 138

Ayurvedic Medicine, 259, 271, 330

Ba, 157

Baba Yaga, 57

Babylonians, 182

Baptism, 70, 217

Barakka, 44

Bast, 57, 312

Bath salts, 217, 222

Beauty, Sacred, 172-190

Belly dance, 105, 181

Bindi, 314

Bingen, Hildegard von, 135, 138, 328

Birthday, 83-86

Birthing Energy, 19-29

Birthing Meditations, 24-29

Blavatsky, Madame, 331

Blessed Mother, 9, 33, 52, 59, 135, 138, 183, 203

Blessings oils, 207-212

Blood pressure, 265, 268, 272, 276, 286

Body powders, 217-223

Brain, 31, 35, 109, 126, 127, 160, 200, 202, 270, 281, 287, 308, 309, 365, 368

Breasts, 35

Brides, 173, 180, 246, 249

Brigid, 63, 65, 67, 243, 256

Brothels, 313

Buddhists, 44

Burial, 44, 331

Cancer, 30, 125-6, 248, 254, 257, 258, 259, 260, 264, 265, 271, 277, 279,

Candle rubs, 229-231

Catherine, St., 12, 188

Cats, 57

Cedar, 50, 55, 59, 60, 62, 66, 102, 198, 200

Celibacy, 12, 316, 338, 366

Ceremony, 81-103

Ceres, 57

Cernunnos, 57

Chakras, 122, 127, 206, 261, 264, 270, 276, 285, 305, 308, 315, 349

Chant, 47, 76, 82, 118-125, 138, 237, 310

Chemicals, 193, 235

Childhood, 12, 137, 200, 347

China, 247

Christianity, 9, 12, 51, 70, 125, 173, 175, 182, 183, 188, 217, 302, 135

Cleopatra, 180

Clitoris, 320

Corn Mother, 57, 60, 244

Cosmetics, 173, 179, 189, 189-91

Couples, 249, 316, 319

Creative Force, 19, 106-7, 120, 314, 316, 370

Creativity, 20, 22, 24, 62, 65, 106, 126, 127, 184, 269, 281, 285, 305, 339, 356, 358, 369, 370

Crone, 96, 111, 112, 238

Crystals, 308-310, 317

Cunti, 321

Cybele, 55

Dargah, 44

Dark Goddesses, 167

Dark Mother, The, 167-170

Daughters, 11, 20, 32

Death, 11, 45, 86, 87, 112, 155, 156, 157, 158, 159, 160, 167, 188, 201, 202, 249, 281, 331, 347

Demeter, 43, 45, 57

Demons, 19, 173, 247

Diana, 55, 60, 129, 242

Dionysos, 45, 55, 57, 61, 242, 245, 250, 312, 340

Divination, 53, 93, 129-154, 193, 242, 244, 246, 330

Divorce, 54, 86

Doppelgängar, 157

Dreams, 21, 51, 70, 90, 158, 160, 161, 162, 163, 185, 243, 269, 274, 288, 296, 304

Drugs, 137-38, 188

Druids, 54, 55

Durga, 9, 58, 124

Dusting powders, 217-223

Earth (Element), 54-62, 334-352

Earth Sister, 334-342

East, 334, 342

Ego, 68, 132

Egyptians, 157, 179, 182, 187

Elements, four, 53, 329-333

Elemental identity, 329-375

Eleusinian Mysteries; 43, 45

Emoto, Masaru, 303

Energy centers (see Chakras)

Envy, 178, 245 (also see Evil Eye)

Eresh-Kigal, 167

Essential Oils, 196-231

Evil, 12, 50, 53, 169, 175, 245

Evil Eye, 18, 51, 177, 178-79, 181, 187, 245, 249

Eyes, 178, 179, 193

Faerie, 58, 61,203, 238,262

Feet, 177, 182, 188, 260

Fetch, 157

Fifth Element (see Akasha), 331

Fingers, 180-81, 182

Fire Art, 145-48

Fire Gypsy, 343-352

Fire, 62-68, 343-352

Food lore, 241-250

Food, 166, 235

Four directions, 331

Fragrance, 187-88 (see Aromatherapy)

Frequency, 120, 124, 183, 186, 192, 196, 197, 198, 199, 203, 205, 235, 252, 287, 296, 308, 325

Gabriel, Archangel, 57

Ganapati, 58

Ganges, 217

Gemstones, 183-87, 308-9

Gender, 13, 317

Gestation, 20-21

Ghosts, 51, 249

Gnostics, 245

Goddess prayers, 113-118

Goddess symbols, 80

Great Spirit, 136

Greeks, 68, 101, 156, 314, 328, 330, 331

Guadalupe, Lady, 60, 203

Gypsies, 105, 174, 242

Hair, 19, 173-176, 177, 194

Heart, 272, 284, 308

Heart chakra, 52, 126, 258, 265, 266, 273, 276, 284, 285, 305, 306, 308

Hecate/Hekate, 55, 167, 201, 244, 245

Henna, 51, 175, 177, 180

Hephaestus, 65

Hera, 242

Herb pantry, 237, 251

Herbalism, 252

Herbs, 101, 236-302

Hermes, 77

Herne, 55, 58

Hestia, 63, 65, 67

Hindus, 44, 119, 124, 314, 331

Holy Child, 45

Hormones, 11, 90, 91, 201, 203, 278

Horns, the, 181

Illness, 131, 156, 179, 183

Incense, 56, 59, 60, 63, 66, 67, 73, 78, 79

India, 9, 119, 170, 175, 181, 246, 313, 330

Initiation, 21, 43, 53, 84, 133

Ink Blots, 151-54

Inquisition, 13, 175, 178

Iris, 71

Isis, 52, 77, 244

Jains, 63, 123, 125, 188, 249

Japan, 36, 43, 55, 67

Jealousy, 178, 270, 360

Jesus, 176

Jewelry, 179, 180, 182, 183

Jinn, 177

Joan of Arc, 129, 173

Journaling, 191

Joy, 16, 282, 309

Kailas, Mount, 43

Kali, 58, 167, 321, 340

Karmic justice, 168

Keyes, Laurel Elizabeth, 125

Kirlian photography, 235

Kitchen, 46, 234-38

Kohl, 179

Kuan Yin, 51, 58, 71, 73, 122, 185

Kumar, Acharya Sushil, 123

Kundalini, 125, 128, 185, 186, 315, 323, 324, 349, 350

Lady of the Grain, 43

Left-handed, 180

Left-Hand Way, 315

Lesbian, 319, 322, 350

Lightning Shamans, 350

Lilith, 33, 65, 167

Love, 318

Lunar rite, 108, 123,

Magdalen, Mary, 52, 53, 60, 175, 203, 204, 213, 244

Make-up, 173, 179, 192, 193, 267, 339

Mala, 182, 183

Mantra, 120-125

Maple, 55

Mari, 72

Matriarchal society, 9, 10, 14, 33, 313

Medicine Wheel, 42, 44

Meditation, 22-9, 122, 206

Medusa, 174, 175

Megahertz, 197

Mehndi, 177

*Men*, prefix, 314

Menopause, 54, 93, 95, 203, 258, 261, 269, 273, 278, 279, 280, 292, 314

Menstrual blood, 19, 250, 314

Menstruation, 10, 90, 175, 274, 314, 315

Mercury, 77

Michael, Archangel, 65

Middle East, 9, 44, 51, 60, 70, 105, 175, 177, 178

Midlife, 93, 94, 345, 357

Midwives, 121, 174

Milky Way, 35, 79, 80

Minerals, 58, 66, 72, 77, 156, 179, 183

Miscarriage, 98, 278

Moon rite, 108-11

Moon calendars, 10, 314

Morgana, 167

Mother Goddess, 157, 246

Mothers, 20-1, 122, 338, 346, 366

Muse, 77

Music of the Spheres, 119

Music, 118-9, 138, 188, 303

Musterion, 45

Mystery Schools, 43, 45, 133

Mystics, 12-3, 16, 120, 136, 158, 170, 188, 346

Mythology, 68, 156, 174

Nail polish, 177

Native American, 42, 44, 60, 65, 237, 269

Navel, 19, 20, 23, 127, 181

Neurotransmitters, 31, 268, 278

Nile River, 71

North Africa, 174, 177

North, 49, 59, 62, 174

Nut, 77, 78

Oak, 54, 55, 284

OBE (out of body experience), 156

Oracles, 132, 136, 137, 139, 142-154

Orgasm, 158, 261, 267, 287, 316, 324

Oshun, 72

Osiris, 72

Palmistry, 330

Pan, 55, 58

Paul, 173

Pele, 63, 65, 67

Perfume, 187-8, 193, 194, 196, 206, 213-217

Perimenopause, 93, 203, 258, 261, 269, 273, 278, 280, 287, 292

Persephone, 58, 60, 115, 247, 248

Phoenix, 65, 68, 347

Pine, 52, 55, 59, 62, 66, 76, 78

Pineal gland, 35, 197

Pituitary gland, 35, 105, 197

Plato, 120

Plants, 236, 252, 340

Plutonian, 43

Pomegranate, 247, 248

Poseidon, 72

Potassium, 166, 254

Power finger, 85, 194, 195

Prayer (see Goddess Prayers)

Prayer pose, 33, 102, 106, 139

Prayer shawl, 114

Pregnancy, 181, 198, 206, 248, 258, 278, 338

Primary Element, 332, 351

Prostitution, 313

Protection, 139-141

Psychic ability, 35, 126, 128, 130-38, 166, 184, 271

Pythagoras, 119, 120

Ra, 52, 67

Raphael, Archangel, 71

Regression, 158, 162-66

Reiki, 197, 202

Rhea, 55

Rhiannon, 58

Rising Element, 328, 351

Romans, 64, 173, 188, 242

Room spritzers, 226-29

Rosary, 42, 182, 183

Rose, 52, 280-1, 287, 292

Ruach, 331

Rumi, 8

Sacred sound, 121, 123, 124, 313

Sacred space, 42-80, 226

Saints, 12, 129, 157, 188, 204,

Salamanders, 65

Same-sex, 317

Second sight (see Psychic Ability)

Self-blessings, 30-40

Self-image, 38, 186, 190, 201, 203, 281

Sexuality, 24, 62, 65, 106, 201, 204, 244, 274, 281, 312-26, 338, 346, 369

Shakti, 65, 106, 122, 185, 313, 314, 315, 319, 320, 324, 349, 350

Shamans, 44, 50, 52, 133-4, 136-7, 251, 350, 371

Shells, 80, 182

Shinto, 36, 43, 44

Shiva, 244, 313, 350

Singing Sands, 119

Sleep, 35, 121, 158, 160, 162-5, 212

Smudging, 53, 55, 227

Sophia, 9

Soul, 156-61

Soul sounds, 120

South, 49, 62, 66

Spirit Elders, 17, 168, 169

Spirit houses, 44

Spirit journeys, 155-166

Subconscious Mind, 70, 121, 161, 164

Sufis, 116

Sumerians, 179

Sylph, 364-72

Tammuz, 58

Tantra, 315, 317, 350, 352

Teas, 288-99

Thoth, 77

Thunderbird, 65, 68

Tiamat, 72

Tomb, 44, 157

Toning, 125-8

Trees, 54-5, 298-9

Tribal Nations, 44, 55, 105, 330

Triple Goddess, 111

Umbilical cord, 16, 19

Urania, 77

Uterus, 92

Vagina, 19, 179, 314

Vanities, 192

Vardoger , 157

Veils, 179

Veriditas, 135

Vesta, 66

Vestal virgins, 173

Virgin, 319

Visualizations, 30-33

Walnut, 55, 62

Water (Element), 68-74, 217, 353-63,

Water Maid, 353-63

Waters, consecrated, 302-11

West, 49, 72

White Buffalo Calf Woman, 58
Wicca, 9, 42
Wind garden, 76
Wise Woman way, 289
Wise women, 251
Witches, 173, 174, 175, 178, 180, 236, 247
Woman of the Wilds, 101
Womb, 244, 247, 248, 258
Yemaya, 72, 73
Yeshua, 53, 176
Yoni, 19, 37, 80, 92, 244, 246, 287, 319, 321, 322, 323
Zaghareet, 102, 105
Zeus, 55, 77, 242

# *About the Author*

Marlaina Donato is an author, visual artist, instrumental composer, and certified aromatherapist specializing in the clinical application of essential oils.

She offers women's meditation classes and co-facilitates women's Goddess day retreats. She and her beloved husband Joe live in beautiful rural New Jersey.

See Marlaina on Facebook or visit
www.booksandbrush.net